SNOBS
And
SARDINES

To the memory of my dear husband
Michael Parnell

SNOBS
And
SARDINES

Rhondda Schooldays

Mary Davies Parnell

SEREN BOOKS

SEREN BOOKS is the book imprint of
Poetry Wales Press Ltd.
Andmar House, Tondu Road, Bridgend
Mid Glamorgan, Wales

British Library Cataloguing in Publication Data:
Parnell, Mary Davies
Snobs and Sardines
I. Title
942.9720092

ISBN: 1-85411-095-0

The publisher acknowledges the financial support
of the Welsh Arts Council.

Cover Illustration — Tom Hutchinson

Printed by The Cromwell Press,
Broughton Gifford, Melksham,
Wiltshire SN12 8PH

CONTENTS

List of Illustrations

SNOBS
And
SARDINES

CHAPTER ONE

The School Bus

Writing an English composition on her first day in secondary school in the mid seventies, my eleven year old daughter began "What an awful place! Tomorrow can only be better". In the mid forties, children were not so forthright; indeed honesty implying criticism of the establishment was positively discouraged. Actually, for me, far and away the worst part of the whole school business was getting there. A special bus picked up the children from the southern extremity of the Rhondda at the Trehafod Hotel for the Porth County, Porth Secondary and local secondary modern schools — so there we were, the Snobs, the Sardines and the Toads, all squashed together in one moving machine. I huddled in a seat with two friends from Hafod juniors going to the Secondary School: Enid Morgan who had boarded at the Bridge and Joyce Bevan who got on with me at the Vaughans Arms. We squashed in three to a seat on the premise of safety in numbers and sat there wide-eyed like alarmed little mice watching the dubious goings-on around us.

"Aah, look at 'im, goody goody County snob."

"Ee was born up a tree."

"Ga'an 'e wasn' born 'e was knitted."

"Nah, 'is mother bought 'im in the Co-op."

The Toads and some of the lesser Sardines found this hilarious and would chortle with glee as the small, overwhelmed boy in his new, over-large green and gold uniform would put on a brave face, attempt a frightened smile then turn his head to look steadfastly at a fascinating bit of passing mountain as the school bus lurched on up the road past the colliery and over the

9

New bridge to Llwyncelyn, bodies hanging off and out of various apertures.

How the Toads had failed to pass the Scholarship exam I could never understand as their wit, quickness of tongue and originality in the insulting reply always amazed me and I felt I could never match them. The odd thing was the more elevated in brain power you were rated, the slower you seemed to be in the quip and smart answer stakes. Perhaps these Toads, of whom little was expected in the way of behaviour, dress (for they wore no uniform, lucky things) or academic achievement had less entramelled minds, and cruel, funny words came spilling out of their mouths with easy spontaneity.

Caps, striped school scarves, rulers, rubbers, pencils, set squares, the occasional pair of glasses, tie or even blazer flew out of the bus windows with regularity, littering the road to the schools. During my first year at the grammar school my lunch consisted of flattened sandwiches, their filling having oozed out, mis-shapen cakes whose cream had merged with the wrapping paper and biscuits disintegrated into crumbs. This was because I had sat on my satchel for most of the journey to school, underneath yourself being the safest place if you wanted to hang on to your possessions. I could well understand the reason for the little boxes of compulsory name tapes bearing "Mary Davies" in black writing — not so much for what was mislaid in school but hurled out of the bus windows on the way there. Named possessions, especially larger items, could usually be reclaimed at the bus depot in Porth, collected by passers-by and long suffering inhabitants of houses on the bus route who had witnessed the passing mayhem and who were no doubt accustomed to it over the years.

My bus stop, the Vaughans Arms at the top of Sants Hill, was the fourth pick-up point on the route so the bedlam was well under way when I boarded. Once on the bus your eyes had to be everywhere. One morning a satchel badly aimed at someone's head sailed out of the bus doorway and into the passageway of a house through the open door to land with the mail delivery on the floor. Manna from heaven indeed!

It was bad on the lower deck where most of the girls and the odd, timid, small boy cowered, but quite impossible on the

10

upper. Harold the conductor, a grey-haired man in his thirties, spent his time between checking passes and selling tickets with his eye on the mirror on the stairs. Many times during the journey he would rush up them to sort out free-for-all wrestling matches involving anything up to twenty youngsters, including tough girls, to demand that a boy's trousers doubling as a flag be returned to him, that they stop hanging out of the windows, performing gymnastics on the poles or playing tunes on the bell. Occasionally rude mis-spelt ungrammatical remarks were written on innocent adverts on the bus walls, "Rinso washes whiter than white! Shuv it up you're jumber", or pendulous addenda added to pictures or drawings of people. Harold must have badly needed a job or felt a desire for martyrdom to be a conductor on that bus. Despite his premature greyness he was always cheerful and welcoming with the civilised pupils.

"Lo 'Arrold."

"Lo luv. 'Ow you today? Orright?"

With the boys, especially the rebels, he was not as charming.

"Aye aye 'Arrold."

"I'll aye aye you my lad. You sit at the back mind, where I can see you in the mirror, and no messin' about."

"Aww, 'Arrold!"

Harold was constantly going to the rescue of one tiny, wiry, bird-like boy called Liam in the dark and light blue uniform of the Secondary School. How this young man had ever passed any exam was beyond my ken as his behaviour, bringing constant wrath on his head from his peers, was unbelievably stupid. He seemed not to possess one jot of common sense. He was a top decker from the start and when Harold was on the lower deck Liam was continually trotting down the stairs to report misbehaviour.

" 'Arrold, John James is smokin' upstairs,"

or

"Ey 'Arrold that ginger boy who got on by the bridge keeps swearing. Jew wanna know what 'e said?"

As a result Liam usually alighted from the bus at the steps near the bus depot at Tynewydd Square minus part of his uniform and most of his school equipment, face blotchy red, sometimes blood trickling down under one ear, strangled with

11

his tie tight around his neck, ink stains on his shirt but always with a blissful unblinking expression on his face, no doubt triumphant to be still alive after the fray.

Fortunately the Sec Mod stop at the Rink Dance Hall on North Road was first. The Toads would troop off noisily, those on the upper deck ignoring the stairs after the bend, some leaping straight on to the platform, while others hurled themselves directly on to the pavement. A favourite game was to push from behind when the stairs were crowded so that all would overbalance and land in a heap at the bottom. Children frequently spilled into the road. Surprisingly, no-one was ever killed though there was an abundance of grazes, bruises and the occasional letting of blood. Harold was always yelling at kids who jumped off before the bus had stopped, but after the Rink the journey was more peaceful and Harold rested his frayed nerves, sprawled in exhaustion on the long seat by the door.

Satchels were removed from under bottoms, and a bit of hasty last-minute homework attended to in the form of copying one's neighbour's answers. Squashed lunch packets were examined and the contents pulled into shape or consumed as a late breakfast. Sometimes they were so mangled the sandwiches had to be eaten on the spot. Finally the bus disgorged the Snobs in Cemetery Road, first the boys opposite the short steep hill up to the Boys County School, then the girls outside the garage opposite their school where other buses deposited friends from the Rhondda Fach and Fawr who had no doubt experienced similar journeys in their quest for knowledge.

Girls trooped up the lane past the grand mansion house serving as a nurses' home and along the drive into the extensive, well tended school grounds, happy in the knowledge that the place could hold few terrors comparable with those of getting there.

CHAPTER TWO

Uniform

We were very small fish in the biggest pond we'd ever experienced — seventy two new little Form One girls, self conscious and wary, if not scared, in uniforms still retaining their packing creases and smelling of cardboard boxes. Everyone wore a white blouse with a green and yellow, horizontally striped, knitted tie. The smart, silky ties with diagonal stripes weren't available until a few years later, but so attractive and desirable were their smooth lengths that it seemed no sooner were they on display in the Porth Hodges and other Valley outfitters than they were around the girls' necks in school and all the shops sold out. Few felt any loyalty towards the cumbersome knitted variety, an extension of war time deprivation, but which, to be fair, had been useful as instant bandages for bloodied limbs, harnesses for follow my leader, blindfolds for various lunchtime games and replacements for lost gymslip sashes for they were stretchable as elastic. No such roles for the silky diagonal, which stayed firmly under the wearer's collar.

The main item of the uniform was the gymslip, everyone's least favourite garment. Two wide straps that buttoned over the shoulder and attached to a flat part under the neck held it on the body. Then, just before the bust, it blossomed forth in three box pleats whose irrepressible wild folds were contained around the waist by a woven sash of coarse material. Below this, all semblance of pleat was usually lost and the navy serge material ballooned around the lower thigh "four inches above the knee when kneeling". Why kneeling was included in this rule no-one knew as this posture was probably the least, if ever, practised during one's school career; we stood in Assembly for prayers.

13

Under and slightly forward of the gymslip's left armpit was a tiny, flat, sewn on, almost totally useless pocket. If you tucked a handkerchief in it you looked as though you had a surplus provision of an off-centre breast, and money kept there fell out once you bent over or ran. The only use I could fathom for it was to conceal small pieces of paper containing test or exam answers, but you could just as easily write these on the palm of your hand with far less potch and ducking and writhing (so as not to be seen by the invigilator) in the testing period.

To wear a gymslip successfully it was necessary to be stick-thin, tall and quite straight. In fact they were garments far better suited to the shape of boys than girls. Fast developing girls and fatties had no chance. Since the garments were cut level at the bottom, the gymslip front hung so high on the former there was a constant danger of navy knicker exposure, while the latter simply resembled a disintegrating Christmas parcel tied up with a hopeful bit of string. If you mislaid your sash you just looked pregnant.

No wonder the prefects were respected and admired, for they were allowed to wear navy blue skirts. Compared with the rest of the school they were models of grace and refinement, Parisian mannequins whatever their shape or size. Naturally their silky diagonals fronting a white blouse could be seen in all their green and yellow shining glory. And why was this ill-assorted, inchoate package of pleats, straps and pockets all in the wrong places called a gymslip we wondered? The first thing we did when we had gym or games was *slip* them off to exercise in our white blouses and baggy navy knickers.

In some way the disaster of the gymslip was compensated for by the blazer — an attractive moss green colour, with silvery buttons and a integral gold badge woven on the breast pocket if you bought it at E.R. Roberts, Kingsway, Cardiff. Blazers bought elsewhere required the badge to be sewn on manually and weren't quite the delightful shade of Roberts's. The badge bore the stern school motto, warning "Ni wyr ni ddysg" ("No knowledge without learning", in other words, no messing about in Porth County) around the shield encasing a few entwined serpents (the symbol of knowledge and discovery apparently), and a pair of daffodils growing out of a shining light. At the top

14

were the letters RCSG in fine, upstanding capitals. The blazer, which successfully hid most of the hideous gymslip, was primarily an outer garment worn in suitable weather. For warmth inside school navy cardigans were donned and feet pattered along in white ankle or three-quarter grey socks and black daps or "indoor shoes", as they were more elegantly and eloquently called in Porth County, worn to keep the building quiet and preserve the revered hush of academe. Black shoes were *de rigueur* for to-ing and fro-ing from home or anywhere else in the outside world.

Navy coats or usually Burberrys also enveloped and protected girls in this coming and going and the new first year pupils in their macs were a sight to behold. It is well known that human growth is at its most rapid between eleven and fifteen and the majority of Rhondda parents, still recovering after being knocked for six by the war, together with the deprived school outfitters, conspired to fit huge rain coats on small girls to last them until they were at least a foot taller. For some, lacking in upward growth, this was into old age, but for most this meant many years on in their County career, sometimes seeing them to the end of it by continual letting of the hem which was always several inches deep in itself. A typical conversation during shopping for some garment or other would go something as follows:

"Oh, Mam, that's a nice skirt. Lovely shade of blue in it and nice material look. Isn't it a smart style, mam? Oh I do like that," (meaning — Can I have it?).

"Mmmm. S'quite nice, you're right. Lovely colours. Go well with your twin set that would."

"It's not very expensive either look, only 12/6d," (starting to simmer with enthusiasm seeing the battle for the skirt almost won).

"No indeed it's very reasonable. Pass it 'ere for me to have a look...Oh yes...oversewn seams...wool..." Then mam's eyes would widen in disbelief and near horror.

"Oh that's no good. There's no hem on this, look. Look at the thing! It'd be too short for you in a couple of months. Cheaply made old thing!"

And the coveted skirt, despite having a hem almost an inch

15

wide, would be cast aside hastily and in disgust as though something nasty might be caught from it. No, hems had to be at least a third the length of the garment to be acceptable.

All this hemmage added great weight to a Burberry, which was long in the first place, so there we were, small girls in coats down to our shoes ("Good protection against the cold and the wet") shuffling along like a troop of miniature Prussian soldiers in greatcoats trailing off to war in Siberia. Hands and ankles weren't visible until Form 3, and so on the school bus it was impossible to check whether you'd put your feet into odd socks on dark mornings or indeed were still wearing bedroom slippers. Gloves of course were hardly necessary, hands secreted away as they were in sleeves.

After Form 4 the Burberry was a desirable garment and looked smart on girls, with its casually flipped up collar, belt coolly knotted around a slim waist and skirt flaring to the knees. Trouble was, it was threadbare by then.

The item of clothing considered most important to one's welfare by the school management, indeed, I almost tremble still to think of it, and then in hushed, reverential thoughts, was the beret or tam. To be seen outside school minus your beret (pronounced berry) was the most heinous crime or cardinal sin it was possible to commit up to the age of eighteen. If you'd come to school naked, provided you were wearing your navy tam with a small version of the school badge perched up front you would, I'm sure, be forgiven. Younger girls, largely uncaring about their appearance, simply jammed these tams down on their heads. Their ears then stuck out like Noddy's friend 'Big Ears' and bits of hair protruded like darning needles everywhere. We sympathised with bespectacled girls as glasses became tangled up in the beret and often unladylike phrases were heard issuing from these normally easy-going people. For some reason placidity went with short-sightedness. Some secured their tam to their head by tying their school scarf above it then knotting it beneath the chin, and one girl, Margaret Booker, had demolished her brother's braces to use as a tam-retainer. Older girls eased them on to their coiffure-conscious heads and others balanced them at various unstable angles, giving a decided impression of the continent, ranging from the French tart to the Shonni Wniwns.

Whatever earth-shattering event occurred, from the death of kings (and we had one of those) to the invasion of inhuman creatures from Space, come rain, hail, snow, blistering heat, electric storm, wild wind, hithering and thithering, tams had to be worn or instant detention ensued. If there was one thing that made a member of the teaching staff snap, purple-faced and swollen with ire, rage and fury, sometimes to the brink of apoplexy, it was to see a County girl on the street, tamless. If perchance one had mislaid one's headwear, there was simply no point going to school as it was quite impossible to avoid the hell flames, opprobrium and ignominy destined for a bare head. One risked eternal school damnation not to mention an indignant letter home with no doubt a promise of suspension, even possible expulsion. Thus we were prepared to guard and preserve the innocuous looking little navy beret with our blood, and on the school bus this was usually daily the case. Without it life just couldn't be lived.

My preoccupation with hats, and that of fellow County pupils, stems from our youthful awe of the humble beret and terror of being found without one. Nowadays when there is a social affair to attend — various church celebrations, theatrical, musical and literary affairs, concerts and garden parties — and you are uncertain whether or not to bedeck your head, there is one thing you can be sure of: if there are any former Porth County pupils present at the event, conditioned as we were from a young age, they will be wearing a hat. One is never alone and outstandingly noticeable with a covered head when another Porth County girl is there. More than once have I approached the other, usually one, sometimes two behatted females at a function with the words:

"Don't I know you? I'm sure we've met somewhere before."

"Well I don't know unless it was in school. Did you go to Porth County?"

"Yes. Where else?"

Good old Porth County providing its pupils with means of instant recognition and friendship. No matter that I had been at the school ten years before my new acquaintance and possibly had never even seen her before in my life, the old school hat was at work. It has, of course, entered my mind that I have probably missed many F.P's (former pupils), tougher minded pupils or "saucy pieces" as some were called, who remained impervious to the career-threatening momentousness of the tam while at school, and who are not dogged in adult life by its reverberations "to wear or not to wear". There might clearly be room for other manifestations of the old school network other than the tam or tie.

CHAPTER THREE

Early Days

So, kitted out in full uniform with name tabs sewn on everything pliable enough to receive a needle (a complication with there being four Margaret Joneses in Year one and quite likely half a dozen more in the school) we were poised to "listen, learn and inwardly digest".

On our first fearful, wide-eyed morning in Porth County, we were initially impressed by grave ladies, unhurriedly walking around in strange, black flowing robes. There were also young ladies, prefects no doubt, wearing skirts but with white blouses and ties like us, but who behaved in a brisk, confident, important manner, looking big and capable enough to be our mothers. These grand calm ladies were the teachers, wearing robes, presumably to show they were clever and had passed all their advanced exams. Or did they wear these ample gowns to keep their clothes clean, like my mother who wore a pinny most of the day when doing her household tasks and looking after the shop which was at the front of our house? Perhaps the teachers used these robes to carry around chalk, board dusters and books somewhere in their vast folds. Perhaps they were simply to keep them warm. Later I discovered gowns were used for all of these purposes and more. They not only transported board dusters but were put into service *as* board dusters and were also convenient for a quick and surreptitious nose-blow or eye-wipe in the event of extreme mirth or sadness. I have seen them used as umbrellas, curtains, draught excluders, instruments of chastisement, cushions, pillows, floor-mats and royal robes in class plays. The range of uses of the academic gown is prodigious. However at the time I was sure I would not learn anything confronted by a venerable lady in one of these awesome garments. I would be too overwhelmed to open my mouth let alone operate my brain, if I still had one, that is.

And what of these queenly prefects then? They were just ordinary girls only six years or so older than us. But what elegance, coolness and urbanity they exuded. I had instant "crushes" on a dozen of them. It was quite unimaginable that before our school career ended we might be like them: tall, slim, shapely, with slender ankles which could be seen even when they wore a coat, with shining hair in attractive styles, and with firmly and properly knotted ties. The head prefect, Arfona Davies, at least the whisper went reverently round that she was so, particularly fitted this category of Goddess, with her golden locks in a smooth, page-boy style, upright confident walk, and smiling, assured demeanour. For the first time in my life I fully appreciated the story of the ugly duckling. That initial morning, while the rest of the school and staff were in the Assembly Hall being welcomed back after the Summer holiday, the new girls were in the capable hands of the prefects who allocated cloakroom hooks which would be ours for the school year. In preparing us for school, mothers had been asked to make green shoe-bags with our initials embroidered in yellow and during the day these were suspended from hooks and contained our outdoor shoes. At night they hung alone in the cloakroom, transforming it from the rich daytime forest of navy blue coats into a sparse one of green shoe-bags looking like baobab trees swollen with water, as they held our black canvas indoor shoes until these were needed the next morning for padding quietly around the building. The place might have been kept quiet at ground level, but it often echoed with cheery, happy greetings and laughter from the upper end at mouth level.

Bessie

Once our garments were deposited and we had learnt our hook number (and repeated it aloud to the prefects) we sat on the cloakroom benches awaiting a summons to the Hall to be addressed by the Headmistress, Miss Elizabeth Hudd; "Is she nice?" asked one forward girl. "Nice? She's a double first!" answered a prefect. Despite our total incomprehension of what constituted a double first, this piece of information was greeted with impressed "oohs" and "aahs" and respectful looks from the shining up-turned faces. No-one asked for further enlightenment afraid of being exposed as a complete ignoramus. Shortly after, clinging unpractised onto slipping satchels which seemed unnecessarily large, cumbersome objects, we filed along the parquet floored corridor into the Hall.

In front of us on a high platform standing behind a lectern was the Headmistress — the double first lady. She too was resplendent in black gown which matched her hair. She peered unsmilingly down through thick lensed glasses, lips pursed as she watched the hesitant, shuffling procession.

"Come along girls, move right across the Hall. Form straight lines, one behind the other, then sit on the floor please. Quickly now. All settled? Thank you prefects."

Her briskness transformed shuffle into scamper and we sat, trying to concentrate on her words of welcome, information and instructions though there was much to gaze wonderingly at all around. Once or twice she stopped in mock patience in mid sentence waiting for complete attention which she instantly got. Finally she swept, or rather stumped heavily, off the platform, down the steps and out through the swing doors, for she had arthritis which deformed her poor hands and lower legs, and unfortunately her carriage didn't match the majesty and authority of the woman when still. Although walking was painful for her, she could move quite fast, if inelegantly and noisily, on splayed out feet.

Was there ever such a Head of a school? Perhaps Doctor Thomas Arnold of Rugby, immortalised in Tom Brown's schooldays. It would have to be someone of almost mythical proportions to match our Bessie of Porth County. As Form Oners we were terrified of her and held our breath at the very mention of her name or the sound of her voice. Silence and order issued out of rumpus and chaos at her approach. She was known to everyone in the Rhondda whether they had Porth County connections or not. Indeed her reputation had preceded her much further afield. It seemed no matter where you went people would declare "Ah yes, Porth County Girls! Miss Hudd! Say no more!"

Some girls remained terrified of her and some hated her throughout their school careers but I believe these were in the minority. She could certainly shout, could instantly summon a sarcastic turn of phrase and from time to time was harsh in meting out punishment. What always turned my knees to quivering jelly was the way she looked down on you as a malefactor even if you were as tall as she, by throwing back her head, narrowing her eyes and considering you down the length of her nose through those thick glasses. Her narrowed eyes could have quelled a rebellious army of deranged deserters and turned them into meek, tremulous mice. But she was never unjust. There was logic in her discipline and fairness in her correction. She had no favourites, mitigating circumstances were rare and, when acceptable, overwhelming in their persuasion. Everyone was treated the same.

With visitors to the school Miss Hudd was the epitome of graciousness, good humour, wit, charm and understanding. As girls developed and matured into young women under her and the staff's tutelage, she relaxed with them too, showing this side of her nature. Of course, to feel the approval and friendship of so respected a person made her Sixth Form pupils idolise her. Once a week she would take the Upper Sixth for a general discussion lesson and it was at such times we came into contact with her wisdom and intellectual consideration of principles, ideals, dogma, current popular thought and world problems. We discussed the establishment of a world language as well as the European Esperanto, a united Europe long before its creation, commercial television and radio, ethnic problems throughout the world, the East/West balance of power, the role of the United Nations and many other topics. No matter what you thought at the beginning of the lesson, your ideas, through carefully guided discussion, would have a new slant by the bell forty minutes later. Miss Hudd would hurriedly stump into the room, gown trailing, usually a few minutes late after a meeting or other appointment, and even before sitting down would gather her gown around her and say "Now then girls. It is better to travel hopefully than to arrive. What are your thoughts on that?" Lessons with the Headmistress had style.

Although unmarried herself, her vision of a fulfilled woman's life was that of marriage and a family. This is not to say she encouraged boy friends for her girls — chatting to boys over the wall or railings of the adjoining Boy's County School was strongly frowned upon. Romance was for women, not girls! However, girls were not to be shy and intimidated by the opposite sex, and Upper Sixth girls were allowed an official Christmas party with their male counterparts from next door. This party took place in alternate years in the Boys' or Girls' School and was always attended by a large complement of male and female teachers, present no doubt not so much to enjoy themselves as to keep an eye on the proceedings. After all there was no knowing what eighteen year old members of both sexes might do after seven years of being kept apart.

In the annual school play in the Autumn Term we performed, as always, in an all-girl version (Bessie's magnanimity didn't stretch to tolerance of co-education in treading the boards). In my Upper Sixth year it was Shakespeare's *As You Like It*. The whole cast blended together and it was the usual nightly sell out and noted success. The role of Touchstone was particularly well played by a young actress with good timing and lightness of touch. The week following the performances we were half way through an Upper Sixth Geography lesson when Miss Hudd came into the class with a visitor introduced to us as the new Director of Education. We rose at their entry and the Director stood smilingly looking around, questioning us about our 'A' level subjects and courses when he suddenly registered that my friend Caryl Williams had been Touchstone. "Oh I recognise you," he said, "you were Touchstone in the play last week. An excellent performance, I might add, not only by the whole cast but by you personally". He looked around again then vaguely recognised me. "You were in it too, weren't you? Now let me see..." "Jaques", I said. "Ah yes, of course, Jaques. All the world's a stage... very good too! In fact there were absolutely no weak links! Not one!" Like a good diplomatic Director of Education, he carried on praising the play, our work, the school, the staff, Miss Hudd, but then returned to Caryl — a striking, dark haired, athletic girl whose pretty, freckled face was further embellished by thick, finely arched eyebrows, which I envied. My own were sparse, pale and ill-defined. More praise for her as the jester, Touchstone. He went on and on and secretly we thought this young, new, rather handsome Director must fancy her. Many young men did. Caryl did not indeed lack for willing escorts. Finally to put an end to his tirade, or perhaps never at a loss for words, Caryl simply felt she had to take part in a conversation hitherto one-sided and said; "Well now, Director, I'm very glad you enjoyed the play so much. We all enjoyed performing in it and rehearsing for the past month and I think here I speak for everyone. But I must say I'm especially gratified to know you liked my interpretation of Touchstone and am very flattered to think you've recognised me today — in civvies, so to speak." Caryl beamed but above all Bessie beamed before she and her visitor affably took their leave.

The next day a still broadly smiling Headmistress came to the Upper Sixth form room; "Girls, I was delighted to show the Director of Education around yesterday and he was pleased with his visit. I must say though there was one thing which delighted me above all and that was the manner in which one of you spoke to him in an intelligent, natural way, not in the least intimidated by his position and at the same time being feminine and gracious."

We all looked at each other. Who on earth could Bessie be referring to? Who was this paragon of enlightened womanly behaviour?

"I am of course talking about Caryl, who answered his praise of her so fluently and spontaneously. She is an example to all of us. I was proud of you my dear."

For probably the first time in her life, Caryl blushed. Yes, Miss Hudd was a fine Headmistress and it was a privilege to have been one of her girls. Indeed, it was a privilege to have been at Porth County.

CHAPTER FOUR

New Friends

There were no tests in the major subjects to place the new girls in forms. The entrance exam had seen to that and sorted the ewes from the nannies so to speak. In no-nonsense manner the first 36 girls in the Scholarship exam were marched off to Form 1A and the second 36 proceeded to 1B. Our form teacher Miss Beard allocated desks in strict order of intelligence. Margaret Thomas, on whom all the eleven year old respectful eyes were focused as she was 'Top of the Rhondda' sat in the first desk by the door, on the right, number 2 was behind her and so on. There were six rows with six desks in each row. The Jones clan had done very well in the exam as numbers two to eight were all of that widespread family. Ann, Barbara, two Margarets, Anwen, Mair and Sheila. There was also a Ceridwen Edith Mary Hicks-Thomas, generally known as Crid, high on the list. I suppose she deserved to be with a name like that! My seat was on the left side of the room, next row but one to the high windows from which only sky was visible. In front of me pupil no. 24 was Mair James and no. 26 behind was Margaret Booker. This must have been the European part of the room, perhaps the draught blowing down our row was the Mistral or the Föhn as all three of us later studied modern languages. The doctors were by the door, the lawyers in the middle and the scientists under the window.

Not all of us had Welsh names. There was a Faith Ffoulkes, (permanently wiping her nose), a Hope Higgs ('Ope 'Iggs or even Oh Pigs) and no, not a Charity, but a Verity Martin. Hope Higgs or Hope Rachel Barker Higgs in full, a small brown-eyed, mischievous-looking girl with brown bobbed hair, a chunk of which had been arbitrarily trapped and tied in a bow with a huge navy ribbon, sat opposite me in the adjacent row. As it was easier to subversively communicate with those alongside rather than those in front or behind, she became my friend. Her main interest after food was football and she was at first rather scornful of me because I didn't know any footballers' names and had never heard of some player called Billy Steele. However we had a race, I marginally beat her and she agreed to become my friend, especially on learning I lived in a shop.

"Are there sweets in it?"

"Yes of course. Lots, and chocolate and sherbert and things."

A delicious thick, chocolate-covered crisp wafer bar had just been invented but with what I thought the rather unsuitable, off-putting name of "Slam". I clearly wasn't alone in these thoughts, as at first, it sold slowly. Customers would say to my father "Slam!? Oh I don't fancy the sound of that Mr. Davies". However, the uninitiated eleven and twelve year old people, myself included, who doggedly sought out and tried all that was new in the confectionery line, thought otherwise. It was quite, quite outstandingly good. Hope was a girl after my own heart.

"Got any Slams?"

"Yes. Boxfuls."

"Great. I'll come and visit you on Saturday. Where must I get off the bus?"

As Hope lived in Cymmer, Porth, the journey caused no problems once she knew to get off the bus at the Vaughans Arms. She duly visited. We had mainly chocolate marshmallow cakes for tea. My mother, duped as ever, thought she was "a sweet little girl" and she finally departed with a pocketful of Slams and an invitation to visit again soon, to which she promptly replied that she was free tomorrow, but that was too soon.

We became firm friends until the fifth form when I, having a September birthday and being one of the youngest in the year, was deemed by Governmental decree to be too young to sit 'O' levels with the rest. Hope continued into the sixth form while I had to while away another year in Form 5, thanks to the then Minister of Education, Florence Horsburgh. I expect she was instrumental in breaking up many beautiful friendships nation-wide. We still considered ourselves friends, of course. Had we not, over the years, played hockey together, suffering bashes and bruises, hidden together under the Geography room (a temporary building on stilts which is still there) when we should have been in Needlework? We'd mutually sympathised when having to eat piles of sopping boiled cabbage, custard with lumps which exploded like powdery bombs in the mouth and platefuls of slimy semolina around the merest splodge of jam. So although similar shared experiences make you life-long pals, (for half a dozen or so years anyway) proximity is encouraging to a close friendship whereas distance is not. It might lend enchantment to a view, but absence does not necessarily make the heart grow fonder. Finally, Hope went off to do Physical Education in Kent while I muttered away in French for a further year before my release into the world of real students, living away from home with grants, college scarves and things.

However, that first year we were mates, primarily due to class position, but also because of shared interests in speed and choco-late. Those, mainly the Joneses, who sat in the far corners of the room, I didn't get to know at all. One or two, with whom I shared the air for five years, I never directly addressed, nor they me.

That first morning we were given rough books: exercise books in which notes were to be taken, mathematical workings-out done, initial biological drawings practised and geographical maps shakily essayed, before all these were neatly put into best exercise books at home. On the first page, though, we copied out the timetable, which to my and Hope's delight had P.T. in it somewhere every day except one which had Games instead. A form captain, we were told, needed to be elected, but as we didn't know each other, this would be deferred for a week or two. The form captain's chief duties were registerial carrying and fetch-ing and to keep class order between the departure of the last and the arrival of the next teacher. Meanwhile, we were to be quiet and well behaved between lessons and, of course, at all other times. We blinked in innocent wonderment. Was there really anyone in this august place bold enough not to be thoroughly virtuous, always? Was there really any need to tell us to be good? No-one was brave enough to speak barely above a whisper and names, when asked for, had to be repeated several times. Even then teachers got them wrong.

"Next girl, name?"

"Maureen Cutler, Miss," in scarcely audible muffled tones.

"What? Speak up girl!"

The name was given, and for her first year, the pupil was known as Doreen Butler to one particular teacher. As the year progressed and the girls got bolder, they encouraged the mistake and participated in the nomenclature confusion.

"Please Miss Williams, Doreen Butler's feeling sick. Can we open the window?"

Maureen would pull a face, not entirely comfortable in the deception, but she would nonetheless go along with the partial imposture.

"If you're feeling ill Doreen, you'd better go and have a breath of air by the outside door."

"S'all right Miss. I feel better now the window's open."

Miss Williams, who taught us English Literature and Grammar, which meant parsing and sentence analysis at which Maureen was hopeless, must have been quite mystified to see a terminal report for a Maureen Cutler in 1A. She clearly had no idea who M. Cutler was, as her comment for the girl's work in English Grammar was "very disappointing exam after excellent work in class during the term".

CHAPTER FIVE

School Grounds and Rules

Playtime was called by the impressively grand name of "recess" in Porth County, and this was one of the reasons I think we had earned the name of County Snobs: using words other people didn't understand. On the bus home from Porth to Trehafod with my friends Enid and Joyce from the Sec, the talk would go:

"Coming out to play after, Mary?"

"I 'spec so, but I gotta go to Ponty with my mother first."

"Wha' for?"

"I gotta get a new fountain pen. I lost mine in recess yesterday."

"Wha's tha?"

"I dunno, t'was a Platignum I think. I'm gonna 'ave a Swan this time. They got gold nibs."

"No, not pen mun, that other thing — re...something..."

"Oh, recess. That's playtime. That's what it's called in our school."

Eyes wide and mouth pulled down at the corners in mock respect. Enid said; "Oh Gawd, there's posh. They say break for playtime in our school don' they Joyce?"

Recess lasted fifteen minutes in mid morning and the first concern for most Form One pupils was the daily intake of milk. Arriving at the Grammar School, I was hopeful of having left my one third pint, often warmed around the classroom stove, back in Hafod School, but no such luck. The Rhondda Education Authority was the first in Britain to provide children with a daily dose of milk and the practice was intended to ensure strong bones and teeth until their owner was twelve. It was, however, now optional. On the first day of term we had been given a slip of paper to be signed by a parent to say whether we wanted milk or not. Personally, I didn't want milk, free or not, preferring to pay for the pop mixtures supplied by Mr. John, the caretaker, when I was thirsty. Besides, it was a great waste of the precious minutes of recess, trekking down to the school basement where the crates of milk were disposed, jostling and pushing for a bottle, drinking the milk and replacing the empty, when I could be tearing around the school grounds with Hope, dodging around trees, playing on the field and rolling down the sloping lawns and grassy banks. For this new school wasn't merely furnished with a tarmacked yard like Hafod School, but surrounded by extensive grounds with much greenery, trees and shrubs. It did have inhospitable outside toilets like Hafod, but at least there was no adjacent boys urinal, so you could walk safely along the lavatory corridor without spray appearing from nowhere when it wasn't raining!

My mother, a farmer's daughter, who had drunk milk straight (or almost) from the cow all her unmarried life, however, would tolerate none of my preferences. Of course I had to have the milk. Not only was it good for me, but the Rhondda Council was kind enough to provide it, and daily drunk it had to be. "Look not a gift horse in the mouth" she kept repeating so insistently. I was afraid she would write something besides her signature on the slip of paper and embarrass me before my classmates and begowned form mistress.

So, the first job at recess for me and for the majority of Form One who also had sensible mothers, was the consumption of milk, slowly, through a straw if you had time, or if it was a cold day. The basement, if gloomy and lit by one bare bulb, at least housed the boilers, and you could linger in the dark warmth before facing the cold, hostile grey outside. The milk was gulped straight out of the bottle in five seconds flat when the weather was fine and there was a game that urgently needed playing or if you had reluctantly to keep an appointment with a teacher to hand in late homework, or lines to give to a prefect for running in the corridor the previous day.

The school grounds provided a blissful playground for youngsters and a picturesque, pleasant environment for older girls who, having out-grown eagerness for speed in forward movement, wanted simply to stroll on the lawns or avenue fronting the school, and chat, or just relax sitting on the steps leading up to the two front entrances at either end of the building.

Being well above the Rhondda Fawr river, the school, like the whole of Mount Pleasant and the ribbon development area of Trealaw, between which it is situated, was built on the hillside. Behind the school was a farm, then mountain, beyond which was Ynyshir in the other valley, the Rhondda Fach. The school playing field was the uppermost part of the mountain to be tamed, levelled off and reclaimed from nature. A steep bank forming a natural grandstand led down to another terrace housing two tennis courts. Sporting activities taking place here could also be viewed from the opposite side, a long, again inclining, shady corridor of grass, nurturing a profuse growth of laburnum trees that yielded pretty yellow flowers in late spring. Years later, it came to the public's notice that laburnum seeds were highly toxic. I doubt if any Porth County girls were fatally poisoned by them, or even slightly discommoded. Not knowing they were poisonous, they wouldn't have tried eating them. Although today R.S.C.G. is basically the same as it was in the fifties — but with a few extra classroom terrapins and extensions. The laburnum trees and grassy corridor have disappeared to make way for a road running the length of the school. It leads into what was the Boys School next door but which now, with the former girls school, constitutes Porth Comprehensive.

A steep wall topped with railings in school green separated the field from school, play from work. A thick laurel hedge prevented pupils at work in the Geography and Art and other classrooms from seeing pupils playing tennis or netball, but one could sit and sigh and dream over a difficult map projection or complicated theorem on hearing the ping of tennis ball on catgut.

The highest point of the school grounds, just inside the boundary wall below the mountain, was known as the Jungle. A few feet above the hockey pitch, it was an area of long grass, bushes, undergrowth, nettles and unpruned trees of anonymous species. It attracted the little girls like wasps to a late summer picnic and at lunchtime, small, giggling females, oblivious to all but the game, were constantly to be seen chasing each other in and out of the bushes, hopping over brambles, dodging around branches or stumbling and falling over in the straggly grass, pealing with laughter. Sometimes, trees were to be seen shaking violently in the still air and voices were heard raised in mirth or argument with no bodies visible at all. Then, the bell would ring for afternoon school and the bank would suddenly be alive like an ant hill with little tomboy girls emerging from the greenery, faces flushed from play, bits of grass and twigs in dishevelled hair, white blouses and socks muddied, bounding, jumping, running, pushing, falling over each other. Their youthful energy was augmented by their anxiety not to be last, or worse, late, walking up the corridor under Miss Hudd's awful gaze. If anything, the most impressive ceremonies of the day took place when the bell summoned us back to class after recess and lunch break for 'lines'.

Morning assembly was also a fairly intimidating affair, but as this took place at 9 a.m., people hadn't properly woken up yet even after the eventful bus-ride, so it didn't register as such. The school sang the assembly hymn as if on automatic pilot and moved about like somnambulists. Miss Harries smilingly and enthusiastically played jolly marching tunes on the piano when classes were entering and leaving the hall, but the reverse effect of that desired was achieved, and the music lulled those still drowsy into an even more soporific state. After a couple of lessons of Maths or Needlework, however, your wits had returned, enough anyway to understand that it was necessary to be prompt and properly garbed for the re-start of lessons at eleven fifteen.

The girls filed into school from the Junior entrance at the Dining Hall end, walked up the middle of the long main corridor until they reached their classroom. They then waited in double lines. Miss Hudd stood outside her room and watched each girl as she passed. A tap on the shoulder as you went by meant the eagle eye had spotted you and wanted to see you, usually for something inappropriate about your person. This signal meant you had to stop walking and stand aside there for later questioning. Few girls dared present themselves at school improperly uniformed, though there was always the mislaid tie or an aberrant replacement, which Miss Hudd could spot at fifty paces. Only prefects were allowed hidden knees. The knees of the rest of the school had to be on display. I never fathomed the reason for the obsession with that particular part of the anatomy. Perhaps it was for cleanliness. My mother often asked "Have you washed behind your ears, Mary?" but never enquired about the knee region. Perhaps a short skirt was to ensure free circulation of fresh air. Fresh air certainly had plenty of space to circulate in the roomy gymslip folds, often with the result of freezing one's thighs.

Hair had to be decidedly off the face. This rule seemed sensible to me, as you couldn't see your work in lessons if you had unruly and untied long hair. Exuberant hair tended to spring out of ribbons and hair clips and sometimes the tormented girl would receive the light shoulder tap, stand aside, and a few minutes later, the errant tresses would be back under strict control and, if necessary, in a 'school brown' elastic band. Their owner would, in the meantime, have received a lecture on cleanliness, neatness, school rules and the high expectations of Porth County girls. One girl with long, blond sleek hair arrived in school one day with her locks tied up neatly in a new fashion — a ponytail. But not for long. Miss Hudd, aghast, had spotted her in assembly and sought the poor innocent out in class. "Child" she bellowed: "Tie your hair up at the nape of your neck. Do not besmirch these portals with a similar coiffure. Such styles are for horses, not humans!"

When all forms were lined up outside their classrooms off the corridor, under the black honours boards with gold painted letters on the walls, and the Sixth Forms stood in a single line outside the Library and the Hall, the staff then filed out of their sanctum to stand facing the pupils they were to teach next, or their form, if it was afternoon registration. When there was absolute human silence and stillness, when you could hear the leaves rustling in the trees on the lawn outside, when you could hear a bluebottle buzz on the ceiling, and sheep bleat on Troedyrhiw mountain behind the field, or a train arriving in Porth Station two miles away, Miss Hudd, holding up the clapper of the school hand bell would let it drop gently against the casing, causing a minute, barely audible tinkle — the signal that all was satisfactory in

Porth County, and that life could continue. Girls would move into their rooms, followed by their teachers, to resume the accumulation of knowledge, good taste, breeding, *savoir-faire,* self-discipline, discernment, perception and confidence that Porth County endeavoured to instil into its pupils before they finally quit its hallowed doors.

Initially, what little girls had inside their heads didn't seem as important as what was concealed inside the rest of their bodies, as we were weighed, measured, examined, tested, and poked and prodded in various parts of our anatomy as never before. Copious notes and strange hieroglyphics were written on coloured, official-looking confidential cards by ladies in white coats and we worried whether we were in line for hospital or dental treatment of some kind or another. The late forties were the early days of the Welfare State, when the Government was largely concerned with the condition of people's health, especially juvenile, after the war years. To judge from the frenetic activity, Porth County figured prominently in their research and compilation of statistics. Small bells were tintinnabulated at various distances from ears; eyes strained to read small letters on optical wall charts; long handled miniature ladles were shoved down throats to allow the cognoscenti to observe epiglottises or whatever; similar straight ladles with smaller bowls were poked around in one's teeth; toes had to pick up handkerchieves and spatulas as feet were examined to see if they were flat; spine curves were assessed; we stood on scales with a swaying balance and weights to find out if we were over- or under-nourished and, finally, our upward growth was determined by having a wooden plank unceremoniously jammed on our heads (taking off a couple of inches with its downward pressure in the process).

So many new impressions on my first day at the Porth County School for Girls exhausted me to such an extent that I fell asleep on the school bus going home. My mother was disappointed that I was not full of energy and enthusiasm to tell her about my first day. She expected me to run up the hill from the Vaughans Arms, bound into the house and bombard her with news. It was all right for Mam. All she had to do was stay at home, listen to the radio, have cups of tea, go and serve in the shop now and then and have a gossip with the customer. On Wednesdays, she closed the shop to go to Ponty where she made a few purchases around the market, chatting to the stall holders, then had faggots and peas and coffee with her sister. Life was a bed of roses for mothers, whereas I, at my new school, had had to run round to-ing and fro-ing, hauling a satchel that gained in weight with books as the day progressed. I was despatched from pillar to post for medical examinations and was continually dressing, undressing, and struggling to achieve something resembling a knot in my tie. I'd had a load of new names to learn and places to familiarise myself with and now, when I had a pile of books to cover, Mam wanted news.

"Did you have a nice day in your new school?" Mam enquired fervently.

"Oh orright" was my lacklustre reply.

"Only all right?"

"Well, it was quite nice, really."

"What did you do?"

"Well we had to go to different places for things."

"Did you learn anything?" Mam's tone was getting sharper as she lost patience.

"We didn't have any lessons really, jes' books."

"If you had books you must have had lessons." (Then picking up *Palgrave's Golden Treasury*...) "What did you learn in English?"

"Um...the teacher is called Miss Williams."

"Oh very good. (A definitely ironical tone was creeping in now.) Is that *all* you learnt *all* day?"

"No. I'm 5 stone 10 or 10 stone 5, one or the other." Then, thinking desperately for an item of interest and little known information. "I learnt that Miss Hudd is a double first."

"A what?"

"A double first..." A slightly prolonged pause followed as Mam, no wiser about double firsts than I, digested this bit of knowledge. "But I don't exactly know what that is. Do you Mam?"

"No, not I — unless she won something twice in competitions for head teachers. Ask your father when he comes home, I expect he'll know. Anyway why didn't you ask in school?"

"I didn't like to. I thought it was cheeky to ask."

"No, it isn't. You must always ask when you don't understand something."

Thus ended my first day of eight years at Porth County Girls. And though Dad knew something about double firsts and explained them to us when he came home, I didn't really understand what they were for another decade.

CHAPTER SIX

Teachers

Miss Lauder

The teacher I remember best from my first year was a tall, thin, dark-haired lady with an outstretched Cyrano de Bergerac-type nose and a large busy mouth (with hard-working jaws) called Miss Lauder. She was Australian and like all people from that continent, friendly and unceremonious. I believe she was on a teacher exchange scheme. I particularly remember her because she seemed to be our teacher for just about everything. We had her first for Arithmetic, then were a bit disappointed when she turned up to teach us Geography, groaned when she put in an appearance for the History lesson and felt positively rebellious when she arrived to take us for Scripture. Occasionally she filled in for absent teachers too. It seemed to me the school was having good value for money out of Miss Lauder, working her to the bone, but if she left Form 1A's classroom with taut nerves she always entered it cheerfully.

By July of 1947, we all had a good mastery of 'Strine' and, forever after, when we read Irish, Scottish, French or West country characters in plays in English lessons, they all came out with Australian accents, it being the only foreign one we'd ever heard in any great quantity. At first, we giggled to hear her talk and with familiarity breeding contempt, imitated her, initially, behind her back or in asides, but eventually, to her face. She was conscious that we might not fully understand what she was rabbiting on about and encouraged us to question her about anything — encouragement she was to regret later, when in Scripture naughty little girls with innocent expressions wanted to know Biblical terms they pretended to be ignorant of such as circumcision, virgin, conception and copulation.

She told us a story to illustrate her point. A woman friend of hers went to a book-signing session with a famous English author at her local bookshop in Sydney. When her friend reached her turn with the author, "Emma Chissett" she said pointing to the book. "Right" said the author, signing the fly leaf "To Emma Chiz..., but how do you spell Chissett?" "Nah, nah" said the friend, "Emma Chissett, Emma Chissett." "Yes dear lady" was the reply "but I don't really know how to spell your surname. Is there a z in the middle or..." "Nah, nah. Moy naime is Janis Regan. What I'm saying is emma chissett, emma chissett...eow much do I 'ave ter paie?"

Eventually, the author extricated some sense out of Antipodean English and, after being told the signing was free, dear lady, but the book was three pounds, Janis Regan duly departed with her book signed to Emma Janis Regan, Best wishes, J.B. Priestley.

We were badly behaved in this easy-going Australian's lessons, coughing around the class, all putting up our hands simultaneously to ask red herring questions, indiscriminately shouting out answers, hiding the board duster and the chalk, and once, lifting out the black boards and concealing them under some desks at the back of the room. In her Geography lessons we deliberately traced Australia inside out and upside down and took it in turn to ask to leave the room. We were heartless, even cruel, towards Miss Lauder and only realised this when one day, to our horror and subsequent remorse, she put her head down on the teacher's desk and wept, deep sobs lifting her shoulders. Silence in the room was absolute and although the next day we collected to buy her flowers as a lame gesture of apology and were never as naughty again, she was clearly delighted when the summer arrived and it was time to return down under to marry her fiancé.

Miss Beard

Our form mistress, Miss Beard, was an altogether different proposition. A tall, fairly young, unsmiling Mancunian of plumpish proportions, she had a pretty face that was always slightly flushed, and a cleft chin. Miss Beard taught us French, rapidly, out of a book whose title, *Apprenons le français*, nobody understood and which she never thought to translate. It was about the Laborde family. They had a house with a floor, four walls, ceiling, staircase, lights and a fireplace. We knew this because they stood around saying so. "La table est sur le plancher — voici le plancher sous la table" and "Il y a une cheminée dans le mur du salon. Il y a quatre murs en tout". They were very fond of artichokes, ham sandwiches and rum cakes, had a son called Firmin who planted celery, and went to Trégastel, wherever that was, for their holidays every year. Apart from reading in the book, all the French Miss Beard spoke to us was "Bonjour mes enfants" at the beginning of the lesson, followed by "Asseyez-vous s'il vous plaît". Then, several times during the lesson she would say "Encore une fois" which we didn't understand either, so we'd say "encore une fois" back. Then she'd get angry and shout at us in English. We understood "Répétez" — any fool could understand that — and we were quite happy to say things after her, though usually we didn't know what it was we were repeating.

It was her pronunciation of some English words, however, which fascinated us. One morning all the girls from Ystrad Rhondda had failed to arrive in registration. It was too much of a coincidence that they were all ill. "Has the buzz come?" she enquired of one of the Joneses from Ynyshir, who looked around in total incomprehension. Buzz? What was this? Some French word or some new disease the Ystrad girls might be suffering from? The only buzz we knew had to do with wasps, bees and bluebottles. "The buzz must be late," she continued. "Did anyone see the Ystrad buzz this morning?" Enlightenment dawned. She was talking about the trauma transport. But what funny pronunciation! We were most amused by this and henceforth did our best to get Miss Beard to talk about buses:

"Please Miss Beard, I've lost my pass to go home. Can you

ask the class if anyone's found it please?" someone, (usually Barbara Jones) would ask her.

"Has anyone seen Barbara's buzz pazz?"

After much repressed class giggling, Barbara would find her pass on the floor under her desk, deliberately put there, hold it up, and, to more suppressed laughter, exaggeratedly imitate Miss Beard and say "I've found my buzz pazz mizz on the floor". Somehow or other, with her straight face and self control, Barbara would get away with it and we assumed Miss Beard was unaware she was being mocked. We found other words for her to say weirdly;

"Miss, there's yellow stuff in the cut on my hand..."

"That's puzz Anwen, leave it alone."

Perhaps the crowning moment was when she marched angrily into the form room one morning and announced; "All the girls who travel from Tonypandy step out here please. There was a fuzz on the buzz last evening and I intend to get to the bottom of it."

We all burst out laughing, so delightfully unexpected was the jewel. She left after our first year, probably to return to Manchester where girls had no puzz in their cuts and didn't make a fuzz on the buzz.

Miss Bird

Miss Bird, who taught Maths, was the antithesis of the previous ladies. She was also at the other end of the age-scale. Although she retired with much ceremony when I was in the fourth form, no suitable replacement was found for her, so at the start of Form Five she was still teaching there, having had no break since her retirement other than the summer holidays. She was a Bristolian who, despite decades in Wales, retained her West Country accent. Short legs, clad in beige lisle hose with wide calves narrowing into delicate ankles, bore a round body nearly as wide as it was long, and it wasn't very long. We could also discern salmon-coloured knickers, which came down to just above her knees, when she sat down carelessly. Her grey hair was swept back into a bun from a chubby, friendly face which had difficulty with severity. Several chins merged into her neck, a fine but perceptible grey moustache ambled across her upper lip and she always wore a hand knitted cardigan. Her progress around the school was slow, not so much because of age and girth but because she was laden with massive wooden mathematical instruments and other impedimenta. The instruments were a protractor, a set square, a 'T' square and a pair of compasses with a stub of chalk in one end. As she was a keen marker of exercise books, she took piles of these around with her. Whenever possible, three small girls were deputed to carry her accoutrements, one for the briefcase, one for the exercise books and one for the wooden instruments. This little retinue was a familiar sight, as it walked along in single file behind Miss Bird. For all the world she looked like a Queen Mother, especially if wearing her gown in cold weather, followed by her weighted-down attendants. These little girls, looking like miniature potentates bearing gifts, walked dutifully along behind her. If there was no-one of note about, they imitated the teacher's slow rolling walk, step for step, on flat-footed feet, giggled and poked out a tongue at passing pupils. They pulled faces at the teacher's back, faces which blossomed into cherubic smiles if another member of staff appeared.

There was always a long delay before the start of Maths by the time Miss Bird had returned to the staffroom from the previous lesson, press-ganged a set of small girls into service, collected another pile of exercise books, organised her tools and briefcase and set off for the classroom. Sometimes, when she'd entered, wished us good day, got us seated ("Good day girls, please sit"), dismissed the retinue and laid down her paraphernalia, she would discover she'd brought the wrong set of exercise books. Off she would go again in her rolling gait, not to be seen for another ten minutes. Once the door was closed, with someone on guard, the wooden mathematical equipment and sticks of chalk were eagerly seized upon. Most of the class would be on the platform in front of the blackboard, disputing possession to draw circles with pretty arcs and petal shapes inside using the compasses. Someone else would be playing hockey with the T-square and a crumpled ball of paper, the wicker waste paper basket being the goal. The protractor constantly proved an inept version of a boomerang but it seemed a vicious weapon when it accidentally came in contact with one's person. The set-square was once put over a girl's head and proved almost impossible to dislodge without first removing her ears. Others would be chasing around the room, over the desks and up and down the aisles. Sometimes, a teacher in the next room, alerted if not deafened by the din, would suddenly appear out of the blue to investigate and quell. If the look-out was not doing her job, we'd be caught in *flagrante delicto* and detained at Her Mistress' Leisure at recess or lunch time. By the time Miss Bird arrived back with the books, the class was in no mood for work and the poor soul had a devil of a job to get the lesson started. Occasionally she gave up and would announce "I shall read my paper until you are quiet. Pat Williams, get it from my briefcase please". Out would come the *Bristol Evening Post* and the chatter and naughtiness would sometimes continue right up to the bell, when there would be a joyful but restrained cheer because Maths was over. Once or twice, no doubt fatigued by the journeys around school, Miss Bird nodded off over the *Evening Post*. It fell on to her lap as her grip slackened, her glasses slipped down her nose and her head fell on to her bosom. Then, we were as quiet as mice, so as not to wake her and played OXO, Consequences or Hangman in our rough note-books.

Most days, the Maths lesson went ahead fairly normally once her attendants had departed, but whenever we were bored or had tired of Geometry, Algebra or Arithmetic, Miss Bird could always be led off at a tangent by asking her questions about Bristol. A dog might be heard barking in the distance. Immediately several hands would shoot up "Have you got a dog in your house in Bristol, Miss?" "Is there a zoo in Bristol, Miss?" "Where is it, Miss?" "Do you like zoos, Miss?" If she fell for one of these questions, and went on at length about the topic, there were plenty more queries with which to keep her supplied until the bell. You could often pack up fifteen minutes before the end of the lesson. She was a good old girl who devoted many years of Maths and Bristol to Porth County and provided the school with one of its memorable characters.

Few, if any of the young teachers were given to smiling, and they never cracked jokes with us as Miss Roderick had done in Hafod Junior School. In Porth County, eight lessons sometimes (apart from Miss Lauder) meant eight different teachers and some of them still didn't know who we were at the end of the school year. Perhaps it was the academic aura of the school, with the Honours boards on the corridor walls reminding us in gold letters of the achievements of past pupils from the beginning of the century on, that induced seriousness and the work ambience. Perhaps the young teachers were afraid that if they gave an inch we would take a mile (which we would). Rarely though were we little girls not immediately silenced by a sharp rap on the desk with a pen or piece of chalk, or a teacher drawing herself up to her full height on the front platform, swirling her gown around her, majestically towering and glowering above us. Some could reduce the class to shivering abject creatures merely by raising an eyebrow in an unflinching stare. Few needed to shout. In any case, the threat of detention after school or being put outside the classroom in full view of the Head's study, was enough deterrent not to continue misbehaviour. Recidivists were rare, once having rebelled and been punished for it.

No doubt young teachers had a career to shape, a reputation to build, they had girls to get through exams, there was no time for frivolity. The exam much talked about in awed tones was the Central Welsh Board, the CWB as it was called. Girls in Form 5 lost weight and colour at the approach of this dreaded CWB in the summer. It seemed the most fearsome and important of exams — as I heard some pale and mournful 5th former mutter "Never mind her double first, what I want to know is — did she pass her CWB?". By the time I was due for the dreaded test it had become "O" levels, probably no less difficult but much friendlier somehow, as passing the awesome Latin and Maths wasn't compulsory to get a certificate. Each subject was taken on its merits, so you received a certificate if you only managed a pass in cookery or Gujurati, for example.

Miss Pennington

When Miss Pennington (Penny, of course, behind her back) who taught us Science smiled (she was an older lady), she was transformed from an incredibly formidable woman into a person more reminiscent of an easy-going and benevolent maiden aunt, the sort who would wink at you when you were in disgrace and slip you a bar of Five Boys chocolate to cheer you up. She was tall, bespectacled and, of course, begowned. There was an air of the grand dowager about her and she was of a certain age, if not past it. There was an aura about her that told us there was to be no fooling around in her lessons. She was there to teach and we to learn. She did not need to put girls in detention or even threaten them with it. Like Miss Hudd, a thirty second held glance through her rimless specs quelled any girl contemplating minor rebellion. She needed resort to nothing further than to make girls stand on the seat of their desk for the slight infraction of the rules which occasionally occurred in her classes, such as whispering to a friend, passing a note, or even borrowing a pencil from Hope Higgs across the aisle. Girls loathed having to stand on their seats for several reasons. You felt so silly way above the rest of the class and everyone could see up your gymslip to your navy school knickers or, worse, unofficial coloured ones which some secretly wore if they had a note excusing them from Gym because of a bad cold or earache. Then again, you were in full view of anyone passing along the coridor who happened to look through the high, but not high enough, window. It was no use sagging your knees, you still stood out like a sore thumb. If Miss Hudd passed by, you were in even deeper trouble. So you stood there like a fool, attempting to look nonchalant, while trying to write or draw buds or birds' innards and things in your hand-held exercise book. At the same time you were praying that Bessie was committed to her study for that hour, busy with someone's mother, the Director of Education, the timetable, the cabbage bill, new pupils from the Outer Hebrides — anything to keep her off the corridor. The desk and seat were all in one wooden frame, the seat folding upwards to give facility of access and egress. Thus you had to ensure you stood at the front of it, as the weight at the back caused it to flip up. You then flopped off on to the floor and were trapped (with scorched shins) in the confines of the structure, behind the seat. One miscreant in the Science lesson, and thus elevated to the heights, was Catherine Morgan, a girl rather on the plump side. She was perched on her seat, shifting and shuffling awkwardly from one leg to the other in embarrassment, casting anxious eyes corridorwards. One badly manoeuvred shuffle took her backwards and suddenly, crash, there was the seat upturned and Catherine sent abruptly to the floor, yelling and vainly trying to get at her shins. This exercise proved impossible, however, as she was stuck fast, her fat knees jammed against the vertical seat.

"Get out of there, you silly girl!" said Penny, brisk in her anxiety, to a now whimpering Catherine.

"I can't Miss, I'm stuck" she answered, pathetically.

By now, a few girls had congregated around Catherine, pulling her arms and trying to lift her out of her prison. All efforts proved futile, however, and the form captain, Margaret Howells, was despatched to find Mr. John, the caretaker. When he arrived on the scene with his tools, the study of spirogyra had been completely abandoned (the fronds already shrivelling up in the waste basket) and the class was more or less in chaos, centred around poor, sobbing Catherine. One of the Joneses was lying on the floor, removing Catherine's daps in hopes of promoting ease of exit; Hope, also on the floor, was applying spit on a hanky to a pair of scraped shins, and Verity Martin was feeding the captive biscuits to help her forget her afflictions. Penny was fluttering about, raising and alternately wringing her hands, saying "Oh dear me" and being of no use at all — if anything, she was a handicap and getting in the way. The caretaker dismantled the seat with his screwdriver to eventually release the unfortunate pupil, who had many solicitous offers of accompaniment to the kitchen, where Miss Simon the Cookery mistress, also in charge of first aid, would undoubtedly administer iodine to the wounds and inflict further agony.

It was the most exciting Biology lesson I ever had. Thereafter, I never remember anyone having to balance on their seat and write in their exercise book at the same time.

Another memorable Biology lesson occurred when Penny

attempted to explain to us the mysteries of human procreation. Everybody, of course, had seen cats and dogs larking about in streets and back gardens, and pretty disgusting the performance looked too. One day at Tydraw, my unmarried uncles' farm over the mountain from us in Trehafod, the vet was due to call and the entrance yard was barricaded off — even from me. My uncles were never too keen to have my help with their agricultural tasks, but this day I was told to stay away. Positive rejection, indeed. Curiosity naturally doubled, I got on top of the hay in the Dutch barn overlooking the yard, lay down flat out of sight, and watched the shenanigans of a bull being made to climb repeatedly onto a cow. Mostly it slipped off. Occasionally, they waltzed around the yard, the cow mooing and with its eyes wild and bulging, clearly not enjoying being taught to dance. I found the whole business immensely boring and went off to find something interesting to do, such as riding my older cousin's ancient, tyreless, brakeless, rusty bike around the field.

This particular lesson, to our astonishment, no sooner had Penny entered the room than she was drawing the bare bottom half of a man, then a woman, on the board. Hope turned to look across at me with an incredulous expression, touching her head to show she thought the teacher had gone nuts. There were suppressed giggles and Barbara Jones asked if we were to copy these half-people into our exercise books, to which Penny answered "No!". She drew an arrow to the man's little pair of bags, labelling "testicles", then wrote "male member or penis" against the other pendulous part. "Vagina" was labelled against the woman, although you couldn't actually see anything, but of course, everybody knew what was there.

"Then," she informed us, pointing at the various bits with a long wooden ruler, "reproduction takes place when that (giving the male member a sharp tap) is fitted into that (ruler vaguely circling the woman's hips). The man's sperm (here she drew a tadpole on the board) unites with an egg and nine months later a baby is born".

That was all. Nobody liked to ask any of the questions whirling around in our heads. What about kissing and things? Did the male member get fitted into the lady's parts while they were asleep? That was rather unfortunate if the lady didn't want babies. Did they know this was happening? Did my mother and father only fit together once because they had only me? Yet they slept in one big bed, not two little ones? Did you have to take your pyjamas and nightie off? Of one thing we were certain, and that was that it happened in bed at night. The rest was all very puzzling.

A few years later, I had an opportunity to puzzle Miss Pennington. One summer's day, sprawled on the front lawn with some friends making daisy chains, I discovered that by pinching the green petal base you could push the stalk through to make it emerge from the yellow sunny part in the middle of the petals. Thus, the daisy looked as if it had grown facing downwards, head upside down, so to speak.

Penny and another teacher were taking a lunch-time stroll along the drive towards the front gates. On seeing her, Hope dared me to show her the inside-out daisy. Never one to shy away from a harmless dare, I approached the benevolently smiling lady;

"Look what I've found Miss Pennington — an upside down daisy. Have you seen one of these before?"

She looked at it with great interest.

"Gracious me! What a strange thing. No, I've never seen anything like this before. Where did you find it Mary?"

"Over there Miss, growing with the other daisies."

"Are there more like this?"

By now other friends had gathered around to listen, contribute and become embroiled in the joking deception.

"No, Miss, we looked, didn't we?" (Nods, agreements and exaggeratedly dumfounded looks from the others.) "That was the only one."

"A pity really you picked it."

"We had to Miss. It was in a big patch of daisies and we wouldn't have been able to find it again."

Finally, Miss Pennington departed with the daisy, looking quite excited and beaming even more widely than usual.

Penny wasn't my Biology teacher at that time, Hope and I had gone down a class for not working. We waited for a few days with mixed feelings, for a summons to be told off for fooling around and deceiving her or, with faint dread, to be praised on a new scientific discovery. We debated on whether to come clean, approach her remorsefully, heads bowed like the poor daisy and apologise for our prank. However, nothing more was heard of the rogue flower. Perhaps one of the other staff apprised her of the trick. Perhaps she knew already and went along with the joke, like a double agent, to turn the tables on us, which she certainly had, as we spent a few anxious days. Perhaps she'd returned to the spot and found it littered with practise upside down daisies. As the weeks went by, Miss Pennington continued to smile benevolently, perhaps pityingly, at us, and the incident passed into the annals of time.

Gym with Miss Jennett

The lesson I most looked forward to was Gym. The Gymnasium was also the School Hall used for assembly, plays, concerts and prize-givings. All the changing necessary for Gym was removal of gymslip and tie. We were already shod in black indoor shoes or 'daps' as they were called by less informed mortals outside Porth County, so Gymnastics were performed in this footwear, and the white blouse tucked into navy bloomers. There was no changing into nylon stretch leotard or nifty little silk shorts and T-shirt as there were none, or they hadn't then been invented. And we didn't have to shower after the lesson as, thank God, there were no showers either. There was enough fuss and anxiety trying to conceal the private areas of one's body when changing, without the added problem of washing them as well. Goodness knows what desperate excuses and panic would have prevailed if showering was compulsory as it is now. Bodies in those days might be heard but not seen. Much embarrassment was suffered by girls made to wear a liberty bodice (as well as a vest for warmth) by a concerned mother. The liberty bodice, with its thick, padded material oversewn with pieces of white tape and its white rubber buttons at the front, must have been the most unglamorous garment ever invented for the female sex, even more so than Miss Bird's peach, knee length knickers. Curious young eyes immediately spotted when a taller, larger girl started wearing a brassiere. Not only would her frontal shape be significantly altered, but these garments could be faintly discerned under the pellucid, white cotton material of the blouse.

Mature girls and liberty bodice wearers usually sought refuge to undress away from not overtly, but definitely prying, eyes, behind the piano in one corner of the Gymnasium.

The less physically developed and more intrepid characters rushed into the Gym, tore off their tie and gymslip — leaving them in a crumpled heap on the stage — and were ready in seconds, running off to hang upside down on the wallbars, to leap on the pommel horse, buck or box or just to chase each other round the hall like young puppies. When everyone was ready in blouse and knickers, Miss Jennett, herself wearing a short, square-necked navy tunic and white, short sleeved shirt, blew on her whistle and we formed four lines in order of height — the tallest girls on the left and the little mites on the right. I was third from the back in the second tallest line, so was in the top half of the form as regards feet and inches. Hope was shorter than me, just managing to squeeze into the third line at the front, but we were always partners in pushing and pulling exercises. As soon as the whistle blew, there had to be silence, otherwise there was running on the spot for five minutes with knees up to waist level, which became painful after five seconds and intolerable the next day! So, after a few lung bursting toots, words of displeasure and frowns from Miss Jennett, whom everyone respected, silence reigned.

I don't know what it is about P.E. teachers, but they always command and get absolute obedience and complete discipline. Perhaps pupils are in awe of their athletic appearance. Perhaps pupils fear they may be omitted from Games teams if they transgress. In my experience, this can only be the case for a small minority as the large majority, of girls anyway, hate Games and have no desire to be in any teams whatsoever. It may be because P.E. teachers, however dainty, develop powerful muscles through day-long exercise and powerful, resounding voices through having to make themselves heard outside in all weathers over large areas. Whatever it is, sporting staff are the most feared and respected in schools, and Miss Jennett was in that category. She would brook no nonsense. Young and unsmiling, aloof and handsome, she had a small head, proud but pretty face, thin, permed, mousey hair and muscular legs. She moved gracefully and athletically. Sometimes, when the home-time bell rang at four o'clock, Miss Jennett was to be seen alone in the Hall, dancing vigorously to music from a record player. Girls on their way home stopped to gape, open-mouthed through the glass doors, watching the unexpected and rather extraordinary free show. Miss Jennett would carry on leaping and cavorting, probably not unaware of the audience, but taking no notice of it at all. Then we would be moved on by the prefects who would take our places at the window but, as more discreet observers, peering round the glass door rather than staring unabashed straight through it.

At the beginning of the lesson we did various stretching, bending and rolling exercises which at first caused agony when stiffness set in on the following day. This was followed by rabbit leaps from one side of the Gym to the other, somersaults, handstands and cartwheels. Many were the head clashes, leg entanglements and splinters in hands and bottoms from the wooden parquet floor. The best part was when it was time to get out the apparatus for the latter part of the lesson. We rushed to pull out bristle mats, springboards, pommel horse and buck, and to release the heavy ropes and hanging bar. What unutterable joy it was (for me anyway) to run, jump on the springboard and soar high in the air over the box or pommel horse, doing various things as instructed with my arms and legs in the ether, before landing on the mat, expertly caught by Miss Jennett. Girls were despatched as catchers on the other apparatus, so you couldn't be quite so abandoned in your vault. As you ran up you could usually see looks of horror on the catchers' faces. Then they closed their eyes, wrinkling up their faces, arms outstretched as they backed off to catch, more in hope than certainty. They usually ended up on the mat in inelegant positions under the vaulter. No wonder the more timid, or the overweight jogged up to the springboard, paused to see if Miss Jennett was looking, climbed up on to the box, scrambled quickly along it and dropped safely off at the far end, needing no catcher. Some would push others in front of them, "Go on, in front of me, 'ave another go..." so that it was never their turn to vault, unless, of course, Miss Jennett was standing at the far end of the apparatus. At such times, if a vault wasn't performed willingly and with enthusiasm, it had to be taken again to much under breath muttering, tutting and eye-rolling.

Five minutes before the bell, a quick whistle blast, followed by the brief instruction "Apparatus away" and small girls would be running everywhere, busily hauling up ropes and the parallel bar, struggling with the heavy sections of box with much puffing, ouches and "Watch out will you? That's my foot/arm/fingers..."

Bristle mats were lugged across the block floor, the girls running as the mats slid faster, gathering momentum on the polished wood for the final energetic haul on to the mat pile. Task completed, girls ran to sit cross legged, backs upright on the floor, in their original lines. When all were sitting, a pointed finger at the winning line indicated they could go and dress; then the others in turn. Ties and gymslips were extricated from the amorphous clothes pile on the platform (or behind the piano for the coy) and there was a rush to dress and appear reasonably garbed for the following lesson or the critical eye of Miss Hudd, should she happen to be on the rampage.

Mostly, the exit was an orderly rush. Some girls were grateful Gym was over and done with for the day and there were not a few long-faced and unenthusiastic pupils waiting their form's turn for physical jerks, but I was hooked. As a result, I admired the unsmiling Miss Jennett and thought she was the most exciting female I'd ever come across, apart from the swimming film star Esther Williams. Had I ever met the latter in the flesh (in the bathing suit, so to speak) I would have been totally dumbstruck with awe and respect. Oddly, at eleven, I far preferred women to men and all my most favourite people were female. This didn't last long, however, especially when the singer Frankie Laine came on the scene. I also thought Van Johnson and Gene Kelly quite wonderful, especially the latter's mischievous smile.

If it was Games lesson day, we changed in the Hall and ran up to the tennis courts at the opposite end to the Boys School. We took footballs and coloured bands and were divided up into teams for netball when Miss Jennett arrived. Not all ran up, a fair number walked, some strolled and dallied, looking over the boundary wall into the lane to see what was going on there and, occasionally, one or two hid under the Geography room or in the bushes, where they consumed sweets.

The first girls on the court would always practise shooting into the net whether they played goal shooters or not. As more arrived, disputes and arguments ensued as to whose turn it was;

"Hey, gi'me the ball...I'm next!"

"No you're not 'Ope Iggs. I was 'ere before you."

"No you weren't, liar."

"I was see 'cos I brought the green bands up and they were 'ere before you."

So usually, one of the many Joneses would reluctantly be allowed to keep the ball and, tongue out, netball perched at the end of an outstretched arm, would aim for the net — provided nobody had first mischievously knocked the ball out of her hand or jostled her — and miss wildly. Several would chase after the ball and one would emerge from the mêlée, clasping the ball, away from the other would-be possessors. These would be shouting, arguing, pushing, pulling, rucking and mauling so that if it were not for the round ball, a passer-by would think it was a rugby game in progress.

Once Miss Jennett came in sight, order resumed and soon, banded and positioned, two games of netball would be under way, one on each court. A non-Games participator, someone who'd recently had an appendix operation, a broken arm, a suppurating ear, or a verucca, would be given a whistle and the unenviable job of refereeing one of the mobs. No matter that she was a little short on knowledge of the rules, the invalid's decision was law and we played in near silence. There were expletives, criticisms and insults muttered under the breath, but the referee was allowed to give a free throw to the other side if she heard any. So we obeyed her as if she were Miss God, for the time being, anyway. Goodness knows what would have happened had anyone used a swear word — expulsion probably. Form One didn't play hockey and during lunch break I enviously watched the older girls brandishing hockey sticks while chasing a white ball around the field. They appeared to have a licence for violence and many were the hacked shins and bruised ankles. The cleverest players, though, were never hurt, dancing nimbly out of the way of a flailing stick, more often than not taking the ball with them and making their opponent look a complete dolt. How I longed to be in Form Two to join that elite, hockey stick-wielding band, to run around dodging and tackling until I was red in the face, then saunter back down to school, stick casually carried over shoulder or under arm à la sixth form who made up most of the 1st XI.

At eleven, the future, as far as the sporting life was concerned, looked promising. Little did I realise that in the second form Gym and Games would be reduced to one each per week as this was when real work began. My indignation and disappointment were hitherto unsurpassed and I was then in the undignified position of envying Form One!

Miss Griffiths

A lesson I was not fond of was Needlework. This was a double lesson once a week, on a Thursday morning, and became known as 'Double Agony'. The teacher, a Miss Dorothy Griffiths, was very pale with blond hair, eyelashes and brows, light blue eyes and white skin with yellow freckles. We were all scared of her: her aggressive briskness, sudden outbursts and, when mildly provoked, her smiling sarcasm. The first large garment we had to make was a bleached calico pinny, the bottom of which was folded upwards to form a wide pocket on which our initials were embroidered. No doubt the pocket was designated to hold a needle-woman's implements — scissors, cottons, tape measure, packets of needles and pins — but in reality was used to hold sweets, chocolate, bubble gum, assorted cakes, crumbly biscuits and other goodies. We used rulers as often as needles in our sewing, as our tacking stitches had to be precisely three quarters of an inch in length with a quarter inch space between. If our sewing was not mathematically accurate it had to be undone and re-done for homework by the following week's double agony. The first item we made was a dinky little pins and needles holder with a flap pocket and embroidered with our initials. It is a comment on the quality of the materials used, not to mention the teaching, and especially, the workmanship employed, that I still use this handy little holder today, forty three years later, although sadly, the initials have departed.

My mother had trained as a seamstress with Gwilym Evans and Co., of Market Square, Pontypridd, so she was immediately recruited for sewing homework. Her three-quarter inch long tacking stitches were indistinguishable from mine except she managed to keep the cotton white while mine was grey. Later on when it came to hemming and running sewing, I constantly fell behind in class. The chief reason for this was Miss Griffiths didn't allow us to use knots to hold the cotton firmly at the start. Consequently, as I proceeded along the hem or seam, the cotton would come merrily along behind like a faithful pet, so as fast as I was sewing, it was undoing.

"Never mind", I thought, "Mam will do it before next week. She likes needlework." Which she did — on both counts. However examining "my" homework, Miss Griffiths decided that it was far too neat and clean to be my work and that it wasn't mine at all.

"Mary, did you do this yourself, or was it your mother or sister?"

"Yes, Miss Griffiths, I haven't got a sister."

"What do you mean, 'Yes'?"

"I did it myself Miss."

"Are you quite sure?"

I faltered under her pale-eyed, stern gaze through blond lashes. (I've always been a bit wary of people with blond eyelashes...). I bit my lip and lowered my eyes guiltily.

"This doesn't look like your work at all!"

Hypnotised by these unwinking eyes in their fair nest, my resolve wavered slightly.

"Well, I did most of it Miss!"

"Most, or some, Mary?"

"Well, some to most, Miss."

"Right, take it out as far as there and hem it again. I don't care if your mother only did one stitch. It's *your* homework and *you* must do it. I'm sure your mother has enough of her own work to do without doing yours as well!"

I didn't tell her she was creating more work for Mam.

So despite my dishonest protestations of honesty, I spent most of my lessons unpicking what Mam had done — and fell still further behind. Most weeks, Mam had double the home-work to do, the unpicked part she'd already sewn once and the new section to catch up with the class. Several times in that first year of Needlework, she said, in a puzzled tone, peering uncom-prehendingly through her glasses at a previously sewn then unpicked hem, "I'm sure I did this bit last week", but would carry on uncomplainingly, provided I threaded the needle as her eyesight was "going".

Fortunately, the previous week's homework wasn't examined so it didn't have to be unpicked a second time — only the most recent bit. With all the practice, I became a far better unpicker than a sewer, and it was a wonder to me that any garment was ever finished despite having been sewn up twice. Not that any we made were indispensable — the short calico pinny which was mainly pocket, a huge spare green shoe-bag large enough to contain a family's weekly wash and an enormous pair of green check gingham bloomers similar in shape to the ones we glim-psed on Miss Bird, which were clearly intended to match the school gingham summer dress, and which we were all terrified we might have to wear. These were inevitably too big for 99.9% of the class as the pattern for them was based on the tubbiest girl, Miss Griffiths not having time to work out a pattern for every individual's needs, so everyone's knickers fitted Ca-therine Morgan, and little Ceridwen Edith Mary Hicks-Thomas when trying on her completed pair, looked as though she was wrapped up in green gingham cinema screen curtains. Mine ended up as half a dozen dusters. My mother had a good laugh when I modelled them for her, offered to take them in to fit me but ended up by taking them apart instead. One normal girl could easily have fitted into one leg, they were so huge. Indeed, a certain enterprising young lady in the form removed the leg elastic, and wore the knickers as a culotte-skirt on her holidays.

One way to have a break from Double Agony was to snap a needle. It was considered far too dangerous to put the pieces in the waste-paper basket as some ususpecting girl poking around in the bin — perhaps to retrieve a confiscated, partially-de-voured packet of crisps or some discarded lines which could be of some future use — might have an accidental injection. As soon as a needle broke — and it took some strength and considerable expertise to do this — you took it in the palm of your hand to Miss Griffiths who sent you to put it in the fire in the range in Miss Simon's Cookery room. In Form One I was a dab hand at snapping needles, and at running and getting the furthest under the Geography room. The Geography room was a sort of pre-fab building which was raised up on brick stilts. It was pretty horrible under there, with heaps of damp, decaying leaves, dust, empty crisp packets, mouldy, half-eaten jam sandwiches and goodness knows what creepy crawlies. I wanted to be best at something, so endeavoured to succeed at scrambling along on my stomach.

Miss Griffiths would say to me incredulously "Another broken needle? If I didn't know better, I'd think you were breaking them deliberately, Mary. You'll have to buy a packet of needles or reimburse the school or something."

"Yes, Miss. I'm not Miss. I will Miss. It's just that sewing is not my best subject and I'm so awkward the needle snaps."

So she would wearily answer:

"All right then, run along to the kitchen with it and ask Miss Simon if you can put the pieces in her fire."

Once out of the room, I would race along the deserted corridor, because the quicker you were disposing of the useless bits of steel, the more time you had to hang around before getting back to class. It wasn't judicious to take more than five minutes, or there would be a minor inquisition which required quick thinking for satisfactory answers.

On the corridor walls were photographs of the casts of plays performed by the school pupils that one could peruse for a minute or two. The girls were dressed up mostly in Shakespearean costume, as gentlemen in tights and velvet puffed-out breeches, with richly embroidered jackets, sometimes with silly floppy caps hanging over their eyes and swords hanging at their sides. Some bore pencilled-in moustaches, and those with beards were barely recognisable as girls. However well they performed on stage, they all looked ridiculous, really embarrassed and ill at ease in the photographs, especially those, got up as ferocious villains, smiling out of pretty faces. If it was a cold day you could spend a few minutes hugging a radiator without being moved along or jostled off by other frozen bodies.

You could have a quick chew on a sweet without eagle eyes threatening detention, or have a chat with some poor miscreant put to stand outside the classroom for some, no doubt minor, infraction of the rules.

One morning, haring head down along the corridor with my snapped needle, I suddenly struck something soft in places, hard in most — and warm. As I was propelled backwards onto the parquet floor I heard an aggrieved howl of "Ooooh!" and to my chagrin, towering above me, giving me the gaze of doom down her nose, was Miss Hudd.

"Child!" she bellowed at my recumbent, horrified self, "what on earth do you think you're doing? You could have knocked me over. Get up this instant!"

An explanantion of my presence *hors de combat* or *au milieu du combat* depending from which angle you view the situation, was demanded. Unfortunately, the two bits of needle, proof of my errand, had been lost in the fray, probably disappeared down the gaps between the wood blocks, or in some little splintery interstice. I offered to look for them but was summarily commanded with a pointing finger on the end of a be-gowned arm, "Get back to class at once," whither I meekly skulked, "and be careful not to snap any more needles" was her Parthian shot. That episode did signal the end of snapped needles, unimpeded runs along the corridor, illicit chats to shamefaced wrongdoers outside classrooms and brief but comforting hugs of the radiator, for who in their right mind would risk a second encounter with Bessie?

The other thing I learned in Needlework was darning up holes in woollen garments. I became quite a good darner, finding the threading and weaving of little bits of wool rather entertaining, besides the pretty pattern which resulted. I can still happily darn for hours, but then I resent people wearing the mended sock, stretching the weave out of shape and thickening the wool with a sweaty foot.

After Miss Griffiths' 'Double Agony' you either ended up reasonably able to sew or vowing never to commit another needle to cloth in your life.

One quiet, sensitive, bespectacled girl in the form, Pamela Nicholls from Cymmer, Porth, was rendered such a bag of nerves one Thursday morning by Miss Griffiths hovering over her, that the bell had gone for the end of the first lesson before she had even managed to thread her needle, she was shaking so much. Whether Pam's glasses were slightly too large for her or whether they slid down her face, pink and perspiring when she was stressed, is uncertain, but she had a nervous habit of automatically pushing them back up her nose. The more bothered she was, the more she had to adjust them. She had been scolded about the previous week's unpicked sewing and what with Miss Griffith's disapproving, Teutonic gaze, pushing up her specs and jabbing thread at needle, Pamela didn't know what she was doing. Clearly confused by the two activities, she started poking the needle at the cotton, missed, and speared her finger instead. This happened several times and soon blood was spurting freely from the attacked digit down over her hand and on to the outsize knickers waiting to be made.

A fellow pupil, Marjorie Woosnam, concerned at the state Pamela was getting into, feeling sorry for a co-sufferer and wishing to see a little sanity in the lesson, piped up. "Excuse me, Miss Griffiths. Can I thread Pamela's needle for her?"

"No!" was the unequivocal and emphatic reply, "She must do it herself. How will she learn to sew if she can't thread a needle?" which was a sensible observation generally, if incongruous in the circumstances.

Pamela's desires to be a needlewoman, even if such had ever existed, were quenched after her experiences and she vowed never even to sew on a button of her own free will. Let the gap flap or the button be fixed with fuse wire pushed through the material. Those less nervous of us having aspirations in this direction took years to regain our confidence in the needle after Miss Griffiths' awesome ministrations.

Miss Simon

Nobody quite knew what to expect of the Cookery lessons which began in Form 2. It seemed to have little credence as a proper subject in an academically minded school such as ours. After all, it was something you picked up at home, mainly out of necessity to quell hunger pangs when your mother was out shopping or talking. A minority of twelve year olds might even show greater interest and be able to cook cakes or, indeed, meals. But on the whole, cooking was something that evolved naturally in you, unlike Geography or Biology for example. Everybody knew how to make a sandwich or toast or a boiled egg (in varying degrees of carbonisation in the former and liquidity in the latter) and if you were really desperate, there was always the fish shop, or a spare can of condensed milk lying around somewhere.

Cookery was sure to be fun as it was necessary to dress up for it. Mothers had been instructed to provide us with the white coat-type, belted overalls and a pattern had been distributed to make a cap — a kind of white cotton tiara. Despite the pattern, no two caps were alike. We donned our cookery clothes in our form room, as satchels and bags couldn't be taken into the kitchen because of germs. One or two pupils had sisters in the school and had inherited their cookery outfits, which looked reasonable on them. The rest of us had new garments, the majority of which were a size too large to avoid the expense of purchasing more next year, so again, as with the Burberry, most of us were legless, some footless and some appeared to move as though on wheels. The new coats were stiff, the belts were difficult to tie and they fitted where they touched. Ears came in handy to prop up the tiara and the lot of us resembled a flock of fat, whitewashed penguins, objects of mirth, as we shuffled from classroom to kitchen.

We arrived to be taught cooking with hope in our hearts, imagining some delicious chocolate sponge cake or chicken pie to be partially devoured at lunch time or afternoon break, before proudly carrying the remains home. But no such luck. There was to be no actual cooking for some weeks. Miss Simon hated germs, waged a one-woman war against them, and before anything else, the troops had to learn how to keep these evil, unseen creatures at bay. First, fingernails — pitiable objects where these monsters took refuge in their millions — were examined and most vilified, especially the bitten variety.

"Child!" she repeated individually to half the class, "you bite your nails! Don't you realise the vast number of germs you're putting into your mouth? Stop the atrocious habit immediately!"

"But Miss," objected Marjorie Woosnam reasonably, "I've got no nails for germs to get under."

"That's because they're all in your mouth, child. And don't talk nonsense!"

Dozens of nail brushes were produced and for a good quarter of an hour we were obliged to scrub and rub at the tops of our fingers until they were wrinkled and red and met Miss Simon's skyscraper standards of cleanliness. Then we discussed soap and how to wash and clean not only ourselves in the interstices, wherever they were, but also dishes, cutlery, (forks, especially between the prongs, harboured battalions of germs), pans and particularly their lids (another hiding place for the fiendish masses) and the wooden work tables where the cracks, knots and chips were breeding grounds for the unmentionables. Household soap needed special treatment, and toilet soap too, if we had any at home. By this time, we were feeling so inadequate in the cleanliness and purity stakes we were beginning to doubt we'd even seen any before. Soap was to be unwrapped then left on a shelf for a month to dry and harden so it would last twice as long. Clearly Cookery was also about things other than food.

In order to practise our scrubbing and develop the necessary expertise, Miss Simon allocated us in groups to several sinks around the room and produced a pile of gleaming steel pans. We had to pretend these were dirty and then we had to wash and scour them for dear life with steel wool and Vim until they shone like newly lacquered mirrors.

After this labour we were all literally boiling under our long, stiff overalls and irrelevant hats. Most had failed to remove their navy cardigans, not anticipating work more physically strenuous than in the Gym lesson. Sweat poured off shining, puce faces and girls didn't smell as sweetly as previously. However, we had the cleanest fingernails ever. Perhaps by building up this head of heat, Miss Simon was also preparing us for the likely, future torridity of the kitchen, should we ever actually get round to cooking anything in the ovens.

Miss Simon was a tall, dignified, bespectacled, grey-haired, serious, lady-like lady. Humour, like germs, seemed to have found no niche in her nature. All the teachers looked impeccably clean, of course, but Miss Simon looked pure with her pale skin, pale blue eyes and never a grey hair out of place. Her smile was a quick narrowing of the austere eyes and a carefully measured widening of the mouth. Perhaps I am doing her an injustice, as I only experienced one year's compulsory cookery tuition. I dropped the subject as soon as I could for something more interesting involving germs, like Chemistry or Geography. Others, who became competent cooks under her tutelage, may have discerned a playful streak in her character, but she never struck me as being devilish or even remotely mischievous for that matter. In fact, to my mind, she appeared straight-laced and too easily horrified by nonentities.

On fine days staff would occasionally take slow strolls along the drive bordering the lawn at the front of the school. Their approach would normally be heralded by a cessation of unlady-like activities — handstands against the wall, rolling in the grass, mock wrestling and jumping piggy-back on each other with Tarzanesque-like yells. Gymslips would be adjusted, grass hastily finger-combed out of hair, mud quickly removed from exposed flesh with a bit of spit on a hanky. Then girls would sit primly and chat civilly in groups, gaze piously at the trees and sky or produce a book to read (with an air of deep absorption). When the opposition was out of eye and earshot, larks would resume.

I had few enemies in school, being more of a mild onlooker at major arguments, rather than a vociferous participator. I never had much to say, and since running, jumping and netball were the only concerns of my life, I didn't have any opinions to get into quarrels about. There was one girl, however, with the unfortunate name of Myrtle Chick. She was in the form below me and despite her pretty face, nice hair, tidy shape and confident personality, was touchy about her name and easily irritated by it. This increased her inborn aggressiveness. You only had to glance at her for two seconds for her to say, "What are you staring at?", and a smart, if unoriginal, reply of "Nothing much", or worse "Something rotten", would provoke a poked-out tongue or punch or even a pinch, if one was within reach of this fiery female.

Staring absent-mindedly into space one day, thinking about Hope's new Slazenger hockey stick, of which she was terribly proud, bought at Roberts', Kingsway, Cardiff, and brought to school every day even when there was no Games lesson, my gaze must unseeingly have located Myrtle Chick.

"Who do you think you're looking at, Mary Davies?" she demanded, arms folded and surrounded by three or four servile cronies. My mind laboriously and unwillingly quit the games scene to grind into action for a clever reply.

"Certainly not you, Myrtle Chick. You're not worth the effort, so there!"

"Yes, you were, you were staring at me for some reason. Wasn't she?" The acolytes nodded.

"Oh, push off, you're barmy, you are, like your name," was my unconcerned reaction.

"Don't tell me to push off," she said, coming menacingly closer, fists clenched. My friends were by now taking an interest in the argument as she continued "And don't say things about my name. I'll punch you. D'you want a fight?"

I pooh-poohed this childish suggestion, raising my eyes heavenwards while my gang said things like "Aw, come on Mary, let's go somewhere else away from silly little kids who want to pick fights", and "You ought to be in the Boys' School *you* did Myrtle Chick or Chicken or Duck or whatever your silly name is. Boys have fights, not girls!" Someone even said laconically, "Duck! Goose more like. She's a silly goose!" but Myrtle's anger was still directed at me, the innocent perpetrator of the fuss.

"Huh, that Mary Davies thinks she's so clever, but she's scared to fight me, see. She's a coward!"

"Oh for goodness sake SHUT UP!" I yelled, heartily sick of the squabble.

Unfortunately, Miss Simon and Miss Griffiths were taking a stroll in the sun and the pupil-beware signals hadn't penetrated our consciousness because of the bitter argument — until then. There was a silence. I looked up and into the face, with its mouth open in horror, of the Cookery teacher. She beckoned slowly to me with a long, pink, immaculately manicured, germ-free finger.

"Was that you using uncouth language, Mary Davies?"

"Yes miss, because..." my spirited defence was cut short.

"Don't try to excuse yourself child. No young lady in this school should speak in that manner, telling another girl not to speak in that rough, common way. I'm surprised at you. I thought you were a different sort of girl altogether."

"Yes miss," I answered, completely shame-faced, as her ally, Miss Griffiths, looked on disapprovingly through white eyelashes and with pursed lips, also bordering on white.

"Don't let me hear any such language from you in future or I shall write to your mother."

"No miss," was my weak reply, as with very reproving looks they continued their glide along the drive. Myrtle Chick, behind their backs, gleefully poked out her tongue at me and sniggered with her followers, pointing maliciously. All I could do was muster a very glowering look back at her.

This incident was mutually non-endearing to both Miss Simon and myself, and this, added to my deficiency of culinary skill, meant I was not one of her favourites. Some time was spent in cooking that year, but not as much as scrubbing fingernails, utensils, ovens and wash-ups. One memory is of making pastry in the second of a double lesson after we'd spent most of the first washing our hands. We had to rub the flour, lard and margarine together holding them a foot above the mixing bowl to aerate the dough. The mixed-in air would help it to rise in the cooking. Also, it had to be mixed with the fingers, as if there were any traces of flour or fat in the palm of your hand you were a bad cook. We mixed for ages, (by which time a fair proportion was on the scrubbed wooden table or on the floor) until the mix resembled breadcrumbs. Disappointingly though, the pastry ended up as small, uninteresting jam tarts which didn't please me at all, not being a jam fan and being spoilt by my mother's weekly purchase of far more tempting lemon meringue pies and chocolate éclairs from Marks and Spencers. It must be admitted, Mam also made boring cakes of the bakestone and fruit variety, which pleased my father, travellers who came to the shop and other assorted adults, but at twelve or thirteen I preferred something more exotic. We must have made batter at some time in Form Two, because that came up in the terminal exam and my partner, Mari Davies, and I had no idea what went into the recipe. After a few blank looks around the class, a panicky discussion and an attempt at interpreting Marjorie Woosnam's silent and covert mouthing of something (probably the ingredients) at us, we tried to proceed logically and imagine batter. It went around fish and sometimes apples or bananas. It was brown and puffy and cooked in fat. Gingerly we assembled salt and pepper, margarine, lard, flour and water. Holding our hands high above the mixing bowl to please an unimpressible Miss Simon, we mixed the stuff together until we had a sort of runny putty. We gathered we were not exactly on the right track because Marjorie had chuckled at us and our efforts a few times and had hissed, "Melt some fat!" which we smartly did. We were about to put the putty in the fat in the oven when Miss Simon, looking uncomfortably dismayed, materialised. "What on earth is that?" she squeaked. "Our batter, miss," Mari and I chorused. She appeared as if she were about to faint. "Where's the milk?" she asked weakly, holding on to the table for support. Her problem, we assumed, was the heat, not angst at our incompetence. I charitably ran to the fridge to get a nice glass of cold milk, which I held out to her. She looked at me dumbstruck. "Not for me child! I don't want to drink milk. It's supposed to be in your batter." Her grip on the table tightened so her knuckles shone like my mother's cream summer sandals. "Didn't you revise the recipes for the exam, either of you?" She enunciated every word clearly, mock patiently.

"I think I must have been away for batter, Miss," I replied, then more uncertainly, vaguely hoping for a bit of sympathy, "er...er...with pleurisy."

"Illness or not, you should have copied up, Mary. Absence is no excuse. And what about you, Mari? Haven't you got the recipe in your notebook?"

"Yes Miss, but I had to go out last night Miss, with my mother, Miss. You can ask her if you like. Her nephew's wife was rushed to hospital in Ystrad 'cos she's pregnant and they thought...."

"Oh all right, all right," she interposed. "But this will mean a very low mark for both of you, you realise that." She sighed, "Put it in the oven then. It'll be an example of how not to make batter. Oh I don't know...".

Her voice trailed off as she departed to torment other hapless girls or germs or whatever. Our batter turned out like a chunk of deflated leather football. Everybody gathered round our oven, grinning at our pathetic attempt at cooking and nudging each other in scornful glee. Miss Simon held the pie dish in one oven-gloved hand while she poked disdainfully at the shiny, grey, amorphous mass with a long handled knife, grimacing and leaning away from it as though it had been injected with a dose of bubonic plague. "Now then, gather round please. You couldn't imagine fish inside that could you?" She poked away at the greasy lump. "The fish simply wouldn't cook. Nor, for that matter, would fruit, which hardly needs any cooking. Batter must be well beaten and light for the hot fat to cook it quickly and for the heat to penetrate what is inside." She droned on and on and turned the demonstration into a lecture on copying up after absence, learning work for exams, not wasting costly ingredients and not panicking in the kitchen, which she said could lead to slipshod work, accidents and an invasion of germs, resulting in illness, disease and possibly death. We were all bored to death by this time anyway and were glad when our "batter" found its way into the bin and we could start washing up. Mari and I were given marks which would have required doctoring on our reports had they been for an important subject. As it was, all Mam did was tut and Dad remarked that it was a good job we had a competent cook in the house otherwise we'd all starve if left to my devices.

CHAPTER SEVEN

Home Life

School did not occupy all my time — only most. On arriving home at 4.30, if I was lucky, or 5 if I was unlucky and had had detention, the first thing I did was to change out of my uniform so my mother could prepare my clothes for the following day. Like all mothers, she took a far greater pride in my appearance than I did. No speck of dirt or hole where one shouldn't be had a chance with her. The offending garment would be banished to the workbox or laundry bin and replaced with satisfactory apparel. Shoes would be polished to a bright blackness so they gleamed like the curate's dark, brylcreemed hair. Occasionally there would be a grumble.

"Mary, what on earth have you been doing with your gymslip today?"

"Nothin'. Jes' wearin' it."

"There's jam or something sticky down the front, look."

"Oh, er. The jam in the roly poly in dinners was awful runny and someone pushed me an' a bit spilled."

"A bit! A plateful more like. They should be more careful." Whether it was the truth or not was irrelevant, as long as Mam had a feasible explanation. Then she'd sigh resignedly, dab away at the delinquent part or scrub it with a nail brush before carefully hanging it up. Mam was always at home as her job, apart from running the home and organising my father and me, was looking after the shop during the day. We lived behind the "corner shop" as it was known, or "Philly's", having been established by my maternal grandmother, whose family originated from Caerphilly. It was a general stores with an emphasis on sweets. My father worked as a carpenter for B.O.A.C. on the Treforest Trading Estate and he took over shop duty after arriving home from work. Mam was always avid for chat and news and as soon as I got home would start with her questions. "What did you do today?" My usual answer was "Nothing really" so she'd change her approach and ask directly, "what lessons did you have today?" "Have you got any homework?" "What did you have for dinner?" "What did you do dinner time?" If my reluctant answers went something like, "English. Yes. Meat and potatoes. Nothing," she'd ask in desperation, "anybody say anything to you today?" I couldn't very well say "No" as that would be considered cheeky and I'd get told off and a bad mood would overwhelm her. She would occasionally sigh and say, "Oh, getting any information out of you is worse than getting blood out of a stone."

As a result, when I got off the Pontypridd bus at the Vaughans Arms, so as to please her thirst for knowledge and quench her flow of questions, I would start thinking of things to tell Mam, inventing most of it, as I walked up the hundred yards of Bryn Eirw Hill to our house on the corner of Bottom Street.

She had been a farmer's daughter before marriage so I tried to get an agricultural slant into my "news". So I'd say, "A flock of sheep from Troedyrhiw farm invaded the school pitch today and we had to round them up," or "The farmer's pigs ran down the lane next to the school and into the main road squealing like anything," or "The cows from the farm got loose and we could see them from school wandering all over Troedyrhiw mountain". To add authenticity, I would put in a few voluntary extras such as "Ten out of ten for English analysis today" (some hope) or "Stodge for afters and damp cabbage for dinners today". I didn't really wish to spread a false reputation for incompetence with livestock for the Troedyrhiw farmer, but had to resort to desperate measures for a peaceful life. I just hoped my farming uncles didn't know him and go and sympathise with him at markets about his errant animals.

It wasn't that I was trying to hide anything much from Mam apart from a certain stupidity in Algebra, it was just that anything interesting or of note rarely occurred, and if it did, I forgot anyway. My brain had enough to do with school subjects, the daily wrangle of life and thinking up agricultural stories to appease my mother's curiosity, without being able to remember unimportant details that parents found so fascinating.

There was the time, for example, when the King died and we were summoned to sit in the Hall to listen to death music and Raymond Glendenning relating the boring events going on outside Buckingham Palace such as the hushed crowds, the weeping people and the arrival of foreign potentates. However, when I arrived home, delighted I had a piece of news to tell Mam, she knew already.

My father received similar treatment on his arrival home, but after occasionally exchanging a wink with me, would do his duty, satisfy Mam's thirst for the facts of the day, then escape to the shop with the *Western Mail*.

Everything stopped at 7:45 for a cup of tea and *The Archers*—the everyday story of country folk. No-one was allowed to speak then without receiving a terse "Sshh" or an irritable frown. Mam listened with a beatific smile on her face, transported as she was to her spiritual home on the land. If someone happened to knock on the counter or shout "Shop", Mam and Dad would both make as if to get up to go and serve the customer. Frozen in indecision, not wanting to miss the vital happenings of the serial, but each wishing to spare the other, it was I who usually ended up going to the shop to attend to the person, while they both thankfully settled back into their chairs. I didn't mind as you could miss *The Archers* for weeks; you only had to listen to one episode to pick up the thread of the story.

It was the same during meals. At a knock, both would half rise and they'd say, "No, I'll go Sal," "No, no, you sit down and finish your dinner Jack," then, still partially on her feet, Mam would ask, "Will you go Mary? Save your father. He's been working all day." More often than not, in the process of serving, I'd have to open the connecting door from shop to living room to yell, "How much are the Doan's Backache Pills?" or "'Ave we got any inch bandages?" "I can't reach the Lossin Dant. They're on the top shelf. You'll have to come." "D'you want to buy any raffle tickets for the Old Age?" Now and then, individuals turned the tables and wanted to sell things to us. Sometimes, it would be a peripatetic fruiterer. "Tell your mother I've got some nice parsnips on today — 4d a pound," or a neighbour, "Is your father there Mary?"

"Yes but he's having his dinner."

"Oh, I won't disturb him then, but tell him old Mr. Morris has died. Funeral next Wednesday, rising at one."

My father went to lots of funerals and when I asked him why, he said,"Well, I go because I've got a black suit. Not many people got a black suit see, love. And they've been good customers." Considering the sombreness of the business, he always returned from these funerals happy and sometimes a little unsteady on his feet. I could only infer that people quite enjoyed themselves at them and that they weren't as morbid and solemn as they seemed.

Very occasionally, if Mam had been exceptionally busy in the shop in the late afternoon, had had a talkative traveller to deal with, and this meant giving him tea and a Welsh cake once the commercial business was concluded, or if she had had a crisis on her hands, such as the water being cut off or the chimney sweep getting his brushes stuck, instead of presenting Dad with a home-made dinner in the evening, we would have fish and chips from Eileen's.

Eileen's fish shop was situated at the bottom of Bryn Eirw hill. It was right by the Porth bus stop and opposite the bus stop for Ponty, outside the Vaughans Arms pub. When you consider the colliery entrance was a hundred yards up the road towards Porth, you can understand that the Thomas's fish shop did a lot of trade. Added to this, the inhabitants of the Tump were keen on fish and chips, so there was always a queue winding back from the high counter around the walls of the converted front room. The queue sometimes spilled out the front door and onto the pavement.

The shop was owned by old Mrs. Thomas, and mainly run by her daughters Maisie and the glamorous Eileen, who was usually in attendance, hence its name. They all lived in the house adjoining. When waiting for the bus or examining the posters on their end wall advertising the films in the Central and Empire cinemas in Porth, with just a sideways glance you could see in their back yard buckets and buckets of creamy potatoes in water. Sometimes in warm weather the matriarch would be sitting outside peeling them or just dozing in the sunshine.

Altogether, there were three fish shops in Trehafod. The one at the lower side of the Rhondda river bridge was kept by a sad faced lady with dyed blonde locks of which, in the likely interests of hygiene, every hair was kept trapped in a black hairnet. She was always full of complaints and moans, mainly about the adjacent river, and was called Mrs. Williams. She made nice, pale chips but wasn't as generous in her portions (nor in her proportions) as Eileen, whose chips were healthily tanned. The other fish shop was at the bottom end of Trehafod, below the Trehafod hotel, and was called, rather obviously, "Chippos". Mr."Chippo" also owned a general store in a room in front of his fish shop, so you walked (or rather queued) through one to get to the other.

There was another shop next to the Bridge fish shop run by an old lady called Greasy Mary. Despite her name, she had nothing to do with chips. Her real name was Grace Mary, a misnomer if ever there was one, as there was little hint of grace about her. Short of temper, matching her stature, yellow-haired, and always clad in the same clothes, or so it seemed — a dark all-encompassing pinny over a greying blouse — it was surprising she had any customers at all with her aggressive manner. Her attitude was quite unequivocal. When you entered her dark, dingy, unwholesome-smelling shop, where everything was jumbled together — cabbages, cakes, paraffin, milk, lollipops — it was she doing the customer the favour of serving. I was very wary of her. She always seemed to be telling the customers off in her abrupt manner: "Yes, next, what do you want?"

"Well, I wanted a pound of carrots, but those look old and wrinkled."

"Well, if they don't suit you, you'd better get them somewhere else and stop wasting my time," she'd say, making the purchaser look decidedly rebuffed and at a loss for a reply. Boys dropped things — books, balls, toy vehicles — down through a grating above a cellar in front of her shop. They'd persuade her to retrieve these objects, and while she was off grumbling and scolding to fetch the errant item, they would steal sweets from the murky glass case on one counter. My Mother, the epitome of tact and charm in certain situations, seemed to get on well with her. I think she felt sorry for her, knew what a hard time she had shopkeeping and treated her like a lady. Perhaps Greasy Mary, recognising a fellow tradeswoman, tempered her tone with Mam and was always pleasant and obliging. Not that Mam called there much, only when she had to go down to the Trehafod Hotel once a year to pay the ground rent or get a postal order from the Trehafod Post Office to settle some commercial bill or other. I always felt safer in Greasy Mary's when my mother was with me, but I couldn't help noticing her grateful intake of fresh air after leaving the shop. Occasionally, wrinkling her nose, she might say "Oh, nice to be out in the open again" or understating "Bit stuffy in there, Mary" to which I'd reply "Smelly, more like."

Trehafod people were always faithful to their local fish shop and many were the arguments as to the relative tastiness and quality of chip, and to the crispness of batter enrobing the fish, produced by the three friers. If their neighbourhood fish shop was for some reason shut, then people would go incognito, turning up their collar, pulling their hat well down on to their forehead, and take their trade, rather than do without their chips, to a rival. Customers in the rival shop queue would peer at the intruder, who by attempting anonymity, only succeeded in drawing attention to himself, would widen their eyes in recognition, smile falsely, nod knowingly, then say, loudly, "What you doing down 'ere then, Joey Jinks? You don' norm'ly come 'ere for your chips. Eileen's shut tonight then is she? Glad to come down 'ere when you can't 'ave chips nowhere else, 'in you? Never mind love, you'll 'ave better chips 'ere than up the Tump. Chippo do use cleaner fat see, don' you Chippo?" Meanwhile Joey or whoever would shrink further down in his coat and stare glumly at the floor, the object of scorn of the whole shopful of customers, many nodding in agreement.

Secretly, I rather preferred complaining Mrs. Williams' pale, dry chips on the Bridge, even if you did get a small portion, but would never have dared voice my preference and be branded a Tump traitor. Besides, I liked going down Eileen's, despite the queue. She was always happy, joking and cheerful as well as glamorous, with her mop of fair, curly hair, dark eyes and long eyelashes, not to mention her ample body, no doubt filled out with chips, usually clothed in a dress with a low neckline, probably to attract male custom as well as counteract the heat. Humming, she would toss a bucketful of raw chipped potatoes into the pan of foaming fat, then briefly step back while they spat and hissed, before the fat calmed down to a gentle sizzle. The range bore a small plaque announcing it was made by Thomas of Cardiff and I wondered if, indeed, these Trehafod Thomases were carrying on a tradition of family work in the chip trade. "Won't be long love. Jes' chips is it you want?" "No, two fish and a pattie an' chips." "Right, three threes is it, two fish and one pattie. Two shillings, please."

People could argue the merits of the Trehafod chip as much as they liked. As far as I was concerned no other purveyor of fried food could touch Eileen's for patties, nor as far as I knew did anyone else make these tasty concoctions. Eileen's did a huge trade in patties — corned beef between two sliced slabs of potato fried in batter, and they were only a penny. I didn't like fish — that was food that was 'good for you', like plain bread and butter or cabbage — so I couldn't debate the relative merits of cod, plaice and hake or the relative expertise of the Trehafod fish friers at cooking it.

When the chips were satisfactorily fried (or not so fried, if there was a big crowd waiting), Eileen, Maisie or their mother, old Mrs. Thomas, who was short, stout and calm and possessed a wry attitude to life, would bang the handle of the outsize chip basket on the range, shaking off the fat, then, with a casual, accurate movement, throw the chips into the hot compartment. The queue would start to shuffle forward expectantly. If the answer was "Yes, please" to the question, "D'you want salt and vinegar on 'ere love?" generous showerings of salt from a tall, battered, tin dispenser descended enthusiastically on the chips and frequently on the purchaser, followed by a fair sprinkling of watered-down vinegar. Then the lot would be wrapped in last night's "Echo" to be whipped away and hurried home.

Children often went in to ask, " 'Ave you gorr any scrumps Eileen?" — beads and balls of batter detached in the frying process. The polite ones would ask for a penn'orth of scrumps but Eileen usually gave them out for nothing. For children she liked especially she would add, with a wink, a small shovelful of scrumps to the order without being asked. These were often devoured before the rest of the meal, inexpertly re-wrapped and going cold, arrived home.

CHAPTER EIGHT

Local Friends

Our shop was regularly a kind of confessional — with my mother as the confessor. Three or four ladies on the Tump, who were friends of each other, would be in the habit of making their purchases at a certain mutual time of day. Often, they didn't really want anything, just a chat or to gossip. However, you could hardly go to a shop and not buy anything, so to Mam's "Now Maggie May, what can I get for you?" Maggie May, suddenly removed from the reverie of summer holidays in Happy Valley, Porthcawl, or the fascination of who was drunk and singing in the street last night, or who was expecting, carrying on or separating, would stare, blink, then, back in the present, say "Oh, now then, lemmee see. I've forgot what I come for gul. Better give me a tin of Vaseline, Mrs. Davies. I'll 'ave to put some on our Tommy's bad knee."

If a lady, not a member of a certain clique, arrived in the middle of a gossip, the women already there would clam up in mid-sentence, change expression in a split second and, former topic abandoned, smile blandly at the newcomer. "Oh, 'ullo Lizzie-Jane 'aven' seen you for a long time. Been bad 'ave you?"

"Yes gul. I been under the doctor for the las' fortnight. Bad leg up by 'ere. 'S not so bad now, but las' week I couldn't put one leg in front of the other, no." Then the gossip would subside into general niceties until the intruder departed, whereupon it would re-start as though there had been no break. "Connie, what were you saying jes' now about Blod, second street's daughter carryin' on with tha' man from down Cadwgan or somewhere?"

Sometimes, if the interloper stayed to chat after making her purchase, the clique members would realise she had come for the duration and, one by one, disappointed their gossip session was prematurely ended, give an excuse to go. "Well, better go and make Willie John some tea or he'll be givin' me the sack."

"Oooh, there's the three o'clock 'ooter goin'. Dan'll be 'ome in a minute wantin' some 'ot water for 'is bath."

"I must go too. I'm expecting the insurance man 'bout now."

Mam enjoyed being the confidante of people on the Tump and, although she would tell my father, who didn't care one way or another, all the gossip, she couldn't have been indiscreet because Tump inhabitants kept coming to the shop for chats and gossip for decades.

If it was too cold in the shop the cabale would assemble in the back kitchen where Mam would make a pot of tea. But the gossipers would only be given Marie biscuits, the Welsh cakes, or mince pies at Christmas being kept for the travellers.

In the first years of being at Porth County, I would always try to get my homework finished before our dinner at six, when my father came home from work. Then, during the summer, I could go out to play with my always available, but not preferred friend, Jennie Hiscox from Top street. I didn't call for her or seek her out if other friends such as Enid Morgan or Joyce Bevan, who were Sec. Sardines were on hand. Jennie was a Sec. Mod. Toad at Llwyncelyn school and her conversation about interesting things was a bit limited. They didn't have detention, uniforms, hockey, French or school scarves at the Sec. Mod. It was more an extension of Hafod school really. I wouldn't have been surprised to hear that the lady teachers wore pinnies like in the Primary school. Jennie had nothing to say but only asked endless, boring questions. If I said something like, "My best friend in school Hope Higgs had detention today for not wearing her tie," her predictable response would be, "Wha's tha' then?" so I would tease her. "Well, it's a sort of long, silky ribbon you wear around your neck, see." After a minute or two it would dawn on her that I was being jocose, a slow look of enlightenment on her face would develop into a chuckle.

"I know tha' Mary. I'm no' tha' daft!" and she would chase me to stick a pin in me. She always seemed to have a pin somewhere on her person, stuck into the edge of her cardigan or in the bodice of her dress, and weak with laughter she'd chase until I let her catch me then, honour restored, dignity satisfied, she'd prick me gently on the hand or bare arm with her pin. "There, that's your July injection!" (or whatever month it was).

These pin incidents appeared to exhaust her vigour and certainly left her devoid of further originality, for after such an occasion she'd have to sit down and perhaps make a daisy chain or arrange small stones in a pattern.

For something to say, I might point proudly to a mark on my leg. "See tha' big, purple bruise? Had tha' playin' hockey today."

"Ow'd you play 'ockey?" she'd ask, so I'd briefly explain it to her and she'd brilliantly come up with another question like "Wha'd you play it for?" or one with an obvious answer like, "Where'd you play tha' then?" or even, now and then a more intellectual one such as, "Did you score any goals?" to which I suppose she couldn't have known the answer. In reply to such a question, I was always the top scorer, though I never went beyond ten. Anyway, if I'd said I hadn't scored any goals she'd only have asked, "Why?"

Thoughtfully, she once mused, "I wish we 'ad 'ockey and detention at our school."

"Don't be so daft," was my natural response, "you don't want detention, silly." Whereupon she got quite cross and stuck her pin harder than usual in me, insisting, "Yes I do, see!"

Jennie could be hard work with all her questions. Half the time, I suspected she didn't really want to know answers but just asked absent-mindedly, to say something and fill up a gap in the air waves. She was all right for roaming the mountain with though, for running through the ferns and having log races with on Coedcae pond. She could beat me hollow at hopscotch which was her favourite game and for which she kept a special round, flat stone in a secret place in a wall.

My near neighbour, David Thomas, was another playmate and I enjoyed his company most of the time because he was lively and behaved in a mad sort of way. He was a Sec. Mod. Toad too, but had the most eccentric and individual way with chat of anyone I'd ever known.

He had not managed to pass the ll+ scholarship exam the year after me, despite my trying to get him to recite the times tables with me, and what is more surprising, despite being loaded down with a lucky piece of coal, a rabbit's paw, the winning half of a chicken wishbone, a red plaster Cornish piskie and a black cat brooch on examination day. David always had a ball in his pocket and besides football and catching we had competitions throwing the ball across the gully on the mountain to each other. If my throw didn't reach the opposite bank, David would launch himself down the steep gulch, roll to the bottom, (getting grass stains all over his clothes) pick himself up and march happily through the bog of the gully floor to get the ball, usually with mud and water squelching up over his shoes. Then, standing in the stream, he'd throw the ball up to me as I peered down. If it rolled back down, he'd be off after it again, chuckling merrily at his incompetence.

David was an expert at crossing the gully via the redundant, rusty pipe. He would sit on it and move forward, mainly by leaning on his hands and easing himself across in a sitting position. Sometimes he would cackle, adopt a horrified look and, in slow motion, fall to one side of the pipe, hurtling the twelve or so feet down on to the hummocky grass of the bank, emitting a ferocious yell of "Geronimo!" that echoed around the ravine's sides. He was never hurt, never even crocked an ankle. "That boy's made of rubber," my father would say, and I believed him. He and his clothes, forever mud-stained and torn, were his mother's everlasting despair.

His major obsessions were making dens on the mountain and damming up streams. He would patiently hack away at the mountain with a broken-bladed penknife, cutting clods of earth, which we would then pile up across some unsuspecting bit of brook. David was always the engineer and I the labourer under instruction in such enterprises. According to him, girls didn't understand building dams. The great thing, once the water had collected profusely in a pool, was to collapse the dam in one push with a branch so the water would gush down the mountainside. Then David would jump up, run round in circles, and flapping his hand over his mouth, give vent to strange noises, ululating like a red Indian.

Our walks were normally aimed at the three mountain ponds,

of which Coedcae was the furthest, highest and largest, as David was attracted to water like a fly to jam. On those occasions when we weren't sidetracked by the other delights of the mountain, and actually arrived there, he was forever getting things out of the water, marching in to fetch his booty with scant regard for his own apparel, comfort or safety. Sometimes, espying a particularly interesting looking, partly submerged log or tied-up sack, he would wade forth, oblivious of the depth and end up in water to his waist.

"Oh, look," he'd say gleefully, using those ingenious expressions common to Sec Mod toads, "Do my little peepers see a sack? Some little doggy or moggy put out with the ashes, I bet." Seconds later, his omnipresent penknife would be sawing away at the sack as I withdrew to onlook from the far bank. I could hear him talking to himself, then, triumphantly, he'd hold up a stiff, spiky object, black, white, grey or ginger.

"Look, Mary, look! It's a stiff little Tibby." (Tibby was the name of the Thomas's cat.)

"Ugh! Throw it back in, David. It's 'orrible." Then he would pretend to be Frankenstein and walk a few paces in monster fashion with the drowned, rigid feline held aloft. "And merry mog's coming to get you. Waaah!" After three or four laps of the pond, he'd weary of chasing me with a cold, wet, dead animal, and hurl it into the ferns for some unsuspecting walker or courting couple to chance upon, wipe his hands on his jacket, stuff them into his trouser pockets and, whistling, march after me up to Coedcae, or across the incline, if we were on our way back.

One time, David suggested we have a picnic of fish and crisps. I was to supply the crisps courtesy of our shop and he would attend to the fish. To my clear lack of faith in his part of the project, discernible by my wrinkled nose, he patted his pocket, "Fried fish as well! I've got matches in 'ere."

I was despatched to collect armfuls of dead ferns on the bank of Coedcae pond while David laid half a dozen old, rusty cans and empty jam pots in the water. He built a neat fire in a stone circle using twigs from the ferns. Several minnows and dozens of reckless tadpoles foolishly swam into the tins and pots. The lot were put on a flat stone in the smoky flames to sizzle. The tadpoles melted and ran away but the tiddlers cooked and curled up like their larger relatives do in a frying pan. David generously offered me some but I hastily declined and watched while he placed one, complete with head and tail, carefully between two crisps and ate it up, rubbing his stomach with a circular motion while rolling his eyes in mock ecstasy. "Great mun. I love fried fish, aye." He disposed of the rest in crisp sandwiches, "And it's good for you. Makes your ears grow and stops you getting 'oles in your socks." I partook of the odd, damp crisp and watched him, unconvinced.

He was adept at crawling up the overflow pipe in the culvert across the road from our pine end. He would squirm up it until he was out of sight and here he would hide from his mother after she'd seen the state of his clothes. "David! David! Come 'ere I tell you, you naughty boy. And get in that 'ouse. Oooh, I'll give you, I will, when I lay my hands on you mind, you flamer.....And don't wipe your nose on your sleeve!" she would add, as an afterthought. David would also hide from his grandmother in the overflow pipe when she was looking for someone to run her constant errands. "David! David!" she would quaver. "Oh, jawl where's that boy gone now? He was here a minute ago. Where's our David got to Mary? Never mind, will you jes' run quick up Terry's for me for a pound of potatoes, there's a good girl? I'll give you a nice cream cracker when you come back."

David was basically a kind-hearted soul, but he simply didn't want to be hanging round in shops when he could be devoting his time to nature — diverting the culvert water to flood lower down Bryn Eirw hill, climbing trees and finding birds' nests over in the allotments, constructing dams or abseiling ropeless down the side of the quarry (creating mini avalanches of rock and earth) and generally devastating the area.

Assorted creepy crawlies, especially snakes, were close to his heart, often in the literal sense, as where else would these creatures find warmth unless disposed at various points about his person? David could spot a grass snake or slow worm at a hundred paces and in no time it would be in his hand. He would stroke it gently. "Now then my beauty, you coming to live with Davy then up 'is nice warm sleeve? Come and have a look at 'is black, slidy eyes Mary," he would say to me as I retreated rather than advanced. I wasn't over fond of small creatures, particularly fast moving ones. I feared the thing might mistake me for David and want to explore up my sleeve, which would have occasioned a spontaneous display of Saint Vitus dancing. I was always wary of David in the snake season and didn't get too close to him. This fascination for reptiles clearly stayed with him into his adult life. When a young man in his twenties he spent a few years in Australia. On his return to Trehafod his tales were not about the wonderful Australian weather, the male-orientated way of life, the tanned, scantily-clad Sheilas on the beaches or even the famous indigenous creatures — the kangaroo, koala bear and platypus — but about snakes. "Cor. They got flyin' snakes in Australia, aye. They nest in trees see, and jump from one branch to another. I was walking down this road and this bloomin' 'uge snake came flyin' through the air. Only jes' missed my 'ead aye. 'Bout four foot long it was and thick as my arm," and then chuckling, evidently relishing the incident, "Bloomin' great mun!". I was only surprised that he hadn't gone after it and given it a warm home in his sleeve.

Sometimes, when he was having tea in his kitchen, hot with the coal fire, the current snake would slither out of his sleeve for a bit of air and wander round among the jam sandwiches. Screams were often heard issuing from the Thomas household followed by shouts of "Ugh, put that damn thing outside David!" or "Oh, get it away from me. I can't abear ol' snakes, no". Now and then David was to be seen making a rapid exit down the passage, arms protecting his head, as his mother belaboured him with the *Daily Herald,* a cushion or the toasting fork — whatever she could get her hands on first.

Smaller animals — grasshoppers, worms, beetles, spiders, caterpillars and other assorted insects — were housed in empty jars or matchboxes with holes perforated in the sides or lids. All the beasts had names, usually peculiar ones, such as Lancelot Poppadum, Sylvester Spider, Clumpy Bill and Horace Hopper. They got fed on food that David liked — orange peel, toasted crusts, condensed milk, sherbet and sop. This latter especially fascinated me, as we never had anything similar in our house, but David ate it by the bucketful, particularly for breakfast. When we were both in the Primary school, I would call for him in the morning. He would invariably be sitting at the table ladling spoonfuls of this stuff into his wide, eager mouth. "He's nearly ready," Mrs. Thomas would say hopefully, "Jes' finishin' 'is sop." Then, in a more admonishing tone "Come on David, 'urry up mun. Mary's waitin'. You'll be late mind!" David would shovel the remaining mushy bits that could be scooped into a spoon into his mouth, then follow that with the liquid remnants tipped in straight from the bowl. He would usually add something silly, to his mother's frowning disapproval. "Orright mun. Jes' moppin' up my poppin' sop and my soppin' pop."

My father knew all about sop. When I first became aware of the concoction, I reported back to my parents, "Mrs. Thomas is givin' David sop. What's sop, Mam?" Dad explained it was a mixture of bread and butter with warmed milk or tea, and sugar. People who were slow in the morning ate it because then they had their breakfast, toast, cereal and tea all in one go, mixed together in one bowl, so breakfast took less time.

David put several spoonfuls of condensed milk out of the tin on the table on his sop too, and sometimes a dollop of jam to add a bit of colour.

Some Monday evenings, Mrs. Thomas would take David and me to the pictures in Porth. The bus from the Vaughans Arms stopped opposite the Central cinema at the bottom of Hannah Street. We'd always sit downstairs in the 1/3 seats but it was 7½d half price for me and David. There was another cinema in Porth, the Empire, but we always went to the Central, regardless of what film was being shown. I don't remember seeing much else other than cowboy films — Gene Autry with his horse Trigger, the mysterious Durango Kid — or silly films with Laurel and Hardy, the Three Stooges, old Mother Riley, the Marx Brothers and Abbott and Costello. David roared so loudly with laughter at the comics' antics in these films he drowned out the words. Frequently, he was so overcome with mirth he'd fall off the seat and roll on the floor or in the aisle. People would look at him in amusement, but his mother would be embarrassed and annoyed at his immoderate merriment and give him a sharp kick, hissing, "Get up you dopey thing. It's not so funny as all that. People are looking at you mind!" If, on a rare occasion, we weren't watching a cowboy or comedy film, David would quickly get bored and want to go to the lavatory. Sometimes, he'd be wandering up and down the aisle to the toilet at the front all through the film, disturbing the people in the row, who'd start tutting and looking irritated. But David was quite impervious to this and to comments of "You want to tie a knot in it lad," or "Got bladder trouble 'ave you sonny?" Then, spotting a perambulatory usherette with a tray, "Mam I want a icecream," he'd announce in a loud whisper. Mrs. Thomas would grumble, "Oh, you're always in your wants you are," but she would fumble in her purse in the dark to find money to buy two ice-creams to save the bother of an argument in undertones that would just incur more angry glares and Ssssh's from the patrons surrounding us.

After the film, we'd wait for the Ponty bus at the stop outside Bertorelli's fish shop. Mrs. Thomas was always relieved when the vehicle appeared promptly or David would pipe up, "Mam, I want some chips. I'm 'ungry." Having no cinema crowd to restrain him, other than perhaps one or two mildly interested people in the bus queue, a bit of an argument would ensue. "No you're not."

"Yes I am. I'm starvin'."

"Well you'll 'ave to wait 'til we get 'ome now. We won't be long."

"Oh Mam, come on mun, Mam. I'm weak with 'unger honest now. Cun I Mam, cun I 'ave some chips?"

He'd always get his way and his mother would hand over the money with a terse "Oh you're a flamer you are!" On the bus home he'd happily gobble up his chips, usually in the front seat on the top deck, while Mrs. Thomas and I sat downstairs. By this time she was always looking fed up, but she was an easy-going, cheerful woman whose pique didn't last long, and I'd chat to her about nice things such as Christmas, the seaside and shopping. On one occasion, I asked if she would take us to the other cinema in Porth, the Empire, a hundred yards further up the road and no extra fare to pay on the bus, as the following week they were advertising a film with my favourite film star George Formby. "Oh no, we can't go there," was her reply, "we always go to the Central. If we went to the Empire, Dai (her husband) wouldn't know where we were and 'e wouldn't like that see."

Early in the Easter term of my second year, I fell ill, more or less for the first time in my life, apart from measles, chicken pox and whooping cough, which everybody got. It began with a cold which affected my chest, causing pain when I breathed, of necessity fairly often, despite practising the control of the pearl diver. Uncharacteristically, I went off my food, had no appetite at all, not even for Marks and Spencer's hot dogs or chocolate marshmallow cakes brought up to me in bed daintily on a tray, so Mam sent for Dr. Clarke.

Normally his presence alone was enough to cheer up a sick person — sparkling bright blue eyes over a not insignificant hooked nose and a "bell on every tooth" as my mother used to say. "Och, what's the matter wi'ye lass? Ye bin runnin' arround in the cold an' wet playin' yer games 'ave ye?" Despite having lived in the Rhondda for almost all his medical career, he spoke in broad Scots through the gap in his mouth not occupied by his ubiquitous Sherlock Holmes pipe.

"Yes doctor," I managed pathetically. Agreeing with him was less painful in its brevity than the alternative. Anyway, I didn't know how I'd caught this cold. It could have been from running round the street playing with my friends on a dark, cold night or I might have been sitting by the fire reading when a passing germ with nothing better to do took a fancy to me. Sitting on the edge of my bed, Dr. Clarke took his paraphernalia from his attache case, put his stethoscope around his neck and stuck the ends in his ears. "Och, let's have a look at yer wee chest then." He put a cold nozzle on my skin and listened for a few seconds. "Doesn't yer muther feed ye? Ye'r as bony as the rabbit 'a had fur ma dinna."

"Oh she's normally got a good appetite doctor, but she can't seem to put any flesh on. Gone off her food in the last coupla' days though, aven' you love?"

I wobbled my chin dismally in agreement and Dr. Clarke listened to my back, placing the cold nozzle in several spots and giving me goose pimples. After a bit more examining, looking down my throat and ascertaining where the pain was, he cheerfully announced, "Och, we'll have yer mended in no time and ye'll be back runnin' rround wi' yer mates. But ye've got ter rest and do as yer muther says and take yer med'cine like a guid wee lassie. I'll come back te see ye in a few days."

It turned out I had pleurisy. Mam said my lungs were sticking together and that was what caused the pain. Dr. Clarke wrote out a prescription for some foul brown medicine that tasted like sheep dip smelled, which Mrs. Thomas, who was forever going to Porth, fetched within the hour. A fire was lit in the little iron grate in my bedroom and, as the days passed and the chest pain subsided, I really began to appreciate the pampered life. I had several of W.E. Johns "Biggles" and "Worrals" books to read, a pile of "Eagle" comics, a jigsaw of rampaging elephants brought by David and an offer of his pet mouse Nibble to keep me company during the day, which I declined. My mother trotted upstairs with tempting food — thin toast and sandwiches with the crusts removed, small portions of dinners with creamy mashed potatoes instead of boiled, and without cabbage, and calves foot jelly, which I didn't like the sound of at all, but which wasn't bad, but not as tasty as strawberry. I wasn't allowed out of the warm room, not even to go to the lavatory, and had to use a commode in the bedroom, after which Mam would spray with a Flit gun, although there were no flies about. The room glowed cosily from the fire in the dark winter afternoons, as I read, drew or dozed. When I got bored, I had a little brass bell, "a present from Aberystwyth", to tinkle and if she were busy Mam would send up a customer who happened to be in the shop, for a chat. They were all friends, though mainly housewives and the aged — the young were at school — and I never knew who would arrive next. The current cat, Paddy, would eagerly follow Mam up when she brought food on a tray, but after begging for and disposing of titbits of meat, that useless article would mew to be let out. It was no company whatsoever and quite ungrateful for kind donations of tasty food, clearly preferring to be downstairs under my mother's feet cadging the least morsel, than to be sleeping peacefully in front of my fire.

Altogether, I missed a month of school. In the evenings, I had my work cut out copying up in the various subjects and, in class, I struggled along uncomprehendingly for some time. Eventually, everything came more or less together — at least to satisfy my fairly indifferent academic aspirations — except in Algebra which increasingly resembled the study of Hieroglyphics in ancient Greek — meaningless except, to judge from pictures, the latter were prettier. Miss Bird was patient, gave me the book of the best in Maths in the form, Elizabeth Voisey, to copy up from and offered to help me at lunch-time, but forgot to turn up. Dozing probably, or engrossed in the *Bristol Evening Post*.

My anxious mother required daily reports on my progress and viewings of my exercise books. Unless she was busy in the shop and I could make a quick getaway, she interrogated me mercilessly as soon as I set foot over the threshold. The upshot of it all was that she decided I must have extra-mural lessons in Algebra. I protested vociferously: "Oh Mam no. We 'ave Algebra three times a week as it is. I'll catch up, honest. In fact, I think I'm getting better at it already."

She rummaged for the book in my satchel and pointed accusingly at a recent page. "Well, look at these marks Mary. Two out of ten here, one out of ten there, nought out of ten on this page. That's hopeless!"

I pouted and took the book off her: "Look there's four and a half here, that's nearly up to half," I reasonably pointed out.

"It's not good enough, Mary. You'll get nowhere with marks like that. Nought out of ten means you had it all wrong," she argued with horrible, undeniable logic.

"Yes, but Mam," I protested, "Miss Bird don' give anybody good marks. She's a mean ol' marker."

"Don't be silly. If someone gets the work all right she's bound to give full marks. What about Hope? What is she like in Algebra?"

"Hopeless. I told you, nobody's much good. Miss Bird gives everybody low marks. She even takes marks off for a blot on your book."

"Well, when I looked at that girl's book you were copying up from, Elizabeth something..."

"Voisey," I interpolated, trying to be helpful and placatory and hoping for a change of subject, but no luck.

"Oh *ware teg* now, she had all good marks, eights and nines and some tens out of ten. If she can do it, so can you," Mam asseverated decisively, at which point I gloomily envisaged a few more hours of freedom down the drain. "There's nothing wrong with your brain and I don't mind paying someone to help you catch up. I'll ask Hilda Melen if she knows anybody. And you can take that look off your face, 'cos I've decided, so there."

Hilda Melen, mother of Jack and widow of Jack the police-man, was a long time friend of my mother's. She lived in Llwyncelyn and was a health visitor. This, and the fact that she was very communicative ("nosy" some said) and talked to all and sundry as she vigorously marched everywhere on her rounds, meant she knew everyone in south Rhondda — their business anyway. It took her two seconds flat to think of a prospective tutor. "Mr. Fudge," she said, "Reg Fudge, Nythbran. I'll ask him for you. Yes...he'd be the one. Painter and decorator he is really, but he's very clever. Musical as well. Rides a push-bike."

I wasn't too keen on the sound of him at all. What was a painter and decorator doing being good at Maths? No doubt riding a bike recommended him to Mrs. Melen, who was a fanatic about exercise. And would he be coming to my house or would I have to trudge across to Llwyncelyn? Visions of warily taking the short-cut through the colliery and across their bridge over the river came to mind, and being shouted at, then possibly chased by the watchman. The thought was wearying. That was an adventure when I was eight or nine but now, at thirteen, I had outgrown such childish behaviour. Well I certainly wasn't going the long way to Nythbran Terrace, down Trehafod and up the road past the waterfall. Apart from these considerations, the thought of yet more Algebra lessons caused my stomach to contract into tight knots of rope. Now if it had been extra Games coaching....

One advantage was that the most convenient time for Mr. Fudge was a Sunday morning, so in the cause of my education Mam agreed for my religious upbringing to defer one service per Sabbath — matins — so I went twice instead of thrice to church during that time. And thus, through an illness in the natural order of things and a chance word to an acquaintance, began a life-long friendship with a family and their relatives and friends and acquaintances.

For my first Algebra lesson, I did take the long route past the waterfall, as it was a Sunday after all and I was feeling self-righteous, diffident and put-upon. My mood improved when I was warmly welcomed at the door of the terraced house by Mr. Fudge, a big man with a gentle manner, slow and old-fashioned of speech like my father, but who constantly made jokes and said funny things without laughing. Half the time, until I was better acquainted with him, I didn't know whether he was joking or not, then I would denote a certain sparkle in his eyes or a slight rictus at his mouth. Mrs. Fudge, May, was also large, but with an open, extrovert manner. She talked and beamed most of the time and often laughed merrily. In fact, she seemed to me the rather up-market epitome of the eponymous heroine of *Mrs. Rees Laughs* the poem set for the *Cydadrodd* in the school eisteddfod.

Like all good Rhondda hostesses, she was keen for people to be fed, and every twenty minutes she would pop in with a cup of tea and chocolate biscuits or slices of cake. "It's only a bit of rough," she would say, "I just throw some flour, fat, currants and milk into a bowl and bake it." Her teisen lap, however rough, was twice as delicious, as it meant a break from wrangling with algebraic computations. When the lesson, sprinkled with a fair dash of chat about school, sport, music, food, radio and the world, lasted longer than the appointed hour, and it usually did, there were offers to have dinner with the family. "Only a bit of pork, spuds and two veg mind, but you're welcome to stay." If some Sundays, I arrived early and the hour became two or three as the months passed, (not all taken up with Algebra, I'm glad to say) I was often offered breakfast. "Oh, our Trevor's only just got up, lazy thing. Still it is Sunday I 'spose. Will you 'ave a bit of breakfast with 'im?" Mrs. Fudge was convinced that learning found its way to the brain via the stomach.

Despite the interpolation of extraneous, more interesting matter, initially, Algebra was the main topic on the agenda and Mr. Fudge strove to illuminate to my reluctant brain the attraction of x for y and the various complicated relationships of a, b and c. Why, I used to wonder, doesn't Algebra run the whole gamut of the alphabet? Let's for a change have 3s-4k-5f x 686i. But no, the chosen a b c x y held sway, whichever page of the text book you turned to. My mind often wandered off during Mr. Fudge's explanations in their front room. They had fascinating interior walls, decorated of course, by my Algebra coach, as that was his trade. Instead of the usual wallpaper, there were painted swirls, feathery shapes and impressionist images of clouds, trees, waves, giving a marble-type effect, all in delicate pastel shades of intermingled pale peach, watery sky blue, off-white grey and tender spring green. The colour combinations and designs varied from room to room but they were always tastefully done, never harsh and were restful to a sore eye. A few classical art reproductions in frames hung from a picture rail going around the room but I had seen these before and far preferred Reg's own murals. There was a quite fascinating opaque and transparent glass globe around the light bulb which attracted my weary brain. It had two gold painted bands circling its middle between which, the glass was frosted and raised in diamond shapes, the facets of which sparkled when the bulb was lit or when the sun caught them shining in through the window. It reminded me of a fat, jolly, pantomime fairy. Gazing upwards at the light fixture was acceptable, as this pose gave the impression of seriously considering the problem in hand, though I never was and never arrived at a solution on my own. But Reg Fudge never showed that he minded, was never impatient or cross at my total incompetence. He just worked out the sum himself then showed me how to do it. Then, I'd go through the mechanics using that particular formula, forgotten five minutes later. There were long periods of silence as Mr. Fudge, head bent over the text book, fathomed out some combination of figures and letters and I would study his face when he wasn't looking — the rather full nose with large pores and hairs protruding through the nostrils, kind eyes below strong, black mobile brows, gentle, if slightly indeterminate mouth, firm chin and short, tough, dark hair above a wide, shiny forehead. I glanced quickly away when he looked up, so as not to appear rude, but when he did catch me gazing at him he'd smile and, sighing, say something like, "Oh Mary fach, this one's got me beat for the moment. Time for a little break," or "I think it's high time we had a nice cuppa tea don't you? I'll just give May a shout....May....May...Oh love we've been working so hard in here, both of us, (that was an exaggeration) we're parched. How about a cuppa...?" His voice would tail off. Five minutes later Mrs., beaming and smiling, would bustle in with a loaded tray. I don't remember improving very much in Algebra. It was really equational practice for Mr. Fudge, but the visits to the family became increasingly pleasurable and continued for years long after I had anything to do with that particular trying branch of mathematics.

Mr. Fudge would accept no payment from my mother for these lessons. "Dear me no Mary! I enjoy them. Anyway it gives me a chance to use my brain, what little brain I have that is, after it's been addled by my work." Undoubtedly, Reg Fudge was mentally and intellectually under-employed in his job as a painter-decorator, but having left school at thirteen or fourteen, like many bright children of poor valley families, had received no professional training to help establish him in life. He was happy, however, had learnt to play the violin to a high standard of performance, and was physically super-fit from riding his bicycle daily to and from his work place in Cardiff. At one period, after his evening meal, he would set off again for Cardiff on his bike to night school classes, returning in the late evening. On such days he would have ridden a hundred miles. Being of an optimistic outlook he would not complain but consider the good all this exercise and fresh air was doing him.

When he discovered I played the piano, and no doubt realising his efforts were having only a minimal effect on my mathematical progress, the algebraic content of the lessons gradually decreased to be replaced by music. We finished the coaching hour earlier and earlier to play a few duets, me hesitantly on the piano and Mr. Fudge masterfully on the violin. I usually made such a mess of the sight reading and created such a cacophony, I didn't exactly enjoy these sessions either, but anything was preferable to Algebra.

The Fudges had two tall, handsome children — Trevor, also a County snob, a year older than me and fair-haired like his mother, and Mary, a Secondary sardine, two years younger and dark-haired like her father. I only glimpsed them at first. No doubt they had been instructed to stay away and keep quiet for the front room workers. There was a charming framed photograph standing on one of the fitted half cupboards in the recesses either side of the chimney. It depicted a pretty child in a romper suit with long blonde curls and an angelic face.

"That's a pretty little girl," I said to Mr Fudge when he came up for air after one of the silent mental wrangles with x or y, a,b or c. "Who's that then? Your daughter?"

"Oh Lord, no. That's our Trefor that is. But whatever you do don't mention that photo to him. He goes wild." He chuckled, "He had lovely fair curls when he was little and May wouldn't have his hair cut. When Trefor went out everybody thought he was a little girl." I could well understand why. "He probably doesn't realise it's in here. He used to keep kidnapping it and hiding it, then May would find it under an armchair or in some other out-of-the-way place and find another home for it. It's been all over the house, the scullery, the pantry, the outside lav, wouldn't have been surprised to find it put out for the ash man. Trefor hated it."

Mr. Fudge always pronounced his son's name the Welsh way, unlike his mother who called him "Trev" when she wanted a favour or fully "Trevor" in an anglicised version. The young man had no resemblance whatever to a girl now. Still blonde, his adolescent head of hair was cut in a short back and sides style with a wave or two on top. With his blue eyes and athletic frame, he looked like a taller version of Lew Hoad (with less chin). Like many other good-looking Porth County boys, he was the object of keen interest to an assortment of County girls, but at that epoch the interest wasn't reciprocated. "Our Trefor gets very ratty if you tease him about girls," his father would say. Indeed, his life was centred on sport. A track-suited Jack Melen would occasionally come to call for him and, to my astonishment, Trevor would announce they were going for a quick run over Llanwonno, miles and miles away atop a bleak mountain. "Be back in about an hour," he'd say and they'd run off together up the street in the drizzle, the wind, hail or sometimes sun. Trevor's other friend, John, was a strange, silent boy partial to wearing his mother's blouses or so they seemed to me. He would scowl, particularly at me, and visit, then not say anything to anybody.

Mary Fudge seemed a far less surprising person — but then she was a girl. She busied about drawing shapes in sketch books and colouring them in, sticking bits of fur, wool, leaf, cord, crinkly paper on a card to make a collage, read girls' magazines or "Famous Five" books, cut out shapes — pretty pictures and adverts — scattering them on the floor to be chided by her mother, potched about in the kitchen pouting when expected to do banal jobs like washing up and generally hung around as girls do. She was far chattier than her brother. "Do you like our Trevor?" she asked me one day.

"Yeh, he's orright," was my non-committal reply.

"No, I mean d'you like him, d'you fancy him?"

Having only recently become a teenager, mad about girls' sports such as hockey and netball and hitherto only fancying glamorous men such as film stars, Gene Kelly or George Formby, or safely unattainable ones like sports hero Gagsa in the Boys' school and the curate Mr Corbett, I had never lost my heart to any boy. I'd been kissed once by a fellow pupil in Hafod school and didn't rate the experience highly at all. In fact, I might as well have been kissed by the cemented side wall of our house, his lips were as rough. Besides, Trevor was very fair and at that time I had an aversion to blonde eyelashes, with the exception of Lew Hoad. My response didn't need much thought. Even if I did fancy him, I doubt whether I'd have broadcast the fact anyway, so "No" I said, fairly promptly. Mary looked disappointed. "Oh why not? Don't you think he's nice-looking?"

"Aye he's quite nice-looking. I just don't fancy any boys all that much."

"My friend loves him," Mary said in a proud, defensive kind of way.

"Oh yeah, does she go with him then?"

Mary sighed. "No. I told him she loved him an' he said she'd better not or he'd bash her."

I wasn't sure whether Mary was trying to set up a romance or a fight, but I was glad my sentiments had erred on the side of safety.

Relatives of the Fudges lived a few doors up the street and were such constant visitors I had difficulty at first knowing who belonged to which family and lived in which house. Front doors in those days were never locked, and usually on fine days left wide-open. Passers-by could see right along the passage and half way up the stairs, into the middle room if you craned your neck and walked slowly. These relations were the Reeses, their father George being May's brother. Betty, the eldest, in her early twenties, popped in so often I assumed she was a resident Fudge when I emerged brain-battered from my lesson. She was a fair haired beamer and smiler too, like her aunt. Her brother, Graham, was a hyper-active, handsome flirt, who never stopped talking, rarely stopped moving and worked in the Lewis Merthyr. His head would appear round the passage door. "Oh 'ullo. Anybody 'ome then?" then spotting me, probably sipping at a reviving cup of tea, "Got visitors 'ave you? Come for your lesson 'ave you love? Well I not stoppin'. In a bit of a rush this mornin', see. Uncle Reg is good mind, innee Auntie May?" Auntie May would be out in the kitchen making Sunday dinner among the boiling, hissing, spitting noises, and so unable to hear clearly. "Whass'at Gray?" She'd appear in the doorway and Graham would repeat, "I was jes sayin' Auntie May, Uncle Reg — he's good mind, innee?" Mrs. Fudge would laugh, "Oh yes Gray, very good, yeah. I *thought* you said something, see." Graham would look mock indignant.

"Well I did mun. I not talkin' to myself 'ere."

"No, I know you're not talking to yourself Graham."

"Sayin' Uncle Reg is clever to teach Mary I was." Then addressing me, "An' 'e 'aven' 'ad no trainin' nor nothin' in school work see, Mary."

Mrs. Fudge would pursue her earlier train of thought. "I had an idea you 'ad a message from your mother for me or somethin' see Gray." During the conversation Graham would be pacing to and from the little kitchen and the middle room.

"Oh yea, tha'ss right, I did. Since I was passing she as't me to drop in and tell you........Oh duw, what was it now she said?" He'd rack his brains for a full half second. "Oh damn it's gone. Couldn' 'ave been very important. Anyway, I not stoppin' cos I gorra be up Ynyshir by a' past. Promised to take this tool up for my mate. 'Is car's playin' up, see, and 'e's gonna fix it 'imself."

Mr. Fudge would appear after sorting his books in the front room. "Oh 'ullo Gray."

"'Ullo Uncle Reg."

"How are you this morning? Orright?"

"Oh we 'ad a good night las' night down the Non Pol, mun, but I'n feelin' a bit delicate this mornin'."

"'Ave a cuppa tea then, Gray. May's jes' made a nice fresh pot for us workers."

"No, I won' 'ave no tea now, Uncle Reg, thanks. I no' stoppin'.

Promised to be up my mate's 'ouse by a' past." He'd glance at his watch. "Oh Gawd, look at the time. Oh well, 'e'll 'ave to wait tha'ss all."

Mrs. Fudge might re-appear out of the steaming, saucepan-bubbling kitchen, wiping her hands on her pinny. "Graham, when you go home ask your mother if she wants some of my Parazone. She's got a white shirt gone pink in the wash she told me." Graham would tap his temple with the base of his hand.

"Oh tha'ss it. I remember now, the message. She said she wants tha' bleach stuff for Dad's shirt and our vests and pants. Mottled puce they've gone aye, 'orrible mun."

Graham, bleach bottle now in hand, would start making his way out. "I berra go then, I'll be a 'alf hour late as it is. S'pose I'd berra take this 'ome first. Ta-ra. See you later Uncle Reg. Ta-ra Mary." The younger sister, Marjorie, was a beauty. She was tall and slim with flame-coloured hair and big blue eyes in a readily smiling face. Slightly puffy cheeks gave her an approachable, humorous aura despite her queenly looks. Much sought after by young men, she had left school as soon as she was able, not being very academically inclined, and worked in a shop in Porth. Although she hadn't been a County snob, somehow or other she had seen, met and developed a crush, like scores of County girls, on the handsome, blonde athlete Marcus Morgan, despite his high colouring which (to my mind) made him look apoplectic and over-heated. I'd heard about him from Barbara Jones in my form, a one time girlfriend of his.

"D'you know Marcus Morgan?" Marjorie wanted to know.

"Oh yes, everybody knows Marcus Morgan. Blonde with a red face. That one?"

"Yes. Isn't he smashing? He hasn't got such a red face as all that."

"Been going out with a girl I know."

"Who's tha' then?"

"Barbara Jones from Pentre."

"Oh, lucky thing. I think he's lovely, see."

"I don't think he goes out with her now though. She said he's fast."

"Oh my gosh, no!"

"An' I don' think she means runnin' either." To tell the truth

I wasn't exactly sure what "fast" meant in a similar connotation but knew it was something girls had to watch out for.

Marjorie continued dreamily, "On Thursday afternoons when it's early closing, I go up to Cemetery road I do, and wait to see him coming out of school."

"You don't!"

"Yeah, I do honest. Pretend I'm waitin' for Trevor see. Well I did. I 'aven' been for two weeks now."

"Does he say anything to you?"

"Oh yeah, says 'ullo."

"Don' you go any more then?"

She giggled and blushed a little. "Well, see, one day he was coming out with Trevor and Trevor laughed and d'you know what 'e said to him? 'e said "Oh there's my cousin Marjorie again. She's mad about you, aye. Comes up 'ere just to see you she does." Well, I didn' know where to look, no. I could 'ave biffed Trevor on the spot. Oh, fair do's gul, I felt awful embarrassed. showin' me up like that. There's a fool i'n it? I went all hot. My face must have been a red as a tomato. I must've looked a sight with my ginger 'air an' all an' Trevor didn' 'elp. In fact 'e made it worse. 'E laughed and said, "Oh look at 'er blushin'. She's crackers on you Marcus."

"What did Marcus say?"

"Nothin'. 'E was blushin' as well."

"No, I don' 'spect he was blushin'. 'E's always got a red face."

"Well, he looked embarrassed too and was sort of smilin', you know. I just said, "Oh come on Trevor", and I gave him a row all the way down Cemetery road for showin' me up like that, then 'e bought me ice-cream in Gambarini's an' I was talkin' to 'im again." She tutted, "Oh I dunno. Boys!", then after some reflection, "I do fancy Marcus Morgan though, I do."

CHAPTER NINE

The Social Side of School

Wet lunchtimes in Porth County were always enjoyable. If anything, pupils preferred wet weather to fine, as when it rained we were allowed in the Hall. Not to run around, play with the Gym apparatus or swing on the wall bars, but to learn ballroom dancing steps. The Prefects were in charge: one of their number — a competent musician — played the piano. The older girls who were cognizant with the dance steps taught the younger ones. Pests were ejected. If your lunch was the second sitting and you managed to be one of the first into the Hall after morning school, you could have a bit of a bash on the piano. Half a dozen girls jostled for position at the keyboard to play their piece. The cacophony of mis-struck notes and arguing voices was painful to the ear. Hundreds of girls learned to play on that piano, using two stiff fingers, the only two tunes they could ever play, *Chopsticks* and *Bells*. However, once one or more of the mighty Prefects arrived, all became calm, ordered and organised. Sometimes an older girl would grab a "Form Oner", hitherto naughty and noisy, for a partner, to find her suddenly coy, blushing and overcome with shyness. Sometimes partners were decided by a Paul Jones. We waltzed, foxtrotted, tangoed and quick-stepped though, apart from the tango, I didn't know which dance was which. You simply tried to follow your partner, not step overmuch on her feet, and avoid getting kicked or trodden on yourself. Some of the uninitiated would anxiously ask, "Is this a foxtrot or a quick-step. I gotta know 'cos I can't do a foxtrot". The steps seemed much the same to me. All that was necessary was to move your feet faster or slower according to the rhythm. Occasionally, an older girl

95

would say, "I can only dance the woman's steps. You'll have to be the man, but I'll lead. Come on, put your arm round me there. Instead of pushing, I'll have to pull you round, O.K.?" This role reversal bewildered me for decades. As far as dancing went I never knew which way up my arms had to go and whether I was to pull or push. Further complications arose when the older girl was left-handed. It was fortunate that by the time I was a Prefect the whole wet dinner time dancing tradition fell into abeyance, as scores more little girls would undoubtedly have emerged as perplexed exponents of the art of ballroom dancing. When the dancing sessions ran smoothly, it was a sight to see everyone moving anti-clockwisely around the floor, more or less in step, even if the younger ones were looking down at their feet, their tongues hanging out in concentration. Random yowls of "Ouch" often rose above the piano. I liked the tango best. The pianists (in my time, Arfona Davies or Rita Woolf) knew two, *La Cumparsita* and *Jealousy*. The first was Spanish and the second, a classical tango. Once you had mastered the steps you were away, or rather "in", as slow learners and dilettantes were ushered off the floor after a practice and only the competent tangoists were allowed to perform. The rejected would leap on to the buck, box or horse standing along the back wall, and comment critically on the rest. At several points you had to "dip", that is, stop suddenly in fast forward motion and lean backwards bending your knees. On other occasions, you had to actually go into reverse, the lady doing a nimble *volte-face,* trip three steps backward and "dip" again. Crashes were maximal during these manoeuvres, causing much merriment. Sometimes there ensued a domino-type reaction — dancers going down like skittles, with legs and arms flailing and bodies rolling on the floor.

Just before the end of lunch break we would have a jolly dance such as the *Vellita,* the *Military Two Step,* the *Okey Kokey* or the *Conga.* This normally turned into a wild free-for-all stomp, so that by the time the bell rang for afternoon school, not only were we puce in the face from our dancing but also too exhausted for the lessons of the second half of the day.

Once or twice a year the junior forms were summoned to hear a recital by the Cardiff University String Quartet. Miss Hudd revelled in visitors, and in her most munificent, smiling and gracious manner, introduced the gentlemen musicians by name to the girls on every visit. Mr. Patrick Piggott played the piano when he was of the group, Mr. George Isaac was the cellist and Messrs. Popperwell and Alfredo Wang, the violinists. A Mr. Mutter played the viola. To we small Rhondda girls it was as though they were from another world. Their names alone were fascinating in their individuality. We were also impressed that they were from Cardiff, not then capital of Wales, but all the same a grand, romantic city where my parents took me once a year on shopping trips. Cardiff was a city with a Lord Mayor, ancient castle and TWO railway stations, where the porter, ticket collector and station master weren't the same man. It had elegant, smooth trams instead of swaying, jolting buses and restaurants with palm court orchestras in them — a place far posher and more awesome than Porth or even Pontypridd for that matter. On top of this, these gentlemen were from the university — a place spoken about in reverent tones — to which the cleverest girls went after they had passed very difficult exams in 6A.

The tall, epicene gentlemen carrying their instruments — one in a black velvet jacket, another wearing a coloured bow tie — would be ushered in by a beaming Bessie. The Bechstein grand piano had previously been pushed from its hallowed place in the adjacent Library to the appropriate spot. It being only a few years after the war, there were not many violins in circulation and I had never previously seen a cello. There were certainly no peripatetic teachers of stringed instruments in the late forties and the school had no orchestra. So when the musicians entered, smiling, casually holding violins and cellos, we were agog with interest and simmering with expectation. One of the group would tell us which piece they were going to play, explain its provenance and talk briefly about the composer. They all had cultured accents and spoke as they did on the radio News, quite unlike anyone in the Rhondda, even our most refined and erudite teachers.

The music was enchanting and far louder than one might imagine from such delicate instruments. Some girls though, were bored beyond measure. They fidgeted and when they got tired of that, yawned deliberately until it was catching, so soon the Hall was full of yawning girls, even those who were enjoying the music. Some even dozed off, or pretended to, and did quiet snores to make people laugh. To me the notes seemed to rise from the group upwards, vibrate back along the ceiling and, in clockwise motion, descend from the back wall, then coruscate forward along the floor until they hit you at the back of the legs, creating goose pimples which spread up the spine in delightful shivers. The performers played the *Eine Kleine Nachtmusik, The Trout Quintet* (adapted for a quartet), the Haydn quartets (*Razor, Lark, Sunrise* and *Frog*) and the *Boccherini Minuet,* among many others.

When the recital ended, the applause was loud and prolonged, though ironically enthusiastic from the philistines. Sometimes the gracious gentlemen would play another piece (to barely concealed groans from some quarters) but welcome to most, not only as an encore, but because it delayed our return to class and some tedious lesson or other.

In later years, I heard them praised as the finest instrumental quartet in the country performing outside London. They must have led a full life and been totally dedicated to music as not only did they visit the Glamorgan schools but played in orchestras and tutored at the university as well.

Miss Harries, the music mistress at Porth County, was one of those ageless spinsters, thin as a scarecrow, with light grey, wispy hair drawn back in a bun. She was probably about fifty going on sixty-five, and had been for most of her life. Her facial muscles worked overtime in displaying pleasure. Her eyes formed narrow slits in her bony, ascetic face and all you could see of their bright blueness was the occasional glint. When she was overjoyed, as when present at the recital, she beamed — and her eyes disappeared altogether. She must have been able to see out perfectly well though, as she made her speedy way around school without mishap, her gown often hanging down off one shoulder and trailing on the floor. Miss Harries was clearly fond of children. This affection was not only discernible by her beams when she saw a particularly affable one, but by the way girls chatted easily to her without feeling the need to stand on ceremony. She trusted entirely and erroneously in our goodness, and in singing lessons in the Hall would play the piano with her back to us, leading us vigorously in the song. Her sublime trust in the virtue of apparently blameless little girls was far from justified as all manner of mischief went on while she concentrated on the music. A girl would leap up from one of the low benches we sat on and do a silly jig for a bet, another might execute a cartwheel, yet another accept a dare to flee without permission to the toilet and return undetected. Sandwiches and chocolate were consumed, lines written and all kinds of barter went on — sweets, foreign stamps, badges, pen-pal addresses, pencils, film-star photos and various other odds and ends. When she turned round to teach us a bit more of the song, purity, innocence and eagerness shone from our faces and the lesson continued with no suspicion on her part. Once or twice she did catch someone in a misdemeanour, and the look of shock and betrayal on her face was such, even for the slightest thing, one might have thought World War Three had erupted. Miss Harries was easily deeply hurt, giving even the totally sinless a guilt complex which weighed considerably on us, to the point of making some girls cry, even though she never scolded or shouted. She simply abandoned smiling, her eyes came out of their slits, her jaw dropped in extreme dismay and her head tilted to one side as if bereaved.

Her favourite songs must have been *Where e'er you walk* and *Who is Sylvia, what is she?* as we lustily sang those at the start of every lesson. Then besides *Jerusalem, Non Nobis Domine, Land of Hope and Glory* and other stirring patriotic songs sung with equal gusto, we also learned most of Handel's *Messiah* in the first year. This was because the Upper School was publicly performing this oratorio with invited male and female soloists and a small orchestra. It is rare for a school to master the *Messiah* adequately for a public performance, let alone a girls' school with no tenors or basses. Miss Harries adapted the music for soprano, mezzo soprano and contralto voices and it was a huge success. Many girls must have been forever grateful to her for this ambitious project, having subsequently been able to appreciate the *Messiah* far more for having learnt it in singing lessons.

Every year, the school English department produced a play, often Shakespeare, with the original sixteenth century tradition of men playing women's parts being reversed. Girls played every role since all unnecessary intercourse between the Girls and Boys schools was discouraged, the latter rarely being invited to tread our hallowed boards, whether on stage or not. Apart from the annual Christmas Sixth Form get-together in the form of a dance with food, held alternately in the two school buildings, the sexes never officially mingled. Unofficially of course, it was a different matter. So girls were dressed up as men in Shakespearean costume, wearing tights, silky knickerbockers, colourful braided tunics and capacious caps. They casually dangled swords from the hip as though to the manner born. Moustaches and beards were glued on smooth peaches-and-cream skin and girls played not only men, but men playing women. They generally looked so handsome and comely, skin bronzed with stage make-up, cheeks flushed with rouge and lips glowing red, that other girls temporarily fell in love with them.

The whole business must have been convincing as the strangest conversations were overheard. "My friend Anne from Pandy Sec. came to the play last night. She'd like to go out with the second Hamlet." (A slightly shortened *Hamlet* was the play one year and three pupils shared the eponymous role, one in each of three acts, the part being too long and strenuous for one girl.)

"Ha Ha. She must be daft! Go on, arrange a date. Pretend Mair James is a boy. Go on. I dare you."

Someone might say, "Cor, my mother didn' 'alf fancy Ferdinand in the play. I'll have to invite Ann Morris home to tea!"

I first discovered the joys of plays in the Form One English lessons. Hitherto, my closest brush with the stage was when I had been reserve mouse in a youth club pantomime in church and I hadn't enjoyed the experience, with people being bossy, arguing over roles, and dressing up in costumes of coloured crinkly paper.

"I'm going to be the chief salmon."

"No you're not, see, I am, Miss said, 'cos my mother's got the pink paper. You've got to be the stranded sprat."

In the actual performance the third frog's costume had unglued on Trehafod Memorial Hall stage and fallen apart to reveal a small, embarrassed boy in white vest and underpants. It was a safer proposition really, on those occasions, to be in the reserves.

Miss Williams, the absent-minded English teacher who had people in her class who didn't exist, announced one day that we were going to read and act out a play, *A Midsummer Night's Dream*. Each classroom had a small raised platform at the front, the width of the wall blackboard. This was to be the stage. Miss Williams was a devotee of reading with expression and expected verisimilitude in acting. Recalcitrants were encouraged to speak up, abandon inhibitions and perform. She would have had an apoplectic fit had she heard a few recidivist years later the polite, mildly interested, feebly disappointed response of Malcolm's "O, by whom?" to Macduff's awful announcement, "Your royal father's murder'd". Miss Williams would have demanded nothing short of an agonised shriek, fading to a pitiful, wailing sob, with the actress falling to her knees in heart-rending despair. She was ingenious and brisk in her provision of props. An old man would be given an upturned hockey stick to wobble along with. A king would have the upside-down bin as a crown on her head — its contents discarded of course. Everyone wanted to be the queen, regardless of whether there was one in the particular play, as Miss Williams lent her academic gown for the regal role. The teacher's chair was a tree, a castle or a throne and an upturned table, a boat, island or royal court. We were all eager to take part. Plays clearly meant play. Shakespeare was fun, a revelation and a delight to us.

In late November of my first year there was much activity going on at the dais end of the Hall, which was being transformed by Mr. John the caretaker and a few brown-dungareed workmen. They were erecting a stage. The area for P.T. was decidedly restricted and not a few girls ventured into the underpinnings of the new construction for warmth, peace, curiosity or simple cussedness, before the front panels were fixed on. The annual school play was nearing the end of rehearsal and occasionally *en passant* one saw bright lights focussed on the stage and girls in declamatory pose.

One afternoon we were summoned to the Hall in doubly great excitement — because lessons had been cancelled and we were to attend the dress rehearsal of *Twelfth Night*. I had been to pantomimes before but this was my first experience of a stage play as it was for most of the younger children. We sat rapt, captivated by everything — the costumes, the backcloths, the scenery, but mainly by the actresses, as for the most part they were the Prefects, other Sixth formers and a few from lower down the school. The Second formers and upwards were less awed however. Derisory laughter and catcalls, which must have been disconcerting for those taking part, greeted the majority of arrivals on stage when they were acting male parts, especially if they had curly wigs, beards, baggy knickerbockers, silly hats or white-powdered faces. Apart from a brief look of dismay though, they carried on bravely. The laughter subsided as the play unfolded, to be replaced by hisses and boos at black attired Malvolio's every entrance, while Sir Toby Belch was ardently cheered. I was following the plot when I could, but confusion set in when Viola, a girl playing a girl playing a boy, rejected Olivia who was in love with him or her, and was herself in love with Orsino, a girl playing a boy, who in turn loved Olivia, a girl playing a girl. The trouble was, that you forgot they were not Carol Lewis, Arfona Davies, Beryl Morris, et al. Almost total mystification ensued when Viola turned back to a girl and her twin brother, who looked nothing like her, arrived on the scene and the idiots thought he was her. You could, I suppose, excuse foolish, drunken Sir Andrew who tried to fight him, thinking he was his sister, and nearly had his head chopped off for his foolhardiness, but I thought Olivia really showed what a fluffy-headed character she was, mistaking the two just because they wore the same clothes. As if grown-up twins, particularly of the opposite sex, would wear similar clothes anyway. I could see inconsistencies in this William Shakespeare's plotting. I hadn't heard of "suspension of disbelief" and wouldn't have known what it meant in any case.

Nevertheless it was agreed that a school play was a marvellous excuse for a romp and many were the small girls who saw themselves as future Sarah Siddonses, determined to play an active part in future productions. My friend Hope Higgs was equally enthusiastic and for days her conversation was anachronistic to say the least.

"By my troth, my lady, we must hither quickly for our milk before the white beverage in yon bottles is all consumed," or "Maria, my friend from ancient days, hast thou written thy hundred lines for aged bag, mistress of Biology? No doubt thou wilt be despatched to detention if they are not produced forthwith, then thy venerable mother will worry and crease her brow with furrows when thou art not on the school chariot." (At some point I think she got a bit muddled up with Latin.) We soon began to get fed up with this mode of speech though. Hope was howled at and lightly battered, so her Shakespearean utterances were soon confined to his plays in class.

One of the most eagerly anticipated events of the summer term was the school outing. There were two and they took place simultaneously. The Senior school, Forms Four to Six, minus a few Prefects, were packed into one fleet of coaches and the Junior forms into another. No Madame Tussaud's, Bristol Zoo or Dreaming Spires for Porth County Girls though. Dear me no, and Lord forbid! Girls might get up to all sorts of mischief in towns or urban areas. They could get run over, be seen eating chips out of newspaper on the street or even talking to boys! The hussies might play on Allwin de Luxe gaming machines, drop litter, or abscond, to end up in the white slave trade in places like South America or even Liverpool. The safest places, doubly recommended in that they weren't too distant, were deemed to be Southerndown and Llantwit Major on the south Wales coast. Pimps, spivs, boys and white slave traders were unlikely to be much in evidence at these resorts, as indeed, was much of anything else. Both places had a beach, albeit rocky in parts, some miles from the nearest civilisation, and apart from wooden lock-up shacks serving as primitive cafés, the only other sign of life was an abundance of cows. Narrow winding roads led from the closest town, and the only other way out was south, via the sea. As bodies were only allowed to immerse themselves in that element from the knees down, there was no real hope of escape that way. So the school authorities decided these were the ideal localities for outings. One year the juniors would go to Llantwit Major and the seniors to Southerndown, in the reverse direction the following year, and so on, probably until the end of Miss Hudd's reign, even if not to eternity. Porth County girls might not leave school as sophisticated women of the world, having an intimate knowledge of the major metropoli of the land, casually and confidently hailing taxis or tipping pages and porters at grand hotels, but they certainly had a more than passing acquaintance with the wilder, more inaccessible parts of the south Wales coastline.

Our one and sixes for the coach had been paid and on a fine, appointed morning in July when school exams — terminals — were over, half a dozen coaches from Humphreys Garage, Mill St., Pontypridd would arrive and line up in the lane outside the school entrance, ready to take the three hundred girls on their annual outing. School uniform was *de rigueur* of course, but at least it was the summer version of green, short-sleeved gingham frock with white Peter Pan collar and cuffs, white ankle socks, brown sandals and moss green blazer from Roberts', Cardiff or bottle green from Hodges, Porth. The ubiquitous school cap had, of course, to crown the lot, but we were allowed the concession of removing it on the bus and when away from all supposedly critical, local eyes on the beach. Not that Rhondda folk cared one way or another whether Porth County girls were be-bereted or not, but the myth had long been established that people minded desperately and anyway STANDARDS HAD TO BE MAINTAINED!

We had been warned beforehand, and more than once, "No swimming. No rock climbing. No litter." Litter, like the beretless heads, was a major preoccupation with the hierarchy. The sight of an empty crisp packet or toffee wrapper thoughtlessly discarded was guaranteed to put anyone over the age of twenty connected with education into a blazing temper. Further warnings about keeping away from cliff edges and going into caves were added without the opportunity being lost for a bit of supplementary educational (in this case geological) information. "The south Wales coast is composed of sedimentary limestone rock layered in the tertiary era. This is not ancient, solid rock of the primary age such as we have here in the Rhondda, but friable material, particularly where it ends on the coast and is subject to potholes and crevices, because it breaks easily. So be careful. If you were to go into caves the roof might well come down on top of you. If you venture to cliff edges, before you know it, you could be on the rocks below with a broken leg, back or even dead, and it would completely spoil the day. Apart from which I have no wish to ruin my nails by having to indulge in some rescue operation with boulders. So, for goodness sake, ACT RESPONSIBLY."

With a fair bit of fuss, frantic pushing for the back seat and ill-contained excitement, girls scrambled into the coaches. As the coaches pulled away at last, there was much cheering and waving: to friends in other vehicles, to the caretaker (grateful for a day's peace), to the surprised nurses in the nurses' home opposite, to anyone who happened to be passing. Possessions, mainly satchels containing food and one or two illegal, but hopefully packed, swimming costumes and towels, were put into hotly disputed space in the overhead luggage rack. In the Junior School coaches, small girls huddled, mostly three to a seat, with something approaching a whole form crammed like writhing bait on the long back seat. Five minutes into the journey, excitement gave way to hunger, satchels were pulled from the rack, dislodging a variety of gear on to groaning heads, and the larger part of packed lunches were consumed, although it was only half past nine. The second breakfast was hungrily gobbled, despite warnings from one of the long-suffering members of staff sitting at the front that it really was not sensible to eat sandwiches now as there were no shops at these beauty spots to replenish supplies. She resignedly finished with a reminder that the driver had a provision of sick bags.

It must be a Rhondda tradition that shortly after boarding a coach for an excursion with friends or neighbours, and settling down (or in this case, being fed), the singing starts. Perhaps it is a national characteristic ("Thank God we are a musical nation"), the Welsh venting their happiness in song. Sometimes the singing starts with one person humming a tune which is then taken up by those in adjacent seats. Sometimes a natural leader or Form spokeswoman such as Barbara Jones would announce, "Let's sing *Alouette*. I'll start," and proceed to organise the parts of the song. Jolly songs were always sung on the outward journey; *Clementine, She'll be coming round the mountain* with a few *risqué* verses, *Daisy, Early one morning* and *Frère Jacques* in rounds, sung so vigorously the latter could never have had a kip in that racket. The teachers sank deeper into their newspaper perusals, chatted more deliberately to each other or slumped down in their seats, eyes closed, pretending to sleep as they recoiled mentally from the day ahead, quite determined to have nothing to do with the raucous, unsophisticated animation of the young. After a hard day at the sea-side, homeward bound songs were far quieter and reflective; *Row, row, row your boat, Dafydd y garreg gwen* and *Ar hyd y nos*. Now the teachers, no doubt mellowed by the ultimately tolerable day and feeling relieved it was over and that no major catastrophes had occurred, would join in too.

On arrival at the beach car park we were re-reminded of what we mustn't do, threatened with extinction or at least thumb torture if we were not back at the coach at 4p.m., and released, our simmering excitement frequently matching the hot July temperatures.

One may travel the world, stay in grand hotels in exotic places or spend happy family holidays at the seaside in this country or abroad. Nothing, however, can compare with those sunny days on trips with like-minded friends of one's own age, when you can say or do anything you fancy provided it's not illegal, immoral or fattening, though for schoolgirls in the forties the first and last didn't bother them over much and they didn't know what the middle one was.

As we descended in our green gingham hordes from the coaches at Llantwit Major beach, the owner of the small, wooden shack-shop-cum-pot-of-tea-take-away came out to his door scratching his head in wonderment at the invasion. He then rubbed his hands in anticipation of a speedy sellout and a quicker than usual end to his working day. It wasn't long before he was sold out of Smith's crisps (the only available ones then), and well before lunch he had run out of fillings for his rolls so that only plain bread and butter was left for those who had already devoured their lunch. As the day wore on the butter got decidedly sparser too.

"Oh, wish now I 'adn' eaten my dinner on the bus. Tha' shop on'y got bread an' butter left."

"Bread you mean," said a disgusted Catherine Morgan looking disbelievingly at a white slice, "You'd 'ave better food than this in jail!"

"It don' matter. Buy some sweets. Look, I made some nice chocolate an' jelly baby sandwiches. An' 'e still got some Marses. Sold out o' pop though," said an enterprising Hope Higgs tucking into her makeshift meal. "If you're thirsty you can have a drink of water from tha' tap over there, see? 'S for washing the sand off your feet. Wanna loan o' my bottle?"

A similar scene was taking place at Southerndown, which I was to witness the following year. There, the coach and car park is in a field on the top of a cliff which slopes alarmingly on the Bristol Channel side. A sheep gap in the dry stone wall takes you on to the road leading down to the little bay, which has a sandy beach at low tide. The powers that be had, of course, chosen a day when for most of it, the sea would be in Somerset or Tasmania, but certainly very little in south Wales to tempt Porth County girls into its idle waves.

Beyond the wall, one needed to pause at the suddenly breath-taking view. Before you is the steep greensward descent to the beach, rocky at the top and sides, which is the culmination of a small stream valley. The road on the other side of this valley wound up to the impressive, crenellated Dunraven Castle, the quartz crystalled rock of which sparkled in the sunshine. A hundred yards from it was the vertical cliff face. This crumbly, sedimentary rock was arranged so neatly in layers, it appeared man made. Then, below it, the shining blue sea in its gentle mood — white-edged baby waves lazily unfurling on the sand or darkening to slate the base of the pale grey rocks and boulders scattered along the shore which had parted company from the cliff in darker, tempestuous days. Sky does not merge with sea in this scene, as the Somerset coast is clearly discernible in the distance, the undulating hills of Exmoor and occasionally, a stream of smoke rising from an unseen train. Wisps of smoke too, out at sea, above a toy ship smoothly and noiselessly making its way up Channel to Cardiff or Barry or Avonmouth. But apart from the view, and no doubt complementing it, was the silence. Voices, of course — animated, happy and laughing — those of our County day-trippers mingled with the occasional bleating of a sheep or distant noise of a tractor, but none of that constant growl of traffic or life going about its tasks as in the valley towns. Sounds were sharper in the quietness and this very sharpness made you more aware of the silence.

"Cor, I'd like to live 'ere wouldn' you?"

"Yeah, but not for all of the time. There's no shops."

No schools, churches, buses, or houses either, as far as we could see. But there was a pub back up on the road which was more than there was in Llantwit Major, whose beach, at the end of the long, wide, shallow valley of Cwm Colhuw, is miles away from its town, and decidedly Minor from the point of view of facilities.

At ten thirty a.m. on a weekday in early July, Llantwit beach is largely bereft of visitors, so the Porth County brigade had it more or less to themselves. The one or two people peaceably walking dogs or themselves soon beat a hasty retreat, feeling intimidated by this green invasion of excited, noisy little girls.

Initially, long treks were taken to locate the far-off and fast disappearing sea to ensure it was real, and, as paddling was allowed, feet got wet. Then groups settled around rocks and ate, gazed, chatted, sunbathed, dozed, played hide and seek, hop-scotch, touch or a ball game on a pitch marked out in the sand, or just went for walks to see what the teachers were doing. Miss Pennington who, all the way from school, gave the impression of wanting to be elsewhere, was sitting in a small deckchair she must have brought with her. There were none for hire at that beach (barely more commercialised than at the dawn of the tertiary era). She sat in the sun under a black umbrella with every part of her body covered except for her mouth. Hands sheathed in lace gloves clasped each other across her front and her eyes, behind their rimless glasses, were closed. And like that she stayed until it was time to go home when she was first back on the coach. Miss Bird, sitting on a flat rock next to her, wore a large straw hat. Beside her were three or four newspapers and she was in the process of reading (I imagine) the previous day's *Bristol Evening Post*. The habitual lisle stockings had been replaced by a lighter summer version and her knickers, discernible just above the hem of her summer frock, were peach celanese rather than the usual cotton interlock type.

Teachers more in touch with their youth removed their shoes and stockings and paddled, with anxious looks or squeals at approaching wavelets. Some sat with skirts delicately hoiked up to their knees to tan their shins and some were seen disappearing arm-in-arm up the only road in the direction of the only pub, a good two miles away, with the overheard declaration they were going to find the much advertised,"Olde Tea Roomes", aptly named "Quaintways" restaurant in the distant village.

Some of the younger staff, relaxed and smiling for once, strolled around the beach keeping an eye on thingsor sat on rugs on the sand, chatting and laughing. Now and then they would be persuaded to join in a game of cricket or rounders and to our amazement ran about and shouted like normal human beings.

Around mid-afternoon there was a bit of a commotion. Some girls had been for a walk along the cliff top path in the direction of St. Donat's castle, no doubt in the hope that they would be seen looking interested and intelligent by someone in charge and invited into the grounds, if not inside the building, owned by the movie mogul William Hearst where, rumour had it, wild parties with film stars took place. Participation in unrestrained celebrations were not to be, however, as a far more exciting event occurred on the way there. Approximately half way between Llantwit Major and St. Donat's is Tresilian House, which stands in a meadow behind a small private bay of the same name. The walkers had sat down for a rest on the grass above the cliff when Caryl Williams espied a solitary man undressing on the beach prior to a swim in the sea. She pointed him out to the others and to their initial shock and subsequent amusement and delight, he removed all his clothing and trotted off seawards, giving them a view of a well-tanned rear. Immediately one of the group was despatched post haste back to the beach. Word soon got around to ball players, sand loungers and rock pool probers, "There's a naked man in the sea a quarter of a mile up the coast". In no time, a mass of green gingham was making its way off the beach and heading for the cliff path.

"Where's everyone going?" a surprised Miss Beard asked my friend Hope.

"Er...I think someone's located a toilet Miss."

"There'll be an almighty queue there then."

"Um...Yes Miss."

The puzzled staff watched, as most of Porth County Junior School streamed westward to see this never before witnessed sight. A naked man! It discombooberated the mind! What magnificences or horrors were to be revealed to us? Our only previous experience of such a thing had been Penny's drawing of a half a nude man on the board with a little dangly in a certain place when she'd baffled us with a lesson on human reproduction. Now we were to put her teaching to the test. Some girls with brothers were possibly more *au fait* with the male anatomy, but I certainly wasn't.

Amid much ssshh-ing and giggling, crawling, writhing and slithering to get a good view on the cliff top, the larger part of three coachloads of young ladies lay on their stomachs on the greensward above the bay, eyes straining to see this creature in all his glory. And they weren't disappointed. He finished his swim, this middle-aged, greying man with a complete covering of brown skin, and strode up the beach to his towel, the unsuspecting target of dozens of goggling eyes. And was Miss Pennington right? Yes, only sort of... more elongated.

As four p.m approached, there was a general drift towards the car park. Food bags and satchels now contained pretty coloured pebbles and perfectly round or oval small stones. A fair tonnage of sand was also departing from the beach and removing to the Rhondda Valleys in hair, ears, shoes and pockets. In an undoubtedly fair exchange, lost combs, coins, crusts, socks and sandy sandwiches were left behind, not to mention the odd sandal stuck between rocks or cardigan caught on the protruding branch of an intrepid tree, half way down a cliff. The remaining beach didn't look so much depleted of sand as unkempt and weary, relieved to see the back of us.

Every year without fail the coach would be delayed: by a dozy pair having no watch or sense of time between them, a group still searching for a lost ball, or girls wearily returning from an over-ambitious expedition, unaware of the setting sun. Invariably those already on the coach would begin to feel restless. "Is there time to go to the toilet, Miss?"

Miss would indecisively consult her watch, "Mmm. All right Pamela but be quick. We're leaving in a few minutes." The last utterance was more in hope than expectation. A desire to go to the toilet is catching. Straight away most of the rest of the bus wanted to follow Pamela and were soon tripping out, hopping exaggeratedly after their sudden urgency. "Oh Miss, I need to go too." "I'm desperate, I'll only be two minutes, promise." or "Oh, Miss I'll never make it back to Porth." Five minutes after boarding, the coach was empty again for all but a few quietly fuming types, superior beings have no truck with weak bladders and late-comers. These would waspishly offer to find the latter and hurry them up. As there was no-one left on the coach apart from them, the teachers and the long-suffering, ever-patient driver, they departed as well. One year, search parties were sent out to look for the searchers. Eventually, everyone got back to school and I doubt they would have appreciated London, Bristol or Birmingham more. Indeed, perhaps we wouldn't all have returned safe in body or sound in mind from those places. When all was said and done, we quite looked forward to invading Llantwit Major again *en masse* in two years time.

CHAPTER TEN

Prizegiving

The School Hall must have been the most adaptable room in the world. Used every morning for Assembly, every day for Gym lessons, every wet lunch-time as a *palais de danse* and once a term as a concert hall for the string quartet, it was also used once yearly as a theatre and then, finally, as a Presentation Hall for the annual Prize Distribution. Again, Mr. John and his workmen were to the fore, carting their wooden planks hither and thither to build a terrifying construction of steps going from floor to ceiling. Gym classes were abandoned during the Hall's transformation and everybody had Games whatever the weather. All the Gym apparatus was stowed neatly away in various form rooms. The wallbars remained, as they were glued to the wall, so you could go in and have a quick, illicit upside-down hang at lunch-time or when no-one was looking, if the desire so took you.

On one occasion when I was in 2B (relegated, I'm afraid, coming in the bottom three in terminals, "spending too much time on your feet and not enough with your head in a book" as Mam put it) we were delighted to find the vaulting box temporarily placed behind the door in our classroom. Girls gathered round, in and on top of it and wondered to what innovative use it could be put. We decided that Miss Beard's replacement to teach French, Miss Davies, (christian name of Mary as it happened) would be the most suitable victim to play a trick on, as she seemed congenial, hadn't shouted at us, wasn't yet sure of our names and, to be truthful, didn't seem always totally in control of proceedings.

"She'll be a cinch," said Marjorie Woosnam, frequently to the fore in terms of harmless mischief. The plan was simply for two girls to get inside the box and gradually move it the four or so yards to the platform. Hope Higgs (also relegated, probably through being on her feet too much also) and Elizabeth Voisey were chosen, among many eager applicants, for the roles of invisible vaulting box movers. "When I cough," said Marjorie, "that's a signal to move it a bit. I'll only cough when she's marking somebody's book or something. O.K?"

"I'll cough as well," offered Maureen Griffiths, "in case you can't hear inside the box."

"No," argued Marjorie, "we can't have everybody coughing. Miss Davies'll get suspicious. 'Part from that someone might cough at the wrong time."

"What if someone has a real cough?" demanded Pat Williams, "I've got a cold on my chest."

"They'll just have to stop it, that's all."

"I'm afraid I can't stop it if I have a cough," said Pamela Nicholls resolutely.

"You'll have to Pamela. Shut your eyes and think of something else."

"No, I can't," she wailed. "I go all red and my eye starts watering and my glasses steam up, then I can't see and I get confused."

Plans were made, protests summarily put down, and the girls got inside the box between lessons after the departure of one teacher and Miss Davies's arrival.

"Don't grin and don't look at the box," hissed the circus-master giving a last bit of desperate advice.

"Bonjour mes enfants."

"Bonjour madame."

"Asseyez-vous s'il vous plaît."

We were a little more *au fait* with French now and didn't incur Miss Davies's wrath as we had Miss Beard's, by stupidly saying *"après moi"* when she said *"Répétez après moi"* instead of the words that followed. In fact, we were advanced enough to recognise a question and give it a brief answer. We were quite good at this.

"Comment vous portez-vous aujourd'hui, Valerie Charles?"

"Oui madame."

Or, *"Qu'est-ce qu'il y a sur le pupitre, Mary Davies?"*

"Non madame."

113

We always began with the somewhat one-sided conversation then continued to a variety of things such as writing down vocabulary at the back of our green, school crested exercise books, writing about grammar at the front, or painfully and painstakingly reading, then pathetically and hopelessly translating, the latest carryings-on of the unpredictable Laborde family and their strange children Firmin and Edwige in *Apprenons le Français Book 2.*

Whenever Miss Davies was writing on the board, marking a book at the further side of the room, or at the teacher's desk following the text and rolling her eyes in disbelief as a girl attempted to read, Marjorie would cough loudly and sharply. Immediately, all eyes except Marjorie's were on the box, which began to shift sideways with a squeak. From the two rows next to the corridor wall, parts of Elizabeth or Hope could be distinguished through the hand holds, and some bold girls even waved to them. They must have moved a yard when Miss Davies said, "You've got a bad cough, Marjorie Woosnam. Go and get a drink."

"No, it's all right thank you, Miss Davies. I don't need a drink."

"Well, don't cough any more then, Marjorie please. You're disturbing the class." Marjorie pulled a face, wondering looks were exchanged round the class and the box stayed put in no man's land for a few minutes. Suddenly there was a commotion at the back as a wooden pencil case, no doubt pushed off a desk, crashed to the floor, spilling its contents. Girls nearby leapt out of their seats to kindly help collect the errant pencils and pens, Miss Davies jumped up to investigate, everybody had an acute fit of whooping cough and the box positively sped sideways, hurtling into the platform with a resounding crack. Silence weighed breathlessly as Miss Davies turned and walked slowly back to the front, eyebrow thoughtfully raised, gaze coldly scanning the class.

"Ah," she rapped, "so we have moving gymnastic apparatus do we?"

She looked around the class nodding. *"Eh bien, le devoir pour ce soir. Copiez les dix pages soixante-douze à quatre-vingt-deux et traduisez le texte.* BY TOMORROW!" she shrieked, making us jump. Then she turned and wrote on the board *"Je ne dois jamais me cacher dans l'appareil gymnastique pendant le cours de français"* announcing loudly, "that's the extra homework for Hope Higgs and Elizabeth Voisey to write two hundred times." The lesson continued in silence and conscientious work for the remaining ten minutes. After the bell, it was two sheepish, stiff, fed-up girls who emerged from their incarceration. Still, we were partly right. Miss Davies didn't rant and rave but she evidently did know our names. It was also the last time gym apparatus was placed anywhere that mischievous hands could get at it unsupervised.

We watched in alarm as the construction of the perilous scaffolding in the Hall mounted to the ceiling, particularly those with a fear of heights, the unco-ordinated and the timid, as we knew we'd soon be up on those steps in morning assemblies. The thing was most frightening before the sand- coloured sacking was nailed on, as you could see the meccano innards of the beast, metal tubes — untrustworthy, slender metal tubes between the planks and the floor far below. When it was deemed safe — and this was a full week before Prize Day, as it had to be practised upon — the junior pupils had to sit on it, filing up the middle to the top in twos, then parting, each making her generally unsteady way to the right or left to fill up the rows.

More girls missed the school bus, lost their way if walking, had early dental or medical appointments or illnesses which miraculously disappeared by 9.30, during the week before Prizegiving than during the whole term. Some threatened to turn Roman Catholic as the Catholics were excused Assembly. Some hid in the toilets feigning faintness or sickness and some just wailed, "Oh miss, do I have to go up there? I don't like it. I'm scared of heights, miss."

Few were excused the ascension, the usual reply being a "Don't be silly, Maureen. Just be careful!" and possibly, a slightly more sympathetic addendum, "try not to look down." One overheard such exchanges as, "Come along, Marjorie. Don't lurk in class. Get in line for Assembly." "I don't have to go any more, Miss. I've gone Catholic. Shall I go to the dining room with the other Catholics?"

"Assembly, my girl, until I have a note from your mother." Marjorie meekly complied.

Various girls of course, whose ancestors were clearly monkeys, attacked the pile with panache, haring up the steep steps sure-footedly and marching along the narrow plank at the top as though it were the extensive area of Horseguards Parade. These were so well-balanced and confident they even had time to look down and see who was watching them, nonchalantly tossing their hair or flicking back a plait from their shoulder as they strode to right or left.

Most girls took it rather more slowly, one arm held out ready to cling on to their neighbour, the other to grab the next beam up in the event of an unsure step or slight movement in the scaffolding planks. The walk to the extemities to fill up the rows was accomplished with much swaying of bodies and arms held aloft like tightrope walkers. Eventually, the whole construction was a chiaroscuro of glowing faces (many with fear), shining hair, and white blouses with green and yellow ties above dark gymslips. Legs and feet couldn't be seen, hidden by the girl in front who had to manoeuvre herself between the knees of the girl behind. Happily, once seated there was no further motion — hymns were sung sitting down — until the assembly was over. Then came the pantomime in reverse of getting everyone off. Now, of course, you had to look down, even those altiphobiacs who tried to descend with a hand over their eyes. Fat girls came down backwards. Some sat on each step before putting their feet gingerly on the lower one, others descended like crabs, sideways with much waving of forelimbs. Big girls stepped heavily, making thunderous noises, and wobbled the entire structure. Petite girls waited patiently, rolling their eyes, while the offspring of the monkeys skipped down lightly like ballet dancers in *Swan Lake*. Things were slightly less alarming when the sacking was in place. It was stretched taut, so its movement was minimal, but chiefly the bonus was that you couldn't see through the steps to the abyss below — a decided encouragement. For the great event though, fainters were weeded out with the swots who were having prizes and the singers who were performing.

A fainting pupil high up on the scaffolding would have been a disaster indeed, as there was no way in or out without further catastrophe. Passing a fainter over heads as practised in international rugby matches was quite out of the question. If she slumped forward and fell she would create a swathe of fallen girls from ceiling to floor. The alternative might be to launch the unfortunate into space shouting "fore" and hope someone on *terra firma* would catch her without too much trouble. Either way it would make a rather undignified sight for Prize Distribution and possibly even invoke adverse comment in the next day's *Western Mail*. Consequently, one morning during registration, before the final positioning on the platform, our form teacher Miss Lloyd-Davies (Biology), without mentioning the big occasion, casually asked, "Is there any girl here who has a history of fainting or who has ever fainted or thinks they might faint in the heat?" We all knew what this was about. Every hand shot up. After a brief blink of amazement she protested, "Oh come along now. You're not all as delicate as that." All hands remained aloft. She paused, then went on, "We'll have to look at your medical records then." In the event, one girl, Anne Jones, was lucky to be selected and she didn't turn up anyway as she was claustrophobic as well. There was a decided advantage to sitting in the main Hall as you weren't as conspicuous as on the scaffolding and could guzzle a few ounces of smuggled in, unwrapped sweets to relieve the tedium of endless speeches.

On the platform were a main speaker with spouse if he or she possessed one, the local Director of Education, a group of unknown, smiling ladies and gentleman with nodding heads — the governers no doubt — and, of course, a benevolently beaming, double first Miss Hudd decked out in all her academic finery. She wore no mortar board — that would have caused giggling — but the turquoise shot-silk lined hood of the University of Wales hung down at her back over her best black, unfaded gown.

Prizegivings were always held in the evening so that the proud parents of the prize-winners, at work during the day, could attend. Not only did we return to school, but came willingly, because the vast majority loved the place and were proud of it, despite protestations to the contrary. Pressed gymslip pleats, a clean white blouse, scrubbed faces with not the merest hint of makeup, shining hair tied in navy ribbons, Persil-white socks and a handkerchief were the order of the evening. Imagine such a situation in the nineties in a town Comprehensive. It is doubtful if all the prize-winners would turn up, even for money, let alone the supporting cast.

Beforehand the school hymn, or at least the hymn we usually sang on special and public occasions, *Thy Hand O God has guided, Thy Flock from Age to Age*, had been vociferously and enthusiastically practised, together with one or two of the other nationalistic, rousing greats, *Non Nobis Domine, Jerusalem* or *This royal Throne of Kings, this sceptred Island* from John of Gaunt's speech in *Richard the Second*.

After leading in the guests, Miss Hudd, in her most charming, charismatic, urbane, super-cool persona would introduce them to the audience. Bouquets of flowers would be presented by sweet, small girls and the Head Prefect to the ladies, and the speeches would start and go on... and on... and on. Chairmen of this and that would propose, others would second the motion and introduce yet more who would want to say a "few" words which ended up being a discourse of several thousand. After what seemed enough time to get to London and back (on foot) it would be the Headmistress's turn to give the review of the year speech. This was the most interesting item of the evening, apart from the actual prize presentation when girls walked up the steps on to the stage for their book, cheque, certificate or hockey stick (for the hockey prize), and there was always the chance someone might stumble and fall, to cause mayhem and reduce the boredom. A beautifully coiffed Miss Orsman, Deputy Head, organised this part of the proceedings, passing the prize to the wife or chief guest to give the prize-winner, with a handshake and a few complimentary words.

The worst part was when the special guest rose to his or her feet to pass on their many words of advice. By this time it was getting dark and the battery of arc lights above the stage were lit so we could fidget even less and not talk at all, illuminated as we were to several hundred pairs of eyes. It got hotter and hotter and faces redder and redder with each passing speech or rendition of *Who is Sylvia? What is she?* or *Where the bee sucks, there suck I.*

The staff, everyone begowned and wearing their university hood of different coloured silk (mainly Wales turquoise or shot-gold for science), sat in rows facing the platform and even they looked resigned to be bored at the onset of the main speech. Religious and political gentlemen came last in order of merit in the tedium stakes of speech making, probably because talking was second nature to them, they were used to ranting on and putting people to sleep. We had Bishops and Archbishops, dry Academics, local MP's and George Thomas from Tonypandy, who made us laugh. The Director of Education was dry, media people told jokes. I remember Alun Oldfield Davies, an ex-Porth County pupil himself, being chief guest once, but the author Mary Fitt, also a Classics lecturer at Cardiff University I believe, was the best. She explained how she wrote crime novels and talked about the crime club to which she belonged and her friendship with the great Agatha Christie.

All chief guests, without fail, asked for a day's holiday because we were such a terrific lot of pupils in what surely, to hear the plaudits, was the best school in Wales, if not the entire kingdom. Polite cheers were called for by the Head Girl, a few more songs performed instrumentally or sung, everyone on the floor stood while the nodders and beamers made their way out and we got down off the scaffolding for the last time. "Thank God for that", Marjorie said, "I won't have to think up an excuse for being late tomorrow."

CHAPTER ELEVEN

The School Sports

The sporting highlight of the year was undoubtedly the Rhondda School Sports in early June when the two Porth County Schools would fight it out on the athletics track with the sardines of Porth Sec and the other Rhondda secondary schools at Tonypandy, Pentre and Ferndale. Occasionally the Technical College took part but they seemed to be wavering participants who didn't enter every event, had no obvious support and wore brown running vests — a no-hope colour if ever there was one! Four shields for Senior and Junior Boys and Girls and several cups and rose bowls were the valued prizes for the winning schools and individuals. Trophies in ancient Rome couldn't have been more keenly contested by athletes at the Circus Maximus or more vociferously encouraged by their followers. In fact at times rivalry was so intense and proceedings so heated and clamorous, an innocent onlooker might have thought the lions had been brought on to consume the Christians.

The summer sports of rounders and tennis were available to the non or lesser sportswomen, but those who had proved themselves to have a modicum of athletic ability had no option but to practise running various distances, relay races, skipping, (for in the forties there was a girls' skipping race, later replaced by the hurdles) and high jumping. There was no girls' long jump as it was considered too strenuous and undignified for young ladies. We rehearsed starts, passing the baton, dipping for the tape, changing the stride pattern. We did various exercises to loosen muscles we never knew we had. Dinner hours were taken up with athletics and you were even expected to stay after school for extra tuition to improve your performance. Once in Form 1, when I told Miss Jennett I didn't think I could stay after four o'clock, she looked at me as though I had told her her hair had turned green and there was mould coming out of her ears. "What?" she cried in disbelief, "I have chosen you to represent the school and you say you can't remain behind! And why not, pray? If you are going to have the honour of representing this school you must practise, practise, practise until you perform to your utmost ability," and she flounced off on her muscular legs, her small face pink with indignation. I stayed.

One of the compensations for having to be a dedicated, single-minded athletics person rather than an easy-going rounders or tennis player was the Boys School. Adjacent to us, they had no sports field, only a concrete yard. This uninspiring asphalt was quite unsuitable for the pursuit of athletics and, as Porth County Boys carried off the Rhondda Schools sports trophies with monotonous regularity, thus endowing them with a fearsome athletics tradition to uphold, they practised on our field.

For an impressionable girl not yet a teenager, seeing these god-like creatures at close quarters running, jumping in various directions, hurdling and throwing elongated, circular and glo-bular objects against a background of dark trees and sunny, blue sky on fresh-smelling grass was like going to Barry Island for the first time and tasting all its attendant delights. The majority of these young men (like most sportsmen) had handsome faces and beautifully proportioned bodies. Their long, strong, sun-tanned legs emerged from brief, green shorts that concealed tiny, sinewy bottoms. They wore green vests and sped along powerfully and easily, their rippling muscular arms and shoulders propelling them forward in long, graceful strides. Only the stars of the senior boys team seemed to use our field and took little or no notice of the insignificant junior girls. Perhaps it would have been different had we been the senior girls, but it appeared cannily arranged that the latter practised at the same time as the junior boys. It was very difficult to concentrate on your performance with a dozen Adonises sprint-ing around and we were scolded several times for watching them and not listening to Miss Jennett's instructions. But one's eyes were inexorably drawn to them and it was at this point I think my admiration was transferred generally from women to men.

So bedazzled was I by these fine young Apollos, I still remember their names four decades later: John Jenkins, Peter Phillips, Ian Davies, Keith Stooksbury, Philip Padfield, Desmond Barnett, John Isaac, David Enoch, Marcus Morgan and the heroic Gareth Griffiths, the latter, tall with crinkly blue eyes in a tanned, mischievous face and distinctive, slightly chipped front teeth — no doubt resulting from a rugby accident — which strangely made him all the more attractive. Everybody knew Gagsa, as he was nicknamed. Girls drooled over him and during breaks girls stood on the bank gazing at the Boys School yard hoping for a glimpse of their idol. I never bothered, as to me he dwelt in the unattainable realms of the likes of Van Johnson and George Formby, perhaps even more so. Two male teachers accompanied and coached the boys and timed and measured their exploits. Neither looked the typical Games or P.E. teacher or in any way remotely compared in stature, physical or otherwise, with their charges. Mr. Bill Morris, head of P.E. was a wry, unsmiling, chain-smoking man of few words, and those barked out. In his forties, dark jowled and with a cambered posture, he had been spotted on a few occasions in a dark green, baggy tracksuit, but he usually wore a shapeless sports jacket and a battered trilby. I suppose he had a shirt and tie, but these couldn't be seen through a festoon of stopwatches, whistles and measuring tapes hanging around his neck. The other master, Mr. Andrew Williams, was reputed to be actually qualified in some other subject but he possessed a great interest in and knowledge of athletics. Rather on the retiring side of middle age, he was a dear man, courteous and patient with the girls whose names he bothered to learn and in whose events he offered advice and encouragement. Mr. Morris, on the other hand, usually scowled at us if we approached within ten yards of him. Mr. Williams wore dark tinted glasses winter and summer and was always formally dressed with an overcoat when it was cold and a beige Burberry when it rained. He looked as though he had a wife whereas Bill Morris had a slightly reprobate, bachelor air about him.

Arriving on the field to practise high jumping with a third former, Millie Ball, I had my first close glimpse of one of these boy deities — hands on firm, tiny hips, spiked running shoes casually hanging over one shoulder — who was listening to Mr. Williams.

"D'you know who that is?" Millie asked.

"Yes, Mr. Williams."

"No, not him, daft. The one talking to him. That's Gareth Griffiths that is."

"Oh, is he a teacher then?"

"No, silly, a boy!"

"A boy! Gosh!"

"Isn't he smashing? Fastest runner they've ever had in the school. 10.5 hundred yards. Goes with a girl in 6B worse luck."

Millie watched him as he ran laps of the track and lined herself up to gracefully clear the bar each time he passed the jumping pit. He took no notice though. Probably had his mind on his sports day races or his girl friend.

As the spring months blossomed and summer arrived with its warmth and luxuriant vegetation, the field was never without pupils athleticising all over it. The sports were getting closer. Prefects uninvolved in the practicalities of the occasion organised sessions with the junior forms to ensure they knew the sports songs by heart. Toiling away on the field, we could hear these being lustily sung in the Hall to the tune, highly appropriate for the Rhondda, of the *Red Flag*.

> The County Flag is deepest green,
> To win the sports we are so keen.
> And though our limbs grow stiff and cold,
> We'll fight for County 'til we're old.
> We'll raise the emerald banner high,
> Beneath its shade we'll live and die.
> Though Pandy flinch and Ferndale sneer,
> To our dear flag we'll be sincere.

This was followed by the more earthy ditty of:

> Y County yw y goreu, (repeated)
> Y goreu, y goreu, y goreu.

— reaching a climax in the final, wild words of the inane, meaningless piece of doggerel redolent of football hooligans:

Zoom zoom zaki, zoom zoom zay.
A bisha backa, bisha backa
Bisha backa bay.
Who are we? County.
C-O-U-N-T-Y. County. Hooray!

This last accompanied by the abandoned and spontaneous hurling of berets and scarves up in the air and a subsequent, mad scramble for their retrieval.

The sports were held either at Gelligaled Park in Pentre or the Mid Rhondda Athletic ground in Tonypandy. Jumping events took place on the afternoon before the track and field. Most years I jumped and ran, apart from the middle years when a sudden growth spurt left me with no strength for the fast pace of the hundred yards, so I only did the high jump. Besides I'd joined Porth Park tennis club, was a devotee of the game, hopelessly in love with Lew Hoad and had no time to practise sprinting.

Once a year, the school sports kit, in the tenacious keeping of Miss Griffiths, saw the light of day. It consisted of a most unglamorous green cotton blouse with a square neck and long, short sleeves, no doubt sewn up by girls, now grandmothers, who had suffered Double Agony at the beginning of the century. They had lain folded for so many years, except for their annual outing, that the fold creases remained in them even after they were washed and ironed. The blouse came in two sizes — tiny and huge. I felt sorry for the large Form Oners who couldn't get into the tiny blouse and breathe at the same time as the huge one was a decided handicap on what was still a relatively small girl. The air would rush in through the gaping square neck, causing the garment to balloon out at the back like a parachute. It was helpful to have thin arms because the wind could blow out through the flapping sleeves but this created such a chill that you raced with chattering teeth and goodness knows how many strained muscles. It was rarely sunny on Sports day even if it had been boiling for weeks previously, so Porth County girl competitors resembled either a running Bibendum or fast moving mini ice floes caught in the Humboldt current.

The over-long, navy serge shorts that accompanied the blouse did nobody's figure any favours either. No gathered waist or discreet pleat helped camouflage a well developed thigh muscle — muscle propagated of course through exercise, not chips — so that they clung unflatteringly to your legs like cyclists' shorts, showing up every little bulge. Two tubes sewn together with a pocket for a hanky, in case someone fancied a nose blow half way through the 220!

Miss Griffiths, a tape measure round her neck, very cheerfully doled out the garb and measured every competitor carefully to see if they were in the tiny or the huge category.

"Oh Mary, you've shot up in the last year. You'd better have the larger size this time," thrusting yards of folded green cotton at me. "And take a pair of shorts. Make sure they're washed and ironed before you return them. They won't shrink, tell your mother. Good luck in your event. Next!"

No wonder we were called County snobs with our team running gear, especially the shorts, as all the other girl athletes ran in navy knickers and any blouse of the right colour, blue for Porth Sec, Ferndale in yellow, Pentre (the most dangerous and feared rivals) in white and Tonypandy in red. We even had jumping shoes — normal spiked running shoes with two extra spikes in the heel for grip — but didn't broadcast the fact or we'd have been considered even more snobbish.

The jumping afternoon, the day before the main Sports, was usually overcast and gloomy with a threat of rain even if it wasn't already spitting a bit. Assorted girls and boys, legs blue with cold and wearing school blazers for warmth as track suits were not generally available, got themselves to the field on buses from various parts of the Rhondda and hung around waiting for the start of competition. There were few supporters for the jumps apart from one or two unemployed or retired parents, the P.E. teachers, other competitors and a handful of mitchers who kept well away from anyone in authority. The atmosphere among the shivering little groups in the empty acres of field was not a joyous one. What with the damp and hunger — competitors had been too nervous to have any lunch — and the fear your legs wouldn't work so you'd let everyone down, come last, and score *nul points,* it was an occasion more like a visit to the dentist than a celebration of athletic prowess, however minimal.

When I was small, in Forms one and two, Millie would put her arms round me (as there were two high jumpers from each school) for mutual comfort and warmth, although in a strange way she was now a rival. Even in the upper school her friendly smile and encouragement was a great support. For several years, when she had left after 'O' levels to go and work in the Porth 'Boots', she managed to have Wednesday afternoon off to come and watch the jumping events and back her old school and former co-pupils.

Apart from being placed, usually in the first three in the high jump over the years, I especially remember the jumps afternoon for two memorable occasions. On the first, the second string long jumper for the Senior County Boys hadn't arrived for the event. "Probably caught the wrong bus and ended up in the other valley, the imbecile!" said an agitated Andrew Williams, worried about the wasted points and annoyed lest Porth County lose its grip on the shield through careless and futile conduct. There was at that time a fine all-round athlete at the school from Llwyncelyn, Porth. Jack Melen was 6'2" at fifteen and the speediest sprinter since Gagsa. With a mop of black hair and eyes almost as dark, he was shy and not over fond of study. His life was sport, and where sport was, so was he. A year or two later he won a sports scholarship to the prestigious Somerset school, Millfield, and also played on the wing for Pontypridd RFC. His father was a local bobby who died suddenly on duty when Jack was ten. His mother was from Lancashire and inherited, suddenly and surprisingly a few decades later, half of Southport, whence the remaining family moved.

On this particular afternoon Mr. Williams spotted Jack with the mitchers and beckoned to him. Thinking he was going to be reprimanded for not being at school, Jack reluctantly ambled across the field with a hang-dog look.

"Jack, here's a pair of shorts. Get changed. You're doing the long jump."

"But sir, I haven't got any..."

"Don't argue. We'll find you some spikes, and just jump in your white vest." (Boys wore vests in those days.)

"But sir, I've never...."

"Look, just run up to the board as fast as you can, don't over-step it and jump as far as you can. That's all. We'll have points deducted for only one competitor and that fool Cummings hasn't arrived."

Jack, no doubt relieved he wasn't to get a ticking off, or worse, reported back at school with all the hassling ramifications that entailed, was happy to have a go. When his first of six jumps came he overshot the board by a foot and leapt nearly as high as he did long. "Measure your run back from the board, Jack" was the advice. His second turn came. He was ready now and knew what to do. His rangy frame sped powerfully along the run-up, took off perfectly from the board, and with arms, head and neck straining forward, sprang high in the air and landed almost out of the sand pit. There were gasps and whistles of amazement. He'd broken the record by two feet. Only one other jump was required to see if he could extend what was now his record and everyone on the field crowded round to watch. Whether he did or not was 'academic', as John Arlott might say, the thrill was in the initial, unexpected feat. Andrew Williams was delighted. Maximum points and a record! "Mitch as much as you like in future, lad," was his concession, "as long as it's to help out the school in sports of course."

The other significant occasion concerned the Senior Boys high jump. There were various styles of going over the metal bar which clanged horrendously when you didn't, and which could give you a spiteful wallop on the ankle if you didn't smartly get out of the sand after a failure. These styles had impressive names, the Western Roll, the Eastern Cut-off and the Straddle. While some of the boys jumped in these more esoteric styles, the girls all did the more homely named Scissors — a jump with no pretensions — right or left leg up first followed by the other and you hoped your bottom would also clear the bar. There was no Fosbury flopping, going over backwards and head first in those days, as the landing was in sand, and that usually damp, not foam rubber as now. Jumpers tried to land on their feet as touching down on anything else could prove dangerous and painful. As it was, with every leap you got a shoeful of cold sand.

A thin, fair haired boy of the name of Malcolm Mudge was one of the County Boys competitors, a not especially distinguished athlete, and being lanky with pale eyes and blond eyelashes, not especially, at least as far as I knew, the object of female worship, apart from doubtless his mother, which is not quite the same thing.

The competition was in the early stages when word went around among the girls, "Go and watch the Senior Boys high jump." People began to wander across, wondering why a bunch of female spectators were getting so excited by this fairly ordinary event with no 'superstars'. It had all begun when a single girl competitor, having finished her event, went to support the boys from her school. As she watched Malcolm Mudge scissor over the bar at a low height, she gasped in astonishment then, doubled up with laughter, hand over mouth, looked round for a friend who in turn was soon reduced to a fit of giggles. Others joined them and as Malcolm sailed over the bar, cries of "Oooh" echoed around and the applause and cheers at a successful clearance were the cause of considerable masculine mystification. Some boys were indignant to see fellow pupils encouraging a rival. Girls, not only disporting the green of County, but the white, red, blue and yellow of the other schools shouted, "Well jumped Malcolm", though they'd never set eyes on him or heard of him previously. As he prepared his approach there were shouts of "Come on Malcolm!" And he did. Never having hitherto experienced such female encouragement and considerably elated and spurred on by it, he surpassed himself, clearing greater heights than he'd ever done in practice.

And why the vociferous patronage of Malcolm? Well, while all boys at that time wore white vests visible through their shirt, they evidently did not all wear underpants, and this day, this certain young man, it was clear to all facing him as he jumped, was not wearing that particular item of clothing under his brief green shorts. Every time he jumped he revealed all his manly assets. Surprisingly, for such a thin lad, all his very manly assets.

Other boys began to tease him and imitate the female encouragement, and at each new round of cheering, he blushed — as well he might. He didn't achieve the memorable feat of Jack Melen but was placed 3rd in quite a strong field. Unfortunately the feminine interest dissolved once he stopped jumping.

1. The Author,
   Form 1 innocent

2. Form 3B, 1950. Author, second row, far right.

3. Porth County School, upper school.

4. Group of friends, including Pam, Marjorie and Caryl (top right) making silly faces in front of school.

5. Same group, more sober (apart from Caryl).

6. From left to right: Marjorie Woosnam, the author, Pamela Nicholls.

7. David 'Geronimo' Thomas at the edge of Coedcae Pond.

8. Porth County teachers, 1953, second row, from left to right:
Miss Davies (French), Miss Llewellyn (French), Miss Watkins (Chemistry), Miss Griffiths (Needlework),
Miss Davies (Latin, 'Dai Lat', Welsh), Miss Williams (Maths & meal manners), Miss Harries (Music),
Miss Orsman (Deputy Head, Geography), Miss Hudd (Headmistress), Miss Pennington (Biology),
Miss Simon (Cookery), Miss Lloyd (History).

9. Some of the L6 talent on the other side of the railings. Porth County boys, circa 1954. Trevor Fudge, extreme left.

10. Porth County girls on school field, 1954. Author, second row, left.

11. Rhondda School Sports, 1953 at mid Rhondda Field, Tonypandy.
Author in Porth County contingent, bottom row, 4th from left.

12. The Hurdles. Author, second from right.

**13. Cast of the school play 'As You Like It', 1954.
Author, centre, in beard.**

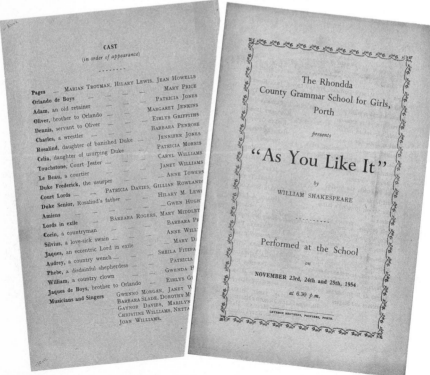

CAST

(in order of appearance)

Pages — MARIAN TROTMAN, HILARY LEWIS, JEAN HOWELLS	
	MARY PRICE
Orlando de Boys —	PATRICIA JONES
Adam, an old retainer —	MARGARET JENKINS
Oliver, brother to Orlando —	EIRLYS GRIFFITHS
Dennis, servant to Oliver —	BARBARA PENROSE
Charles, a wrestler —	JENNIFER JONES
Rosalind, daughter of banished Duke	PATRICIA MORRIS
Celia, daughter of usurping Duke	CARYL WILLIAMS
Touchstone, Court Jester —	JANET WILLIAMS
Le Beau, a courtier —	ANNE TOWERS
Duke Frederick, the usurper	
Court Lords — PATRICIA DAVIES, GILLIAN ROWLANDS
Duke Senior, Rosalind's father —	HILARY M. LEWIS
Amiens —	GWEN HUGH
Lords in exile BARBARA ROGERS, MARY MIDDLET
Corin, a countryman	BARBARA PE
Silvius, a love-sick swain —	ANNE WILL
Jaques, an eccentric Lord in exile	MARY D
Audrey, a country wench —	SHEILA FITEPA
Phebe, a disdainful shepherdess —	PATRICIA
William, a country clown	GWENDA
Jaques de Boys, brother to Orlando	EIRLYS G
Musicians and Singers GWENNO MORGAN, JANET V
	BARBARA SLADE, DOROTHY M
	GAYNOR DAVIES, MARILYN
	CHRISTINE WILLIAMS, NETTA
	JOAN WILLIAMS,

The Rhondda
County Grammar School for Girls,
Porth

presents

"As You Like It"

by

WILLIAM SHAKESPEARE

Performed at the School

on

NOVEMBER 23rd, 24th and 25th, 1954

at 6.30 p.m.

LEYSHON BROTHERS, PRINTERS, PORTH.

14. Programme from 'As You Like It'.

15. Girl Guide camp in Porthcawl, 1954.
Author, third from right.

16. Assorted Porth Rangers and Girl Guides.
Miss Orsman in centre. Guide Captain,
back row, second from left.

PALAIS DE VERSAILLES

17. School visit to Paris, Easter, 1952.
Teachers hiding at back.

HÔTEL JEAN-BART

Près le Jardin du Luxembourg e l'Institut Catholique

PAUL LEQUESNE

PROPRIÉTAIRE

9, Rue Jean-Bart
•PARIS•

Métro: S.ᵗ Sulpice et Vaugirard

~~Pension~~
~~Table d'Hôte~~
Confort Moderne
Chauffage Central
Électricité

Situation
Exceptionnellement
tranquille
Téléph: Fleurus 29-13
R.d.C. Seine 195.474
LIT

Maison Recommandée aux Familles et à M.M. les Ecclésiastiques

J. Meyer Grav-Paris

18. Card from Paris Hotel.

Whether Malcolm ever learned the reason for the spurious support of the fair sex is unknown, but his fame certainly spread through the Girls' school and on passing him girls would giggle.

Morning school finished earlier than usual on the main Sports day to allow pupils to get to the ground for the 3 p.m. start. Excitement abounded among the programme-waving supporters, and nervousness among the participants. But what a contrast to the day before when there were only a handful of spectators isolated in the vast, green acres dominated by the bleak, empty grandstand. Today the place was packed with young people, their school colours dominant in their allocated sections of ground. School were kept apart as otherwise civil war would have erupted, so intense was the rivalry and passion. Each school proudly displayed its Banner. Pupils waved flags, pennants, scarves, sweaters — anything they could lay their hands on in their colour. And the noise! If one school started to sing their song or intoned their chant, others would try to drown them by singing or yelling theirs. Strangely the sun, despite the previous day's sulks, normally deigned to grant an appearance. It sparkled on the silver shields, cups, trophies and rose bowls standing on a small, velvet covered table in mid-field, high-lighted the white running tracks, and bounced off the white painted metal of the hurdles aligned in neat, inviting rows.

When the races began, you could feel the buzz of excitement as five people with different coloured shirts lined up for the off. Indistinct shouts from the starter, presumably "On your mark", "Get set" as the runners crouched, then leaned forward, was followed by the quick report of a starting pistol and the runners springing forth like frightened rabbits. Supporters' cheers were even more deafening during the races: "PentRE. PentRE. PentRE."

"Oh look our girl's winning."

"Come on Marian, come on! Oh flip, the red girl's overtaking her. Aw! Pandy's gonna win. Oh, easy. Blow and damn! Third!"

"Never mind, we 'aven' been doin' so bad. Still got a chance to win the shield."

"You must be joking! Ferndale will win the relay. They got first and third in the 'undred an' second in the 'urdles, and there's double points for that."

"Oh well, it don' matter. Wanna jelly baby? Oh, look at tha' little tubs in the blue. 'E's never runnin' the 220!"

After each race, appropriately coloured flags denoting the first three places were raised, to more cheering, chants and rapturous applause.

The final events were the 4x100 yards relays. Runners stood anxiously just inside the line marking the 'box' for the change-over and practised taking an imaginary baton in their out-stretched left hand, running a few steps then transferring it to the right for the next person. No-one could keep still, but trotted on the spot, ran a few yards or shook their arms out as though trying to get rid of slimy stuff on their fingers. Some looked tensely back at the start or just hugged themselves in an attempt to control their shaking and nervous goose-pimples. Few spoke to their rivals in the adjacent lanes but just glanced surreptitiously at them from time to time to ensure that they too were scared stiff. Officials, holding little flags and trying to look sporty in open- necked shirts and flannels, stood importantly at the front and back of each box to disqualify anyone who overstepped the marks.

The starter's gun fired and the first legs were on their way. Some hesitation a hundred yards further on, perhaps a dropped and hastily retrieved baton, and the coloured shirts were strung out down the back straight. The third set of runners were in position, left arms reaching back well before starting to sprint. Spiked feet thudded on turf as girls urged their legs to move faster and faster. The panting of the runners could be clearly heard above the surrounding din of cheering. You start to run, build up speed, metal is thrust into your hand. Hooray, you didn't drop the wretched thing! Transfer it to the other hand and go, go, go! Adrenaline gives you power, your legs feel strong. You glimpse one or two moving colours out of the corner of your eye — then the bend — they've gone. The face of the last girl to run, Caryl, is visible now, head anxiously turned back, arm outstretched for the baton. She's beginning to move — quick before she's out of the box. Caryl takes the baton — she's gone. You slow down, eyes on the last runner. "Come on! Come on!" you urge between clenched teeth. Yes, County are in the lead. It's close. The white tape flutters and falls. The yellow shirt is there too. A green flag is raised. "Hooray, we've won!" Ecstasy, leaps and cartwheels. The green and yellow scarves on the bank are in the air, people are jumping up and down, the Banner's waving wildly, the cheering's rapturous.

Finally, all events completed, points added up, everyone, spectators included, invade the field to surround the trophy table. It's impossible to see what is going on. You could only get to the front if you had a mother whose razor sharp elbows (honed at jumble sales) you had inherited, or better still, had her with you. Most of the athletes were in the changing rooms anyway, hurrying to dress and rejoin their friends for arguably the best part of the day — the triumphal march back to school. We always marched in triumph whether we'd won the Sports or not. In fact the Boys usually did, the Girls usually didn't.

Crowds of excited youngsters streamed through Tonypandy under the vigilant eyes of one or two extra policemen. The red throng headed north and the mingled bottle green and moss green blazers of the County snobs, south, keeping apart from the blue sardines also making for Porth. Over the bridge by Central Hall we cascaded and up into Partridge Road, singing the school songs and chants, linking arms, eating bits of squashed sandwiches and chocolate someone had thoughtfully brought to compensate for a missed tea, taking swigs out of a peripatetic bottle of pop and getting horribly in the way of the occasional car which had the temerity and foolishness to claim the road. Miss Hudd would have been stiff with disgust and narrow-eyed with contumely if she could have seen such a display, public or otherwise from her 'gels'. As it was, she had probably emigrated to Cardiff for the evening and sought refuge in the theatre in order to dissociate herself from the goings-on.

Although violence and vandalism couldn't have been further from our minds, rivalry and high spirits weren't. Snatches of animated chat could be overheard. "Oooh, did you see Algy Griffiths in the 440? Hasn't he got nice legs?" or "I think Trevor Fudge is gorgeous. Lovely blue eyes. Awful shy though." "Did you see Margaret Booker overtake that girl in the relay? Cor, she went past like a bomb and the Pentre girl nearly stopped in surprise aye." "Wasn't Mair Davey disappointing? She can run much faster. Came close to the record in school, see. Terrible nerves she's got though. Sick before her race she was."

Gradually a message filtered through the marchers, walkers and stragglers. "We're going to get Porth Sec's banner and stick it in our school field." Idle chatter died away, people walked faster or ran to catch up with the control group, always the boys. Expressions changed as a sense of mischief and delicious naughtiness replaced fatigue.

Porth sec sardines were our keenest rivals, purely and simply because of geography — they were just down the road. As a result, in spite of some of us having close mates, relatives, boyfriends, girlfriends, even brothers and sisters there, on Sports day they were our enemies. The prefects of both County schools, and the more responsible, tried as best they could to inject a sense of propriety and orderliness into the triumphal procession. The idea was to march the banners and flags to the school gates and disperse from there. Every year, however, the precursors of the football hooligans of three decades later had other plans. Keyed-up and excited by the day, their energies had to find an explosive outlet. The march surged, then cantered, then ran. In the confusion, Hope Higgs lost her sandal as someone trod on her heel. The errant piece of footwear was irrecoverable in the stampede so she had to wear one dap instead. "Get Porth Sec Banner" was the password. Down Cemetery Road, green blazered boys and girls ran, anxious if not to be part of, at least to witness whatever fray was going to occur. In fact, no banner as far as I knew was ever captured. The procession de-materialized, dispersing in disorderly fashion with groups wandering hither and thither looking for the action but finding none and eventually catching the bus home in great disappointment and anti-climax but with a bag of chips as consolation.

One year a largish crowd decided to finish the celebrations on the school field with a sing-song and all sorts of mixed goings-on in the jungle at the back and among the trees on the front lawn. The following morning we were harangued by a fearsome Miss Hudd in assembly. "The school is private property, not to be invaded by a bunch of desperadoes and ne'er-do-wells who think they can trample the grounds and leave their disgusting litter all over the place. If I find those responsible they will suffer the consequences." At this point there were worried looks, grimaces and sideways glances throughout the school. Half of us could clearly expect expulsion, especially Caryl Williams whom we knew had a bit of red Tonypandy flag she was going to auction in her pocket that very moment.

"It will not happen again," Bessie continued. And it didn't. The following year, the rusty main gates that hadn't been moved for decades, were dragged and forced shut and padlocked across the gap where they couldn't quite meet. Behind them stood Mr. John and the vice-caretaker, Bill, both in their riot gear of boiler suits. So we invaded Porth Square instead, running around the red brick toilets in the middle and rather befuddling the gummy old men who sat on the bench outside watching the buses go past. Some Sec sardines were involved in this happy tarryhooting but they were bannerless and it was all quite friendly, simply those who hadn't taken part in the Sports showing they could sprint and race too. Apart from the confused old chaps on the seat, other passers-by seemed to enjoy the high jinks. Customers in Mann's cafe opposite crowded into the window to watch, letting their coffees go cold. Some missed their buses which departed empty as they gaped at the noisy revellers. Distracted motorists narrowly avoided accidents as they mounted the pavement or swerved, swearing and shaking their fists, to avoid a County snob darting across the road. The jollity was again denounced by the Authority in Assembly the following morning. "I was horrified to learn of the participation of some of our pupils, seen in their blazers, in the disgraceful display of rowdyism in Porth Square last evening. If I find those involved etc. etc..." It was the last post-sports-tournament-roistering of my era, but then as one grew older one tended to go for a stroll with a boyfriend or to a café with friends to discuss serious matters over coffee, such as the latest Frankie Laine record or the staff's love affairs, rather than run around fatuitously with kids.

CHAPTER TWELVE

School Dinners

School dinners were a constant source of interest and discussion. There were two sittings and naturally everyone preferred the first. Re-fuelling was then out of the way and you had the rest of lunch time to skylark around the school; there were bigger helpings and more choice in 'first dinners'. Seconds were reserved for the following sitting of diners though, unless one of the dinner ladies was your aunty or you lived next door to one of them and you ran errands for her. Come to think of it, they often announced there were seconds of cabbage in the first sitting, but there were rarely any takers. In fact, nearly as much of the cabbage that was put out was sent back for the future lunch of some lucky pig — that is, unless Miss Williams (Annie) Maths was on dinner duty. She was a stickler for perfect table manners and for eating up all your food. It was she who was on dinner duty during my first week in County. The wide-eyed, blameless, small girls filed in through the unbelievably narrow doorway and were made to sit at already laid places at the seven or eight long tables arranged along the width of the room. The end place was sacrosanct — reserved for a prefect who was to preside over the diners to ensure there was fair allocation of the food (which arrived in tureens) and that the whole lunching process was carried out in the seemly fashion expected of the young ladies of Porth County.

On this first day there was no food until we'd had a lesson in eating. We were all rather surprised at this initial announcement by Miss Williams, "Now girls, before the dinners arrive you must learn how to eat properly". Puzzled glances were exchanged. Had we missed out on some secret method of food intake? After all, we'd managed to find the right facial orifice for solid and liquid nourishment for eleven years. We sat expectantly. Porth County was clearly going to instruct us in many new things, but in eating? Surely there was only one known way. Were we going to have to shove food up our nostrils for example?

"Now girls, pick up your knife in your right hand. Now, a knife is not a pencil..."

"Dear me! She does think we're stupid! Doesn't she know we passed the scholarship exam?"

"...and mustn't be treated as such," she continued, "so don't hold it like a pencil. The top of the knife must nestle in the palm of the hand with the index finger resting on the back of the blade. Hold your knives up correctly please." To her satisfaction, a forest of blades flashed dangerously in the air, with a few adjustments needed here and there for those with short, stubby fingers or thin, bony hands.

"Now pick up the fork please." At this point a few dreamers who had put their knives down had the forks in their right hands. Annie Maths looked dumbstruck. "Did I tell you to put your knife down? Do you normally hold the fork in your right hand? Really, child! Are you an American girl?" she asked irascibly. This last question, which seemed totally irrelevant, baffled all of us.

"No Miss, Welsh Miss, from Porth Miss," was the contrite reply.

It was not until ten years later, eating in a student canteen in Tours in the Loire valley with a new friend from Washington, Barbara Fazackerly, that the sense of the question suddenly struck me with joyful force and a click of the fingers. "That's it!" I said and explained to a surprised Barbara, who had just cut up her food into manageable chunks to negotiate their transport to her mouth with her fork held in her *right* hand. Illumination evidently comes to those who wait.

Miss Williams carried on with her tutelage on alimentary matters. We had to hold the fork in a similar fashion with the top of the handle in the palm and the forefinger delicately arched to guide the prongs. This method of eating was indeed new to most, if not all of us, and for a few seconds we happily jabbed and speared imaginary food on the table and, surreptitiously, not-so-imaginary neighbours. The spoon instruction followed but was briefer. "We don't have soup here for dinner but you should learn how to drink soup from a spoon. You move the spoon away from you and drink from the side. Never put the bowl in your mouth." At this point peeved glances were exchanged. Put the bowl in your mouth! Did she think we'd been brought up in caves? Anyway you'd have to have a pretty big mouth to get any sort of bowl, apart from one out of a doll's tea set, into it. "And don't slurp. That's very bad manners. On the other hand when you eat dessert you take it from the front of the spoon, but again don't put the whole of the bowl in your mouth."

There she was going on once more about putting bowls in your mouth as though we were peasants.

"Only put the amount on your spoon that you can get into your mouth without difficulty."

At this point, tongues were hanging out, taste buds agog and groans at the mention of food, barely stifled. Tummy rumblings were making noisy intrusions into her attempt at instructing us in good breeding. Mouths watered, minds wandered and eyes gazed longingly in the direction of the busy dinner ladies. However, Annie Maths had not finished with us yet.

"Never put more in your mouth than you can comfortably deal with. It's appalling table manners to have your cheeks bulging out with food."

Our eyes rolled skywards in hungry despair. "If this goes on much longer, not only will we have bulging cheeks, we'll be scrummaging for the peas and potatoes and gobbling them up like starved convicts if you don't finish preaching now."

"But possibly," the voice droned on, "the most important thing is that once you have food in your mouth, you chew it with your mouth shut. There is nothing worse than someone eating with their mouth open. It makes a most odious and vulgar slapping noise. Finally..." Children sat up at this point and expressions became more hopeful. "Finally, once you have eaten everything on your plate, lay your knife and fork neatly side by side on the plate, not crossed over one another and not placed haphazardly just anywhere."

At last the trolleys rumbled up the aisles and a pile of warm dinner plates, tureens of vegetables, a dish of sliced meat and a boat of gravy arrived on the table. The Sixth formers too had arrived and each stood behind the chair at the head of the table. Hands motioned us to stand up and when all scuffling ceased, Miss Williams intoned, "For what we are about to receive, may the Lord make us truly thankful, Amen. Thank you, sit." At last we could eat and even all the cabbage was consumed that day. We were so famished we ate with cutlery digging into our palms and with our mouths mostly shut, chewing away like rabbits tackling unhusked corn.

Staff were not omnipresent when on dinner duty. Apart from their voices saying grace at the start you scarcely realised they were there. Some wandered around reading a book, some leaned against a wall and stared into space in extreme boredom, while others went and chatted to the dinner ladies: but not our high priestess of table manners, Annie Maths. She arrived with her constant companion, Rufus the Ruler, and if her eagle eye spotted, at a hundred paces, a child mishandling her knife and fork, she was at the unfortunate's side at the speed of sound to rap the offender on the knuckles with her weapon. She watched out for the cabbage leavers too, as she prowled. The only way to avoid her ire was to pass your plate quickly up the table when she was at the other end of the room for the presiding prefect to scrape off the leftovers on to the top one. Sometimes though she would bound up, eyes gleaming behind thickish glasses, and utter the fateful words "Stop! Whose plate is that with uneaten cabbage? Pass it back please." And the poor girl would be faced with half a plateful of cold, soggy, stringy brassica that she had somehow to convey the eighteen or so inches down to her protesting innards while the rest tackled their semolina and blob of jam.

Pamela Nicholls, she of the unthreaded needle, found herself in this position once or twice — grounded by the greens. One time she sat there, cheeks bulging with cabbage, tears streaming down her face and into her plate, so the cabbage was even damper than usual. "I feel sick," she kept saying, accidentally spitting out bits of cabbage. Miss Williams' heart, however, was pitiless as far as food went and there Pam had to stay until it had all gone — but she was excused the semolina. Whether she rushed out to sick it all back up in the nearest toilet, I don't remember, but as she had promised never to thread another needle when she was finally mistress of her own life, she now vowed never to eat cabbage.

In my estimation, school food wasn't bad. Perhaps this judgment comes from having an insensitive palate and strong stomach developed over the years from having to run and serve in the shop during meals. I could eat virtually anything and didn't suffer from extremes of dislikes. Not so the majority, especially Hope Higgs, who grumbled at everything but ate it up nevertheless and often went for seconds, still grumbling. The mashed potato was occasionally lumpy but it was covered with thick, savoury gravy. Peas tended to be hard, dry, flaking and difficult to transport from plate to mouth without most ending up on the floor. There was one vegetable concoction they served which I thought quite delicious, and pretty too. This was cooked, grated carrot mixed with grated parsnip. It was bright and cheerful, didn't dart all over the place and escape like the peas, and wasn't sloshy like the cabbage. The meat dished up was much the same every day, same colour, same taste, so we never knew or cared which former beast we were eating, except that sometimes he came in a pie or rissole. Approximately once a week we had cold, round, or sometimes square, pink, floppy meat which looked worse than it tasted. In the summer this was accompanied by a lettuce leaf, a tomato and two pieces of cucumber, and sometimes a bit more meat in the form of a slice of slug, or if you were lucky, a whole, juicy maggot. In the winter, diced beetroot lay alongside, staining the pink meat purple, and in both seasons we were presented with two scoops of the ubiquitous mashed potato.

Semolina with a smear of jam in the middle looking like a bleary eye, was the dominant dessert. In first sittings it was quite palatable as it was hot and runny, but by the second, for some reason, it was cold and came in viscous slabs easier to eat with knife and fork than a spoon. After a second sitting, when sticky semolina was served, it was difficult to speak as one's mouth was glued up. Teachers then had a peaceful, if unprofitable afternoon. Now and then, macaroni or rice pudding, both with the bloodshot eye, replaced semolina. Girls looked forward to macaroni, as if you sucked all the milk out of the little tube and it didn't disintegrate in your mouth, it would whistle if you blew gently through it. On macaroni days, the sitting went on and on with strange noises coming from all over the room. A rather pleasant trifle, though mangled in appearance, completed the chief desserts along with something very dull and uninteresting called *teisen lap*. This was a slab of cardboard cake covered in jam or coconut. Gallons of custard were needed to soften this tough bun to render it eatable, and there was a continuous file of girls going to the servery to have custard jugs replenished. Complaints about the custard were never-ending.

"Ugh! This custard's burnt."

"Aaagh! I've got all the skin."

"Oh, this custard's not been mixed. I've got a mouthful of powder," and the speaker would spray fine grains of custard dust around as she spoke or choked.

Some pupils did their best to put others off their food. A particularly messy helping of trifle would elicit a comment such as, "Ugh! I can't eat this. It looks like a dish of cold sick." The prematurely ejected contents of various kinds of stomach figured prominently in comparisons. If Annie Maths was not on duty, left-over cabbage might be mixed with potato purée erring on the liquid side. "Ah, look at this. Isn't it nice? Our cat sicked up a yellowy green mush like this yesterday. School food is cat sick." There were cries of, "Oh, Oenwen, don't be so disgusting," and someone would throw down their knife and fork in mock horror. "Oh God. You put me right off my food you do. I can't eat any more of this now." "Oh go on," someone would say, "don't be like that. I'll get a nice glass of cold, congealed blood for you to wash it down with."

Rissoles were ripe for insults. "Cor, minced rat for dinners today," and pointing to the hard-as-marbles peas, "and there's the bullets they shot it with, look!" If the rissoles were slightly overcooked and browner than usual, a bright spark would chip in, "Huh, rat indeed. Dog's droppings more like!" The so-called wit flowed.

Vans brought the food, already cooked, in big, round vats on detachable wheels, or in steel boxes. All that it required was heating up and dishing out into tureens. The shiny-faced dinner ladies all wore white coats and caps, more a token to the concept of hygiene than an efficient deterrent to dirt as these strips of white material were perched rakishly on their hair like white, starched linen tiaras. They busied about in an atmosphere of steam and heat, surrounded by gleaming steel: deep sinks, vast draining boards, long taps, ovens, hot plates, cutlery containers, the servery and gigantic waste bowls. The latter provided the only splash of colour among the white and gleam, as the ever increasing pile of uneaten scraps of dinner grew into mounds of beetrooty, cabbagey, carroty pig swill — that is, when Annie Maths wasn't overseeing affairs.

Horrid stories were invented about the food containers. "Guess what? One day when they'd dished out all the potato from that vat thing, they found half a dozen cockroaches crawlin' around in the bottom, yeah," said H. Higgs. "Gerron! I don't believe you, liar," was the response from several anxious, horrified faces.

"No, honest now. Cross my 'eart an' 'ope to die, one of the dinner ladies is the sister of the woman next door to us an' she said, she did."

"Well I don' believe that anyway," Pamela announced with a touching trust in logic, " 'cos how would they breathe under a pile of spud?"

"They could've got in there overnight an', when they were putting the spuds in, p'raps they didn' notice the cockroaches."

At this point Hope would be overwhelmed by unfaithful friends covering her mouth with their hands in order to quench her unsavoury information. Other uncharitable ones would pretend to bludgeon her head with their spoon. Those who had finished their lunch and were enjoying the fun, would pipe up "Huh cockroaches! That's nothing! Ethne Davies had to take her *teisen lap* and custard back because there were too many big currants in it. But, guess what? They weren't currants. They were mouse droppings."

By this time white-faced, sitophobiac girls who had overheard the conversation were on their way out to buy a glass of mixed pop and a packet of crisps from the caretaker in the basement.

The prefects exerted a kind of control on the tables, each of which seated ten girls on either side, and as they walked in there were loud whisperings and hand beckonings to the popular ones — the athletes or games players, the actors and those whose favourite sentence wasn't "Take a hundred lines!"

"Oh Arfona come and sit here!"

"Look there's Betty Hooper. Betty, Betty, over here."

The few miseries, martinets and moaners among them were not in demand and filled the vacant end places, often to glum looks, tuts and eye-rolling from the prospective diners. They underwent the daily mortification of a display of non-popularity at lunch. I vowed that if ever I reached prefect status, I would quit the colourful dinner scene and bring sandwiches to eat so that I wouldn't have to bear the risk of running a similar, humiliating gauntlet.

CHAPTER THIRTEEN

The Eisteddfod

In February every year, strange goings-on were noted all over the school. Small groups of girls sporting round, coloured badges held meetings in various little corners, spoke in low tones and looked furtively about to thwart any unauthorised onlookers. Was this the beginning of the Porth County secret society to campaign for the abolition of berets, compulsory Needlework or limp, school cabbage? A Rhondda version of the Ku Klux Klan to hound swots and toadies? No, these were simply preparations for the great intellectual and artistic efforts of the annual March 1st eisteddfod.

On arrival at the school every girl was allocated to one of the school houses named after the four major peaks guarding the valley — Penrhiwgwynt (green) above Porth, Troedyrhiw (red) behind the school and Trealaw, and Penrhys (yellow) further north overlooking Gelli, both the latter bestriding the ridge between the Rhondda's Fawr and Fach rivers. The fourth was Craig-y-llyn (blue) miles away — the mountain barrier across the head of the valley somewhere above Blaenrhondda and Blaencwm. Girls who lived up there still came down with snow on their winter coats in April when the rest of us were in blazers, so blue was a fitting colour for this house. In my day, I seem to remember Penrhys being the clever house and winning most of the eisteddfod competitions, and Penrhiwgwynt having a bent towards sport — carrying all or most before it in that department — though I'm sure many will hotly dispute this. I was in Penrhiwgwynt house.

Preparations for the school eisteddfod began with a house meeting. Ours always seemed to take place in the Biology Lab, near the junior school entrance. Every available space was filled. Girls sat on the stools, the benches, and some in the crush accidentally slipped into the white china sinks or got skewered on the bunsen burners. Some even clambered up to sit on the high window sills from where they had a magnificent view of the valley and so paid little heed to proceedings. There we were, among the pickled rats in jars, dismembered dogfish, desperately transpiring and photosynthesising plants under glass, exhorted to enter all the eisteddfod competitions as everyone entering everything guaranteed valuable points. We were encouraged to display the green house badge on our gymslips to show solidarity and pride in the house, and if anyone didn't have one, or had mislaid it, or wanted two, they could buy them after the meeting for 2d each. These were sweet, little, shiny, plain but brightly coloured badges with tiny gold pins on them so you could attach them to your clothes. I was always rather disappointed in mine though, not proud of it. First the colour was blotchy with a few blueish or darker dots in the green; they would fade to a pale colour of sea-sick maggots after a week, giving rise to rival house members' insulting comparisons with rotting vegetables and the like; finally, the laminate and cardboard underneath would usually unpeel from the metal leaving you with a bit of useless rusty tin. Still, you could hardly complain for 2d I suppose.

The house captain, a prefect and her deputies, would demand proof that you were indeed entering competitions and you had to bring your incomplete maps of Patagonia, architectural style sketches of Castell Coch or some mediaeval Welsh castle, drawings of dragons and essays on "A visit down a coal mine" to school for their brief perusal. It didn't matter if it wasn't very good. Entering, in the British spirit of 'fair play' and 'cricket' was the thing. House prefects wandered around as if on auto-control, muttering the words of the American, Grantland Rice, who no doubt had American football in mind when he wrote:

> When the one great Scorer comes to write
>   against your name,
> He marks not that you've won or lost —
> But how you played the game.

Similar Kiplingesque and Newboltesque sentiments were to the fore in the pre-eisteddfod weeks:

> If you can keep your head when all about you
> Are losing theirs and blaming it on you.
> If you can meet with Triumph and Disaster
> And treat those two imposters just the same.
> If you can talk with crowds and keep your virtue
> Or walk with Kings — not lose the common touch
> If you can fill the unforgiving minute
> With sixty seconds worth of distance run,
> Yours is the Earth and everything that's in it,
> And which is more — you'll be a Man, my son!

Or,

> The sand of the desert is sodden red —
> And England's far and Honour a name,
> But the voice of a schoolboy rallies the ranks,
> "Play up! play up! and play the game!

The Sixth formers didn't, of course, spout poetry at length at you on a chance meeting in corridor or in grounds but I quote them here because their stirring expression was apt for the occasion. The utterances are all geared towards boys: the last thing anyone in Porth County Girls wanted was to enter the German recitation for example, and become a man.

Lunch-time hockey and netball games were temporarily renounced as girls gathered in various rooms for house choir practice, English group recitation or Welsh *cydadrodd*. As March 1st approached and rehearsals became more frantic, they became more futile too. Space was increasingly limited as panic-stricken practices proliferated. Frequently a group would be howling, "I must go down to the seas again, To the lonely sea and the sky," trying to be heard above the belting of a choir singing, *Gently awakes my heart* in the next door. *Quinquireme of Ninevah* spoken in chorus would unwittingly match the rhythm of the 'dawnsio cymraeg' being stamped out on the other side of the partition. Some rehearsals even took place in cloakrooms and cupboards.

Preliminary heats of the solo efforts took place during the dinner break in the last week in February. Contestants, books open on their laps in the bus, learned poems in various languages — Welsh, French, German and English — as they travelled to and from school. As Pamela, Marjorie, Hope and I walked up to school from Porth Post Office where we met, classmates would go by in buses, gazing out of the window into the middle distance, their lips silently moving as though they were speaking to some airy sprite only visible to themselves. We would wave, but to little avail. They were soundlessly reciting their eisteddfod poem, *L'homme et la mer* par Charles Baudelaire or *Erlkonig* von Johann Wilhelm von Goethe or verses by the ever-present John Masefield who turned up annually in some poetic form.

The Welsh recitation held few learning problems for us, as that was mainly the way we learnt the language — by learning a Welsh poem every week for the Thursday lesson. As far as the other Welsh lessons went we wrote lists of things like, "Yr wyf i, yr wyt ti, y mae ef, y mae hi, yr ydym ni, yr ydych chwi, y maent hwy." It sounded very rhythmical to me and for months I thought it was a poem too, as we recited it altogether. Great was my disbelief when after a term someone said it meant 'to be'. All those words for just 'to be'! "Welsh must indeed be a difficult and ponderous language," I thought. There was another similar load of words we recited, but with "gennyf, gennyt and ganddo" coming first, but I never got to the bottom of what they meant. Sometimes we wrote vocbulary at the back of our exercise books in lists labelled 'Cymraeg' and 'Saesneg', 'Caerdydd:Cardiff', 'Sir Forgannwg (Occasionally Morgannwg): Glamorgan County', 'Y mae'r bwrwr glawr: it's rainging' — a useful expression in Wales, especially in the north where the people spoke no English — and 'Modrib Mair: aunt Mary' — puzzling because in that case, what was Aunt Mair?

We were taught Welsh by Miss Davies Latin, Dai Lat, an unhurried, late middle-aged, affable soul with short, straight, dark grey hair in a fringe, and an air of not quite knowing where she was. If you hadn't learnt your poem off by heart though, she was overcome with irascibility and would yammer on crossly at us in Welsh like a demented woodpecker. At least we assumed she was cross. Nobody knew what she was on about. In order not to aggravate her normally placid demeanour, the girl sitting in front of the one chosen to recite would prop her book up against the back of the girl in front of her who would fluff out her hair so Dai Lat couldn't see the book peeping over her shoulder. As a result, the poems were recited with downcast, maidenly eyes which we hoped Miss Davies would interpret as humility.

We did learn poems, or parts of poems. Dai Lat, being rather absent-minded, would give us the same poem to learn twice or occasionally, three times. We never diabused her of her mistake. If someone copying the poem from the board, and getting to the fifth line or so, might say, "Hey, haven't we had this one before?" the room would so resound with "Ssshh" you'd think the tide was coming in at Trealaw. Dai Lat wouldn't notice. She was probably hundreds of miles away, mentally wandering around the forum in Rome or imagining the people going about their business in pre-volcano Pompei. We had a vague impression of not being taught Welsh very efficiently. But Latin was her first field of expertise, Greek her second and she taught us Welsh because she was a native speaker. So we could all recite several poems in Welsh despite having a minimal idea of what they meant, but could scarcely string together three words of the language.

Long suffering staff gave up their free time to listen to pale, nervously shivering children stutter out a few lines at the back of a classroom. Now and then there were confident competents intoning the poem in a loud, assured voice, some even managing to smile simultaneously while others stared at the ceiling in forgetful embarrassment, biting their lips and waiting for the prompt. Friends waited outside the door to give moral support. House colleagues might escort a reciter or soloist to the appointed room to ensure that her unsteady, trembling legs took her to the right place. Physical support was usually needed here to hold up the wild-eyed but willing competitor on the verge of collapse, or alternately, restraining arms to stop the unwilling one from taking to her heels. It was worse than a visit to the dentist or a practical music exam.

After the test the girl would emerge tottering, still pale but glad the ordeal was over, lean her back against the wall and slide weakly to the floor, looking aghast.

"How did it go?"

"O...o...oh," the martyr would croak, head in hands.

"What was it like then? Did you remember it all?"

"No..o..o," would be the plaintive reply. "Did you forget much? What did they look like? Did they smile or frown?"

"O..o..oh.. it was just awful."

"D'you think you'll qualify? (The least worst three were chosen to perform in front of the whole school.)

"Oh....No chance. I hope not anyway. I couldn't go through that again. Especially not on the stage. I'd rather die. I'm sure I made an awful fool of myself."

I was once foolhardy enough to enter the piano solo competition. The prelims were held in the Library where the grand piano stood impressively in one corner. This initial round wasn't too bad as the only judge was dear, smiling Miss Harries who never frightened anyone. The test piece was Schubert's *Warum?* Search as I might, I couldn't get hold of the printed sheet, so in the last resort had to borrow another girl's and copy the music out by hand. This took a few hours of work in the evenings after homework had been summarily done, dinner consumed and *The Archers* listened to over a cup of coffee. I really deserved several house points for accomplishing this marathon task, painstakingly copying multi-tailed, black and white notes on to a few pages of staves, not to mention the dots, circles and stripes that danced before my eyes for hours after each copying attempt. If ever a version of the modern photocopier, so taken for granted, and much maligned, cursed and kicked when its innards get jammed, was needed, it was then.

To my amazement and horror I was selected for the stage. I think Miss Harries was impressed by my pencilled version of the music. Her mental images of faithfulness, support and dedication to a cause must have been stirred because I really was not a very accomplished pianist, usually only managing to bash out something approaching the tune while paying scant regard to the finer points and nuances of the music.

The dreaded afternoon of February 28 or 29, when the individual items were judged, arrived faster than the normal run of days. I spent the morning feeling sick, could eat no dinner and visibly wore down the wood block floor in the corridor leading to the toilet. The school had been simmering with excitement all morning. Competition standard might not have been all that keen, but rivalry had been honed to a razor edge. Close friends in different houses became dire enemies prepared to kill for their colour.

"Ah ah. Craig-y-llyn's gonna win. We're ahead in the written," said my best friend Hope. "Huh, Craig- y-llyn! They're hopeless. They never win anything — only the Form One netball once. Anyway how do you know?" was my ripost.

"Miss said."

"I didn' hear her. All she said was there were a lot of entries."

"She's in our house see. And she told us something else as well..."

At this she annoyingly tapped the side of her nose indicating she knew something I didn't and wasn't going to impart the information either. The impulse to flatten the little proboscis was restrained with difficulty.

"Oh God. You get on my nerves you do, 'Ope 'Iggs, with your silly secrets."

"Aaah, you're only jealous 'cos we're winning an' we're a better house than the ol' greenies in Penrhiwgwynt."

Speechlessness poured out of my mouth and indignation distended my eyeballs and with a final stinging dart, "You ought to have been called Hopeless, not Hope 'cos you're like your stupid, old hopeless house you are." I marched off, ever to withold my discourse from my secretive, irritating, hateful, former best friend — until the next day anyway.

Pupils filed into the Hall straight after afternoon registration and sat in house groups. The scene was gaudier than usual, the strict school rules of uniform having been marginally relaxed to allow for ribbons, rosettes, handkerchiefs and gymslip sashes in the house colours, if you could get your hands on one. Miss Orsman, Deputy Headmistress and school Geographer-in-chief was the M.C., and Annie Maths, the totter-up of marks. They sat at a table alongside the dais together with the judges. Teachers, according to the event and their particular field of expertise, were the judges. Miss Hudd sat to one side of the stage as the Goddess Majestic in her habitual posture, leaning back in her chair, one elbow resting on the chair arm, fingers lightly supporting the side of her face. A slight disturbance in the audience during an event would prompt her to lean forward in the chair, frowning. Her eyes narrowed as she looked over the rims of her glasses, scanning the rows for the saucy piece who dared cough, sneeze, breathe too loudly or, dare I say it, whisper, thus interrupting the competitor and preventing fair play from holding sovereign sway.

Girls in various stages of fright mounted the steps to recite or sing, hoping some sort of audible noise would issue forth from their parched throats. Between items, winners of previously judged static competitions were announced in reverse order by Miss D.K. Lloyd, chief Historian to the premises. Competitors used *noms de plume* to avoid bias or favouritism.

"Results in the Art competition Forms One and Two. Third, *Wee Willie Winkie* Craig-y-llyn. Second, *Cymro Lil* Troed y rhiw. And first, *Olive Oil* Penrhys. She paused after each name to allow the winners to stand shyly and acknowledge their applause and cheers.

Then it was the piano solos, junior, middle and senior. I sat through the three junior solos wishing I'd never been born, with all my blood in my feet and my heart trying to knock down my chest wall, escape and bounce off down the corridor. Stage competitions were in alphabetical order of surname, so mine, — D, being high on the list, I was called first. Silently cursing my ancestors for not being Zachariah, Yashmak or at least Williams, I stumbled towards the grand piano, clutching my dog-eared, copied music in my nerveless fingers. By now I couldn't exactly remember how to breathe. The silence was terrifying and awesome as the assembly waited for me to produce sound. How I did I shall never know, as my fingers had as much life and sensitivity as a pound of pork sausages. Perhaps it was Miss Harries's kindly smile and wink as she whispered, "You'll be all right. Relax and take your time." Somehow, I got through the piece — much too fast, Schubert's question, *Warum?* (Why?), was answered that day, as far as I was concerned, practically before he'd asked it, certainly with indelicate dispatch. I didn't seem to see the notes or need Miss Harries to turn the pages, as my whole being had switched to automatic and the real me was elsewhere — sitting with my mother in the kitchen on an early winter evening with the fire glowing, or lying in the odorous, scratchy hay in the Tydraw loft. Then, 'o blessed release' the last half dozen bars were coming up and I was back at the piano suddenly concentrating on the music which adagioed softly to the last note which had to be played after a slight pause and very gently but firmly with the little finger of the right hand, so that it caressed the air sadly on a dying fall. I paused and touched the key lightly. Seconds passed. No note came. They were all waiting for the end. "Damn, it had always sounded on our Kaps at home in practice". I touched the note again and this time it clanged out like a drum roll giving quite the opposite of the required effect and completely ruining the end which was my best bit. Applause. Miss Harries's beaming, bony face. Slits for eyes. I rose as in a dream and floated back to my seat quickly in slow motion to start breathing, eating and living properly again. I was placed third of the three finalists but it was OVER and I couldn't have been happier if I'd won a hundred pounds.

The rest of the eisteddfod on the morning of St David's Day was even more competitive but the atmosphere was less tense as the solo events had been completed. Lots were drawn by the four house captains when everyone was seated in the Hall to decide the order of competition in the various senior and junior choral speeches, dances, unaccompanied three part groups and one-act plays. The last event was the house choir competition, the most important because of the high marks awarded. A house trailing in last place could win the eisteddfod by coming first and getting the maximum twenty points for a superlative performance by their choir.

Depending on the previous month's weather, the Hall was more reminiscent of a greengrocer's or florist's shop than a school, as every girl wore a daffodil or a leek, occasionally both, pinned to their gymslip. If it had been a wet, cheerless February, Florence Wilton, whose family ran fruit, veg and flower shops in Porth, which always had daffodils for March 1st, was everybody's best friend. Girls in her form and in others, to whom she'd spoken perhaps twice in three years, and that the previous St David's Day, would approach, "Allo Flor, want a sweet?"

"Oh, thanks."

"Got any daffs in your shop Flor?"

"I dunno. I 'spect we'll have some in for March the first."

"Will you get one for me Flor?"

"Oh I dunno — if I can. P'raps they'll all be sold out." The 'friend' would put her arm persuasively round Flor's shoulder.

"Oh come on Flor, only one— a little one, a bud, a scruffy one'll do. Come on, best pals?"

"Ooh, O.K. then. I'll try I s'pose."

By the end of the morning the Hall reeked of leeks and it was noticeable that the winning choir — the one in best voice — was that whose members' leeks had considerably diminished in size since their arrival in school a few hours earlier. Is the consumption of the national vegetable the reason the Welsh can sing? The choir results were announced to a breathless audience, then after rapid totting up, and to much cheering, punching of the air, and waving of house colours, the final placings were given in reverse order. It didn't matter if your house was last, you still cheered. As Miss Hudd annually proclaimed to a new batch of Sixth Formers, "It is better to travel hopefully than to arrive." The most frenetic applause and hurrahs, of course, exploded as soon as the second house was announced. Frequently the winner's name couldn't be heard in the hullabaloo, which reached its crescendo when the house captain mounted the dais to receive the shield. Then gradually, after singing *Mae hen wlad fy'n nhadau*, calm regained control, we dispersed to all corners of the Rhondda valleys to enjoy our half day holiday, 'cawl' dinner and Welsh cakes.

CHAPTER FOURTEEN

Exams

Though the vast majority liked school, we naturally looked forward to the fortnight or three weeks holiday at the end of term and especially to the one and a half months' summer break. End of term did not, however, bring joy only, but considerable worry and distress to many in the form of 'terminals' — end of term exams. Normally, those who worried weren't distressed as well. Worriers worked and usually did reasonably well, getting high marks and high positions. Some, like Ceridwen E.M.H. Thomas and Margaret Howells, naturally brilliant girls, didn't need to work and appeared to sail through the whole procedure smiling and unperturbed, taking the whole exam week in their stride as if it were no different from usual. Then, in prize-giving the following year, they would sail up to the rostrum to receive their prizes as top of the form, taking that in their stride too and showing no sign of nerves whatsoever. Girls like these and the women they become probably sail successfully and imperturbably through life, enjoying every minute of it, untouched by the trials and tribulations that affect the rest of us.

We were given our exam time-table a week or so before the fatal event. There were three exams per day, two in the morning and one in the afternoon. Whatever its composition, the time-table provoked adverse comment.

"Crikey! Have you seen Thursday? Science first, then cronky Arithmetic, then History."

"It's pap compared with Monday," moaned Pamela, "Frog first with bloomin', 'orrible Needlework followed by Algebra. Ugh!", as if she were talking about some prison-type menu she would be forced to eat. "I can feel a stomach ache coming on for

Monday. I'll have to go to the doctor's to see if I've got appendicitis I expect," she said as she planned evasive action for her worst exam combination.

The termly lecture which, in her school career, each girl received at least fifteen times, ensured that you were not only intellectually prepared for the exam with thorough revision, but manually ready as well, with sharpened pencils, pens full of ink, rulers, rubbers and other necessary equipment. Then in hushed, horrified tones, with an expression to match, one's form teacher, looking over her half frames, would say, "I need not remind you," (but she did all the same) "that any girl trying to contact another in the exam, whether it be by note or speaking, or anyone caught concealing exam information on their person will be most severely dealt with — most severely dealt with indeed." During the pregnant pause that followed, girls had visions of being frog-marched through the Rhondda streets, barefoot and in chains, wearing sackcloth, booed by hostile onlookers and whipped on by masculine women jailers as they made their way to ducking stools specially built for exam cheats over the inky Rhondda river, or to tight stocks full of splinters by the toilets in Porth Square. Even worse, one's mother might be summoned and public humiliation would be total as the whole school would see her on the drive or waiting outside Miss Hudd's room. One's mother might, faced with such devastating shame, conceivably even dissolve into tears and that, together with suspension of pocket money and outings for a year, would really not bear thinking about. So any thought of intra, extra-mural help was definitely out.

The evening before the particular exam was spent anxiously reading through exercise books and desperately ransacking one's memory of the recent revision lessons for any clue as to what questions might be asked. Question spotting was rife.

"D'you think Penny will put a question on the eye or the ear or both?" Hope might ask in lunch time before a Biology terminal.

"God knows. But she spent two lessons going over the ear last week and only one on the eye," Marjorie would butt in.

"Oh blow. That prob'ly means the ear then. I can't draw that as good as the eye." Then handing me her folded open exercise book, "Test me on the ear, will you Mary?"

"What's the inner tube called?"

"The Eustachian tube."

"Right. Now then, the round thing in the middle. You've got it 'ere looking like jam roly-poly."

Rolling her eyes skyward and giving me a gentle, retaliatory push, she'd bite her lip and think. "Umm. Umm. The.. the cock..something."

"Oh, don't be rude 'Ope," someone would say.

"Oh aye, I know, the coccyx."

"No ya daft thing, that's not in the ear."

"That's in your 'ead though, innit?" Pamela might say.

"No you daft ha'porth, it's in your bum," Marjorie would chuckle.

"It's the cochlea and the cochlear nerve."

"Oh well, I wasn't far wrong."

"You were in feet and inches," from Pamela.

So we'd revise the ear and there'd be a question on the paper about the eye.

If revision wasn't all that thorough, preparation of equipment was. Pencils in pencil cases were sharpened to a pin point. Sometimes new pencils were purchased, and so anxious were their owners about a satisfactory point, they'd be sharpened down to half their length before being deemed fit for usage. Tightly screwed small round bottles of Stephens, or cuboid bottles of Waterman's blue-black ink were carried and constantly checked in the front pockets of satchels, with packed lunches if you weren't school dinners, or biscuits for recess. If the bottles spilled, far better the ink spoil food than eradicate vital exam information in books, besides which you got a terrible row if your exercise book had a blot let alone an inky mess. Heads were constantly bent over these small bottles, worried fingers manipulating little gold or silver levers on fountain pens, checking that they were full of ink for the exam. The ink went back and forth from the bottle into the pen as the depressed rubber sac sucked up an amount to satisfy its owner, or squirted back that amount to prove it was working properly. Wooden rulers and rubbers, hard, grainy, dark grey for ink at one end and soft, light grey for pencil at the other, were endlessly inspected as no equipment borrowing was allowed once the exam started. Geography and Geometry exams were a terrible strain, as you had the responsibility of more well-sharpened pencils, coloured ones this time for the former (blue for rivers, red dot for towns, brown for mountains and all labelling in lead pencil — HB please) and for the latter, a pair of not too loose compasses, dividers, set squares and a protractor — often wooden or stiff cardboard in those days.

Once everyone was settled in their desk with two sheets of foolscap in front of them, the dreaded question paper would be placed face down on the desk. When everybody was served, you could look at it. It was normally a small slip of paper with the cursory rubric, "Answer four questions". There'd probably be five on the sheet, six if you were lucky and the subject teacher had been in a good mood when setting it. Modern pupils would not believe these slight bits of paper, often smaller than a parking ticket, could be examination question papers, faced as they are today with anything up to four booklets of several pages per exam. But nowadays children are not expected to write essays or provide their own maps, drawings and diagrams learnt out of exercise books and copied in by their own hand. Students of this decade have all the art work drawn for them and all they are required to do is label items on dotted lines — each dot corresponding to a letter. Frequently, not even a sentence is necessary to answer a question, a brief phrase or just one word will do. No doubt today's papers are far easier to mark, but the tonnage of former south American forest being transported by the Post Office around the country each summer from examining board to school to examiner and back to examining board must use up enough fossil fuel to supply the needs of a street of terraced houses for a lifetime. And for what? So some fool of an examiner can give a question as in an nineties Sociology exam: "Name an educational establishment", and mark the answer from an educationally unstretched child, "A school." Correct. Tick. One mark. Other equally futile questions to follow. "Down with Forests!" is the motto of the age.

In the fifties we did a great deal of comparing and contrasting in most subjects. "Compare and contrast the Bronze and the Stone Ages (with diagrams)". "Compare and contrast Photosynthesis and Transpiration in Plants (with drawings)", "Compare

155

and contrast Eastern and Western Australia (with maps)". We were always having to compare poems with each other, *The Isle of Innisfree* with *Sea Fever* or *The Twa Corbies* with *The Three Ravens*. In French and Geometry, where you couldn't do a lot of comparing and contrasting, the question papers, when placed face down, were often a frighteningly large foolscap page. In Welsh we normally had to write out 'Yr wyf i' and 'Y mae gennyf i' and their retinue and a Welsh poem of our choice, illustrated, if we had time.

In the third form we were given TWO papers for the Geography terminal, the question paper *and* a map of the world. This mappamundi had been hand rolled from a curved stamp with a raised outline using an inked pad. Doubtless, the teacher manually performing this operation had tired and the pad dried after a score or so because some were faint and some blurred with countries having a double or, if you were lucky, a treble coastline a millimetre apart. But this was progress indeed and proof Porth County was keeping up with twentieth century innovations. Girls labelled it enthusiastically, some upside down, putting Scotland in France and the Atlantic Ocean in the middle of Russia. We knew most of the world belonged to Great Britain but where exactly was Great Britain? On some maps, to be fair to the examinee, it wasn't. As a result, Ceylon and Japan won most votes, with New Zealand a close third.

Older pupils in 2A, old hands at terminals and all of thirteen years of age, whose classroom we shared for exams, would look benignly and sympathetically across at us pale-faced, younger ones, nervous lest all relevant knowledge flee our addled brains. The younger girls looked in awe at the bigger, confident Form Two pupils placed on either side in alternate rows. This 'mixing' for exams was also socially beneficial as you made the acquaintance of girls you normally wouldn't come into contact with. A black-haired girl called Shelagh Burke (her Christian name was spelt in that interesting way as I spied it on her answer sheet) bolstered my first exam efforts with her winks, smiles and nods as she detected from three feet away, drawings of hydrae with madly waving antennae, a Roman centurion or a geometrical shape for a theorem, Q.E.D. On my map of Australia I drew the Murray-Darling rivers watering the vast interior, so my new friend shook her head, drew an imaginary map on her English essay and outlined them going north and south just behind the coast. Her friend Mary Norman, whose father owned the fascinating emporium on Tynewydd Square next to the bus depot, sat behind her and passed her sweets through the gap in the chair between the back and the folding seat. Once, it was a wine gum which she didn't notice or feel, evidently, as she sat on it and it squashed, melted and stuck to her gymslip.

Perhaps the worst part of exams was getting the results. The teacher would enter the room more purposefully than usual, clutching a sheaf of bobbing, foolscap sheets. The sadists among them would distribute the corrected, but markless papers to be gone over, in order of merit. As you were made aware of your foolish answers, you were not so much thinking of the corrections in hand, as excuses to tell your mother, as your percentage mark visibly diminished with every question. Some teachers put you out of your misery straight away, giving the mark in alphabetical order while some apprentice sadists gave you the mark and position in order of merit. "First 87, Ceridwen Thomas. Second 85, Margaret Howells...." The voice would drone on, getting slower and more emphatic to stress one's shame and stupidity, unless she thought a deliberate manner was needed to ensure the bird-brained understood. "Hmmm... twenty-eighth 32, Hope Higgs.....Hmmm...thirtieth 28, Mary Davies."

Reports were the final and biggest problem. These were posted home, as clearly some wouldn't have arrived with the original information intact. All the marks, position in class and comments were on the single sheet with, fortunately, only a small space for the reflection on one's ability or, sadly as in my case, the lack of it. Posting of reports was a callous act, causing bad nerves, but mainly disturbing the sleep of multitudinous girls who felt compelled in some way to intercept, kidnap or do other nefarious things to this terminal bulletin. Some chatted up the postman, pleading with him to deliver a certain buff, handwritten envelope by mistake to a friend's house up the street; others took to early morning walks, catching their death to waylay him; yet others sat up half the night on the stairs to be first to greet the post; some suffered stress fractures of the brain waking up to honking alarms at an unearthly hour in the holidays, sometimes when it was still dark. Finally, those with a front outlook on the world kept watch at their bedroom window for the fateful delivery.

I would hear my father go off to his work at the B.O.A.C. Test Beds at about 6:30 and instead of going back to sleep as usual, would force myself to stay awake, listening for and interpreting the merest sound. Living in a long, terraced house meant that from the back kitchen where Mam would be busy making the fire, talking to the cat and feeding it, preparing our breakfast or generally potching about as mothers do, she couldn't hear the post being pushed under the shop door at the front, as we had no letter box. As soon as I heard the swish I would hare down the stairs on winged, gossamer feet, carefully open the door to the shop (wincing at its creaking, sighing protest), tip-toe along the flagstoned corridor to the front door and scan the mail for the long, light brown, hateful envelope. Once or twice I kidnapped business letters and bills which after being steamed open and re-sealed crumpily with 'Gloy' had to be furtively replaced the next morning. Usually though, I successfully managed to appropriate the wretched school report and get back to bed undetected.

During the day when Mam was busy in the shop — fortunately she loved to chat — I would smuggle the envelope down to the kitchen and, under the pretence of a caring daughter making a welcome cup of tea for her hardworking mother, boil up the kettle. Steaming open the flap, I would push the envelope under the chair if Mam suddenly appeared and smile charmingly to conceal my guilty actions and impure soul. In those first days of the school holidays, Mam had a few unsolicited and unexpected cups of tea — a gesture which disappeared once the report had arrived.

With an assortment of pens and inks, strategic words were added which mitigated the hostility or brutality of the teacher's remark and mollified my mother's reaction. On those occasions when I couldn't get my hands on the report first, Dad, being the more intellectual parent, oddly didn't seem to mind an inauspicious comment. He evidently had more faith in me and would merely say, "Never mind. Stick at it and try to do better in future." Mam, however would go mad and be in a bad mood for days, barely talking to me apart from, "Yes", "No", "I don't know", and that in a formal tone of voice as though she were speaking to the tax inspector.

I got better at the alterations as the years passed and the arrival on the scene of the ink eradicator was a decided bonus, so "Rather unsatisfactory" instead of being changed to "Not rather unsatisfactory" as in Form One became "Rather satisfactory" inForm Three just by a flourish of the little glass stick with its drop of colourless liquid which magically swallowed up the "un". A slightly yellowish blob was left in its place but the report pages were yellowing around the edges anyway, probably pre-war production, and no-one would notice an extra bit of discoloration. Difficulties were encountered with words such as "Disappointing" or even "Very disappointing" which tended to end up as "Not very disappointing". "Weak" became "Was weak" and "Poor", "Poor no longer". I could always rely on a commendable report for P.E. and Games — a subject which sadly held little credibility for Mam. One term, in my haste and to my later disgust, I discovered I'd perversely and mistakenly put a "Not" in front of my usual "Very good" for this subject, confusing P.E. with R.E. But on this occasion P.E. and Games was important in my mother's estimation.

"Look at this. 'Not very good' it says here for Gym."

"No it doesn't."

"Yes it does, look. And I thought at least you'd be all right in that subject."

"I am. I'm very good at it. It's a mistake."

"How can it be a mistake? The teacher's written 'Not very good'. There's no mistake."

"Aw. She must have muddled me up with someone else. Mari Davies or Irene Davies p'raps. It's wrong anyway."

But she wouldn't be placated and left me cursing my own incompetence in counterfeit.

Marks had to be changed on the report too as 36% could hardly be an accompaniment to "Not disappointing", so 3's were altered to 8's, 1's to 7's and 2's, with the addition of a squiggle up top, to a 5. So with a mixture of watchfulness, speed, deceit and ingenuity, I got through my first five years of school reports with pocket money only being withheld on two occasions, but I did overhear some puzzled conversation between my parents.

"Oh, not too bad, Mary's report, Sal."

"No, perhaps she's not doing too badly. Some funny comments though."

"Yes, I agree with you there. It makes you wonder if some of these teachers are any good at English themselves."

CHAPTER FIFTEEN

Parties and Open Day

The best parties I ever went to were those in school. They were held exclusively for the junior forms at the end of the Christmas term, to celebrate the end of exams, the approaching holidays, the onset of the festive season and probably as an antidote to the greyness of day prevalent at that time of year. The senior school would be at work as usual and Forms 1-3 plus all free staff would take over the Hall-Library for the afternoon. They were massive parties of over two hundred and ran on smooth tracks as did everything in Porth County, as though arranging a vast entertainment for the masses was merely the blink of a calm eyelid for the organisational skills of the Deputy Head Miss Orsman and her team.

'Mufti' as the aforementioned lady, Girl Guide Commissioner and J.P. called it, could be worn, so some girls went around for weeks obsessed with what they would be wearing for the annual shindig.

"I've got a new saxe blue twin-set. I think I'll wear that. D'you think it'll be too hot?"

"I don't know. I suppose you can leave the cardy off. I had a red check Gor-ray skirt for my birthday. I'm gonna wear that I am."

"My mother's gonna lend me her pearls to wear," another might chip in, "and I'm gonna put my hair in bunches instead of plaits."

Brown paper carrier bags were more in evidence on the school buses on party day than satchels and were carefully guarded against the ravages and rampages of the Toads and Sardines. By the end of the Autumn term even the shy, bespectacled intellectuals had emerged somewhat from their timid shells and were prepared to give nearly as good as they got.

"Wha's tha' in tha' brown bag?" sardine Liam would demand, his grubby hands grabbing at the carrier.

"Oh, gerroff you stupid bone brain. Mind your own business, fry your own fish," the offended would spit out, smoothing the precious package.

"Orright, orright, keep yer 'air on," Liam would shout, scowling and swaying on up the bus looking for someone else to annoy.

After lunch girls would emerge shyly from their form rooms, changed into their civvies and unrecognisable. One year we had been told to prepare a drawing on a piece of paper depicting a town or city for the first game. This drawing had to be pinned to our blouse, dress or jumper. Provided with paper and pencil, we had to wander around for fifteen minutes and jot down as many towns as could be fathomed from the drawings. My own uninspired, easily guessable sketch was of a matchstick floating on the waves (Swan matches). Miss Orsman, the organiser, had the most original drawing, which no-one could work out, of an old woman boarding a ship (Marseilles) while Annie Maths, typically, had one to do with food. It depicted a whole pork pie (and no doubt its owners would be verbally harangued if they didn't eat it all up) and cleverly worked out to be Nuneaton. A man gasping at an open window turned out to be Ayr. And so it went on. The winner was the girl with most names — duly awarded a prize of a 'Gem' dictionary, some coloured pencils, a pen, book or some other small, sensible item. Being prizes, these were sometimes kept pristine and treasured for years, defeating the aim of usefulness.

When a game requiring partners was on the programme, a game to find them had been devised. Teachers would issue cards with one name of a pair on it. So 'Laurel' had to look for 'Hardy', 'knife' for 'fork', 'Romeo' for 'Juliet', 'curds' for 'whey' and so on. Complications sometimes arose. Did 'salt' look for 'pepper' or 'vinegar'? 'Dido' had no idea who he or she was looking for.

Active games such as Flipping the Kipper, Statues, and massed Musical Chairs alternated with intellectual ones, so we were never tired or bored. Not that 'bored' was allowed into Porth County vocabulary. "If you say you are 'bored' it's because you are a boring person. You have a mind, don't you? Then use it!"

Food had been brought in to school by each girl as instructed and consisted of sandwiches, cakes and orange or lemon cordial as no other flavour was available. Normally some bossy person in the class, or the form captain, would organise the sandwich fillings.

"Hope Higgs, tinned salmon. Mary Davies, you've got a shop, cheese. Pamela Nicholls, egg. Marjorie Woosnam, cucumber. Marlene Edwards, your father's a butcher innee? Beef, O.K.? Shirley Hopkins, pressed veal, Cynthia Hughes, grocer's, tongue. Florence Wilton, greengrocer's, tomato."

Objections were frequently raised, as much to the bossiness and lack of choice, as to the designated filling.

"Oh no, not pressed veal. I can't stand tha'."

"Can't make egg sandwiches, sorry. The smell makes me feel sick."

Cake was in the form of Angel, Madeira, Jam Sponge Granny, Fruit or Fairy. On one occasion my mother gave me a packet of Kunzle cakes — delicious coloured cream with truffle and light sponge filling in a chocolate shell, but they all got eaten on the way to school, walking up from Porth Square, by our quartet of me, Hope, Pamela and Marjorie — a sort of breakfast dessert as it were. I knew full well that once handed in at school, that would be the last I'd see of them. In the mid-party break for refreshments, when everyone trooped into the dining room, it was amazing to witness the apparent affection that had built up between a girl and her sandwiches, now piled with hundreds of others of the same ilk on large white school dishes bearing the legend 'Meat', 'Fish' or 'Salad'. Some, in any case, had been cut up in a more genteel manner from their original shape.

"I'm gonna have some of my red salmon sandwiches I am. Ah! They'll be on the fish plate over there. I put real butter on the bread I did and cut the crusts off," said Hope, "C'mon Mary, come and have some of my salmon." Then, after some hopping round and close examination of the contents of dishes, "Where are they? I can't see them. Is there another plate of fish sandwiches?" Then, not being able to rummage through the pile to find her special sandwiches, gingerly taking a stranger and warily biting into it. "Ugh! This is mashed sardine this is! Ugh! I can't eat this. It's vile." She did though, being far too well brought up to ditch a half eaten sandwich, if not to suffer in silence.

Food and drink was consumed, toilets visited, and it was back to the Hall for the second half of the entertainment. While the hordes had been re-fuelling someone had been hard at work in the Hall. We were greeted with the colourful sight of pages of advertising adorning the entire area. The idea now was to move around in an orderly manner, with pencils and paper, naming the product, as the advert only bore the manufacturer's name. So for 'Pepsodent', it was toothpaste, 'Lux' soapflakes, 'Dame Wales' flour, 'Lyons Red Label' tea, 'Jantzen' swimwear, 'Players' cigarettes and 'Kayser Bondor' petticoats — a hundred or so altogether. When the winner had been presented with her geometry set or whatever, it would be time for massive pass the parcel. Massive in two senses: a circle of two hundred and thirty people sitting on the floor around the perimeter of the Hall and Library, and a parcel the size of a beehive. If dropped, it might well have crushed a person and was rolled rather than passed from girl to girl or teacher. Miss Harries played jolly tunes on the piano and when she paused, hands tore at paper and fingernails scrabbled at string. This game lasted a long time, as it was a parcel, in bulk and impenetrability, the like of which the Post Office had never seen. The prize was worth having too — a ten shilling voucher to spend in Boots.

The party wound up with ballroom dancing and singing. Red were the faces and shy the tongues of those lucky or unlucky enough to land a teacher in the Paul Jones. Finally, after a bout of singing *Clementine, She'll be coming round the mountain* (polite verses only), *Alouette,* or *A'r hyd y nos,* it was time to link crossed hands for a rousing *Auld lang syne.* A few cheers for the organisers, for Christmas and goodwill and we were homeward bound in the darkness — no special buses, no parents in cars or on foot — protection for youngsters wasn't needed then. We left knowing that, however many parties we went to during the holidays, even mixed ones, none would be as enjoyable as the one we'd just left.

I only ever remember one Open Day, at the end of my first year at Porth County in July. Open days are showcases for prospective students and their parents and, as the school was one of the best in south Wales anyway, it didn't need to advertise. Parents were only too eager for their offspring to be pupils of the renowned Miss Hudd, and Open Days were supererogatory. Nevertheless, that sole afternoon sticks in my memory. The form's exercise books in every subject had been collected and laid in piles in alphabetical order on desks throughout the room for parents' perusal. The form room, of course, was what parents wanted to see first. I tried to steer my mother away from the French and English Grammar piles as in the first subject Miss Beard was fussy (or fuzzy) about not wasting paper. I kept forgetting to write on the top line and on several nonconformist pages she had written boldly in bright red ink, "Use the top line please," then on the next page, "Use the top line," followed a page later by an increasingly irritable, "Mary, I've told you to use the top line!" Then came a plea, "Will you please use the top line?" and finally there were pages where she'd just put "U T L." In the second, English Grammar, I was ashamed of my low marks, totally bewidered as I was about parsing and analysis. I couldn't tell a predicate from a complement, barely had a mark above 50% — with comments to match. 3/10 'poor', 2/10 'poor once again', 1/10 'very weak', 2/10 'feeble'. Most of the class was in the same boat, except Hilda Lewis whose mother was an English teacher, and she had hardly any redeeming defects anyway (and a new best friend every week).

Fearful of disparaging comments about work and inattention, I vainly tried to navigate Mam away from Miss Beard, also our form teacher, by overwhelming her with introductions to parents, nearly all mothers, it being mid-afternoon, who were with other girls in the class.

"Mam, this is Sheila Marston and her mother, Mrs. Marston."

"Oh, hello Sheila and Mrs. Marston."

"Well, I'm actually Mrs. Hayward, Margaret's mother. We live next door to the Marstons in Pentre and came down together."

"Oh, hello Mrs. Hayward then." Hurrying my mother away from an encroaching Miss Beard, I would find someone else for her to meet.

"Mam, this is Shirley and Mrs. Hopkins."

"Oh hello. How are you? Nice day isn't it?" Mam would say in a well practised manner.

"Well no. I'm Mrs. Price, Shirley's auntie, in fact. Her mother's waiting to go into hospital for a little op you see and didn't feel up to it today. And Shirley had to have someone here, so I came. Yes, lovely day for it." I did mostly get the introductions right though, and my friends, especially Hope, loved meeting Mam as she always carried sweets in her pocket or handbag to give them.

Nine or ten of the class had come to my house the previous November as I'd been allowed to have a fireworks party. Being born at an awkward date early in September, my birthday often fell on, or just after, the beginning of the new school year, and in my first term at County I didn't know anyone to ask to a birthday party. I often bemoaned my unfortunate circumstancial birth date and that year, probably weary of my bleating, my father suggested, "Why don't you have a belated party? Early November. You'll know girls to ask by then, love. And p'raps you can have fireworks an' all." "After all, they are Porth County girls. Young ladies really. They'll be no trouble at all," said Mam hopefully. So a belated birthday party with fireworks was arranged for November 5th. About six Margarets were invited: Howells, Booker, Thomas, Jones and Hayward, Hope, Crid, Pamela, Shirley Hopkins and Marjorie. David, two doors up and still in Trehafod school, knew something in the partying, eating mode was afoot and kept turning up looking optimistic, so he was invited as well on the proviso that he washed, didn't let his nose run and didn't rugby tackle the girls. He was the only boy guest or semi-permanent resident really.

The shop was shut early for the party. Mam had made salmon and ham sandwiches, trifle, custard and chunks for those who didn't like jelly and blancmange, fairy and rock cakes, a Victoria and a chocolate sponge and a special iced non-birthday cake. There were also my favourites, chocolate marshmallow tea-cakes with a blob of jam in the middle. All the food got eaten, as David polished off all that was left when the girls had finished. He also had trifle as well as custard and chunks. Our dog, Peter, had died of distemper a year earlier, to my great distress at the time, but my father reckoned David

166

was as good as, if not better than, any dog at clearing up any leftovers, so there was no waste.

The party games started quietly enough, with things like 'Consequences' and 'Dead Man's Wink'. It must have been the fireworks and the night air which excited the guests. As soon as it got dark, we trooped up the back garden where David and Dad were in charge of the pyrotechnics. Dad lit and ordered people to withdraw, while David put rockets in milk bottles and hammered Catherine Wheels on to the bakehouse door. The girls 'Oohed' and 'Aahed' on cue.

Back inside after the display the guests bustled with a new energy. All wanted to play active games such as 'Hunt the Slipper', 'Hide and Seek' or other games involving ransacking the house. Parents and a few adult sympathisers warily sought refuge out of the way in the kitchen, probably cringing every thirty seconds at the bangs, crashes, thumps and thuds echoing from all the rooms, shop included. To judge from the Saturday morning scene of havoc, guests had found their way behind settees and armchairs, under beds, into wardrobes and cupboards, and behind a fire screen into a grate, as the fire basket was in two pieces. Sweet wrappers, lollipop sticks and chewed bubble gum left a guilty trail, and the boxes of jelly babies and coconut mushrooms in the shop window were rather depleted. My friends fondly recalled my firework party for several years after the event, frequently suggesting a repeat, but Mam wasn't so keen on the idea. Her response to my annual request, "Can I have a party this year, Mam?" was a quick, wide-eyed, mock horror, "Ooh, Jawlch Mari fach, no indeed."

But, 'revenons à nos moutons'. Despite Mam's fascinating conversation with Shirley's auntie about the state of the Rhondda population's insides, my mother was nabbed by a hovering Miss Beard and all I could do was look on with fingers crossed, hoping she wouldn't say anything to ruin my pocket-money chances, which she didn't. I also hoped she might say something about making a fuzz on the buzz or someone's puzzy finger, as Mam didn't believe my hilarious tales about her weird (to Rhondda ears anyway) pronunciation, but she didn't do that either.

Fortunately, I had no fear of Mam meeting Miss Hudd as she

didn't know me. Apart from the one, brief but painful encounter in the corridor, we had never come into contact and she was in her Mistress Bountiful, smiling-at-everybody mood in any case. So after the unnecessarily dreaded meeting with Miss Beard, I proudly led Mam in her tan tweed, prickly suit, her brown business woman's hat with a brim and her real ostrich leather, London made handbag, off to see the Gym, where I did a quick upside-down hang for her on the wall bars, and to the art room where a painting of mine was on display. "See, Mam, that one up there with the sun in the right hand corner."

"Oh, that's nice. Very pretty. Our garden with flowers is it?"

"No! It's supposed to be an erupting volcano with people fleeing. See, they're people, not flowers. They've got legs, look." She put her long-sighted glasses on for better enlightenment.

"Oh, say so. Oh well, very pretty anyway."

"It's not really supposed to be pretty Mam."

"No, I meant colourful, very colourful."

After refreshments, the highlight of the afternoon was the programme of dancing and gymnastics held outside on one of the tennis courts as it was a sunny day. Girls not partaking in the displays sat on the grassy bank, the natural grandstand overlooking the courts, while parents sat on chairs at the side or on benches set out at the top of the bank on the perimeter of the games field. I am able to set out the entire programme for that July afternoon in 1948, coming across it as I did, decades later, a precious, carefully folded, half sheet of paper with deep thirty year old creases, tucked away in a pocket of Mam's London made, real ostrich leather handbag. This is what it says:

Programme of Dancing and Gymnastic Display

1) Gymnastic Team	Exercises and vaulting
2) Form 1V	Rob Roy
3) Junior Eisteddfod Winners	Migildi Magildi
4) Form 1	Gymnastics
5) Senior Eisteddfod Winners	Pant Corlan y Wyn
6a) Form 11A	Rospiggspolska
Form 11B	Gymnastics
7) Gymnastics team	Highland Fling

8) Form 1VA,B	Tatra Dance
9) Form VA,B,V1	Varsovienne
10) Form 111	Clapdance
11) Form 1VA	Skating Ballet
12) Form 111	Little Man in a Fix
13) Finale — Form V & V1	Waltz Country Dance.

Not much is recalled of the other displays, overawed as I was by the largely adult audience and ranks of pupils sitting on the bank. I remember feeling envious of the Gymnastic Team seniors who were wearing pale green fitted gym dresses with short flared skirts and wide shoulder straps instead of sleeves, while we in the Form One team had to perform in our white school blouse and navy knickers.

We had practised the routine for weeks in the Gym. On Miss Jennett's command we did cartwheels or handstands in pairs, leap-frogged, bunny jumped and tumbled head-over-heels on the coconut mats or sat cross-legged in rows awaiting the next brief, brisk but quiet order to move. All went perfectly. To end, we stood facing the Gym teacher awaiting her "Right Turn" which we had rehearsed to miliary precision. Then she would raise her arm and the first girl led off through the Gym doors. So there we were, routine perfectly executed, facing Miss Jennett, expecting her final command. "Left Turn," she said. The majority, myself included, relaxed now the performance was over, unthinkingly turned right as usual. A few alert girls had correctly obeyed the order. To my horror, I was looking at Margaret Howells' putty nose when I should have been facing Mair James' back. She frowned, moved her head slightly and mouthed "Right," so I quickly rotated and was now looking into Mair's blue eyes. Beyond her I could see some faces and some backs. Girls started turning in all directions, looking round to see what others were doing. By now the audience was laughing and chuckling and Miss Jennett was red-faced. Precision had devolved into chaos. She tried again. "LEFT Turn," she shouted, all calm now lost. By this time some of us were giggling in embarrassment, others, who had got it right, raised their eyes in mock patience to the summer sky, some were still turning, brain-locked, and the rest just looked shame-faced. Eventually, the girl who was normally last out, led the way sheepishly off the court through the exit on the left and we had the most applause of the afternoon. There were even a few cheers! Relief, I expect, after the fiasco of the conclusion.

CHAPTER SIXTEEN

Girl Guides

Friends in my form, Pamela, Marjorie and Margaret Algate, were constantly huddling in small groups and having private conversations, particularly on a Thursday, of which one would overhear such things as "See you Porth Square quarter to six", "Bacchetta's afterwards girls?", "Subs are going up to ninepence" and "Captain's gonna be late tonight. She said Margaret Howells is in charge." The last, of course, was the clue to it all — even to my brain, indifferent to institutional organisations and secret societies, unless it was to do with sport. They were talking about the weekly Girl Guide meetings.

As the years passed and the huddled chats persisted, I began to feel I was missing out on something diverting, perhaps entertaining, possibly important. As I was now fourteen and certain of persuading Mam to allow me to go to Porth on the bus, even on dark evenings, and despite the demands of time taken up with piano and piano accordion lessons, homework and the Sunday algebra coaching, I began to show more than a passing interest in their confabs. They were keen for me to join the company and be one of them. Perhaps they got extra points or a badge for a new recruit. "Oh, s'great mun. We 'ave a bit of fun, an' it's not 'ard tyin' knots. You'll soon get the 'ang of it," said Marjorie, "And afterwards, some of us go and 'ave a cuppa coffee in Bacchetta's," Pam added, "That's the best part really."

When I was six years old with a sickly arm still bent from repairs to a three year old fracture, my mother had shown enthusiasm on my behalf for the Baden-Powell organisation and deposited me at a Brownies meeting in St Catherine's Church Hall, Pontypridd. She was keen for me to partake in anything that might conceivably have any strengthening effect on this thin limb. No doubt she had pre-supposed ideas of strapping females in the Guide movement and hoped I, and particularly my arm, might develop to join their ranks. That afternoon was not a happy experience for me, however. I knew none of the other little girls who were all clad in horrid brown dresses and wearing tams indoors while pretending to be gnomes, elves, sprites and nymphs. A large, rough lady with a whistle picked me up and sat me on a large, shiny, wooden mushroom painted white with orange spots, and it was so hard it hurt my bottom. When I covertly slid off on to the far more comfortable floor, I was constantly and firmly replaced. The last straw was when another little girl was told to stick something in me. Looking back, in actual fact, she was trying to pin a badge on my jumper, but clumsily only succeeded in drawing blood and occasioning an unstoppable howling. When Mam suggested going the following week, I went and hid under the bed in the spare room, getting myself covered in fluff, until it was too late to leave. Now, eight years further on, I was prepared to give it another go.

The company, when all were present, numbered about 32, but the normal attendance averaged around 24. The girls were divided up into four patrols named after flowers and each patrol had a leader covered in badges. A sharp-faced, efficient but pleasant lady from Cymmer was the overall boss — to be called Captain. Her deputy was Jane Evans — ex Secondary Sardine — a shy, quiet girl who rarely spoke, only opened her mouth to smile, did a lot of onlooking and now and then uttered a non-committal "Mmm". Nearly all members wore the guide uniform, except recruits and those whose mothers were assiduous washerwomen:

"Why aren't you wearing your guide blouse, Gillian?"

"It's in the wash, Captain."

"What, again? It has more washing than wearing!"

Some, whose fathers were on the dole, were accumulating uniforms piecemeal — a belt passed on, an unclaimed beret, a spare tie abandoned by an overheated, apathetic adherent with infrequent attendance.

A lot of the time we sat around learning how to tie various knots — sheepshank, reef, slip and granny. What for, I could scarcely imagine. To kidnap and tie up some ancient female person perhaps, or lasso the legs of some hapless sheep while practising for a visit to the Wild West where they did such things. Perhaps a flair for tying up bits of cord would one day come in useful for tethering one's boat or horse, or making a passable raft should one be shipwrecked on a desert island after, of course, lashing together a few planks to construct a tree house. Guiding, it seemed to me, was largely concerned with getting oneself out of unusually difficult situations.

We learned how to make a fire outdoors with twigs and leaves; which berries were fit for human consumption (should we have to face Hansel and Gretel-type abandonment and be left foraging for nourishment in the wild). We also learned how to recognise various animals' footprints, though here I wasn't sure whether this was so we could track and slay them for food, or so that we'd know which animals we were fleeing from, which was the likelier alternative. Not that there were many wild animals in Porth Park, our practice ground, where we ventured on fine, light evenings — perhaps the odd, mangy, stray cat, or a few playful puppies ignoring the sign 'Dogs must be kept on a lead'. At most, the fiercest was the occasional field vole. The only berries we found were green blackberries which we'd been familiar with from infancy anyway, and the only footprints we came across upon were those of little boys, so there wasn't much chance of survival in Porth Park.

During one Thursday session in July, we made our way excitedly up to the top, less civilised part of the park. We were going to make a fire and cook on it. Water, orange squash, cardboard cups and plates, boxes of matches and spatulas were distributed among the patrols to be transported thither. Frying pans were borrowed from worried mothers, together with any spare food (but not eggs), although beforehand we'd been told the chief ingredients for the planned feast were fat, bread and cheese as we were going to cook Cheese Dreams. Where no cheese was available in a particular household, however, a tin of spaghetti, a bottle of beetroot, a bar of chocolate, even a box of plasters was brought, the latter no doubt sent by a wise mother, wryly accustomed to her daughter's lack of prowess in the kitchen, let alone in the wild.

"Look Captain, there's plasters among the food."

"Plasters? Who brought plasters?" Captain echoed.

"Me, Captain," answered Hope. "My mother thought they might come in handy."

"I always bring a first-aid kit, you know."

"Yes, but we didn' 'ave no cheese in the house, an' the shops were closed an' I had to bring something."

"Going to put plasters in the bread instead of cheese are you?"

General merriment ensued at this suggestion and comments of, "Cor, Plaster Dreams with pickle. Nice!" and "Roll up! Roll up! Hope Higgs' plaster sandwiches available free to all comers."

Hope protested feebly, "Well, our motto is 'Be prepared' you know!" It was all taken in good part and there was enough cheese to go inside everybody's Dream even if some did crumble on cutting and found its way into assorted mouths, including that of a friendly, lively dog who thought the party was for him. Four fires, one for each patrol, were built with twigs and leaves in the stone circles and eventually lit, after using up several boxes of matches. Chunks of lard were melted in pans and the cheese sandwiches manoeuvred into the crackling fat. More crackling ensued as the crumbly cheese escaped its inadequate prison between two slices of bread and sizzled in the hot utensil, or missed it altogether and spat and flared in the fire. Various ideas were forthcoming.

"Why don't we use Hope's plasters around the edge of the sandwiches to stop the cheese falling out?"

"You're joking! Ugh!"

"Well then, is there any string to tie them up with? Darro! I've only got a bit of cheese left in mine, look. That bloomin' dog 'as 'ad my cheese. Go away dog. Shoo, shoo!" wailed Marjorie.

Eventually my turn came to transform my grubby, well-flattened cheese sandwich into a delicious Cheese Dream. The company leader, Margaret Howells, was sitting on a boulder nearby clearly enjoying the one she had made — crisply browned, crunchy fried bread enclosing melted Caerphilly cheese over which she was spreading home-made tomato chutney. My mouth watering, I lowered my bread into the pan where it protested initially, but quickly settled down to cook over the glowing twigs.

"Drinks ready!" announced Captain, "One each. You can have

more if there's any left when everyone's been served. Come and get them *now,* come on!"

There was an immediate response from all but the current cooks, torn between hunger and thirst. "Oh, get mine Hope, will you?" I begged, "My Cheese Dream's cooking. I've got to watch it."

"I can't. I bet she won't give *me* more than one," was Hope's reply. Perhaps Hope was the wrong person to ask, as her enthusiasm for putting things into her stomach was legendary, and she wasn't above a touch of harmless cheating either. The upshot of this bad timing was, that while I was in the queue, the lard dried up, the lower slice of bread fried itself into the metal of the pan, the cheese ran out from the middle and cooked to a knobbly, lacy blackness, while the top slice remained unchanged white — well, grey — but hot. The frying pan was in a state of ruination and I burnt my hand on the handle, so Hope's plasters were put to good use. The dog seemed to enjoy the foul mess that was left, and he was more than welcome to it.

Other activities of the Guide sessions were teaching the recruits the rules, the salute (two fingers up, straight like soldiers, side by side) and the promise to do one's duty, whatever it was, to God, the King, the country and anyone or thing else that demanded it. Then, when you had a uniform, you were inducted at a special ceremony to receive the 'Be Prepared' trefoil badge which had to be brassoed every week. The Guides' goal was to cover as much of the deep blue blouse as possible with badges. There was the company name and colour flash to go on one shoulder with the patrol emblem beneath. A smart, silky Welsh dragon also paraded somewhere on a shoulder, superintending the armful of potential badges for trekking, cooking, swimming, writing, drawing, bird-watching, train-spotting, stamp collecting or whatever. If something was humanly possible to achieve and at the same time not illegal or immoral, there was a badge for it.

To get the blood circulating after learning and knotting, there were competitive team games between the patrols involving dashing around the Guide hut, passing, or accurately throwing bean bags, hoops, rubber rings or soft balls. Jumping on to strategically placed cork mats in a game called 'Islands' was a favourite, as was 'Statues' in which, if you even breathed or blinked, you were out. The session ended with everyone in a circle singing *Taps* after a few short prayers.

This was a giggling affair if Miss Muriel Orsman, Guide Commissioner for south Wales, J.P., former Welsh hockey international and head of Geography at Porth County, who'd studied under Professor Demangeon at the Sorbonne, was present on one of her occasional visits. A very worthy woman, devoted to her local church, she had eccentricities of both character and appearance. Whether leading troops of Geographers on expeditions over moors and mountains, or groups of Guides and Rangers through city streets, she cared not one iota about the impression she gave of herself and her party to passers-by. She would march proudly ahead, in her uniform, if it was a guiding event, umbrella or walking stick held aloft in crowds so we could always spot her and docilely follow trailing along behind in twos. Then, chancing upon a monument or edifice of rare interest, or wanting to impart some vital information, she would stop and do a smart heel turn often causing a pile-up in the dozy followers dragging along after her. A sharp blast on her whistle, making startled passers-by to leap into the air, meant we were to gather round in silence and listen.

"Remember gels/guides, no more talking at the whistle. Whistle, and listen," she would say, holding forth in a voice loud enough to be heard above the traffic and general city hubbub. If possible she would elevate herself on to a step or convenient base of plinth or pillar so she would be visible to all her gels/guides and, by this time, to all the other people who had stopped to find out what on earth was going on plus the gaggle of cheeky little scruffs we'd collected on the way. Her explanations that, from this point in Piccadilly Circus, we were going to march down through Marble Arch, along Whitehall and up the Mall to Buckingham Palace Road, where we were to have our tea in the Guide headquarters, were listened to and applauded by hundreds of people gathered round. On such occasions, attracting the attentions of the world, the Guides or Geographers would try to shrink and look anonymous as though we didn't belong to this unorthodox lady who thought she was at Speakers Corner every hundred yards.

"Cor, she don' 'alf show us up, do she?" Pamela would mutter, "I feel stupid with everybody looking at us like this."

"I know, an' she don' care a bit. Look at 'er now. 'Oldin' up the traffic she is. Mus' think she's a policeman. Oh come on, we better 'urry or we'll be stuck on this side of the road," Marjorie might answer.

"Look, there's her umbrella going through that archway," and we'd shuffle off after her like chicks after the mother hen.

Miss Orsman's proudest possessions seemed to be her dog, her car and her gas stove, named in that order: Ianto Full Pelt, Minnie the Morris and Gertie. The first two accompanied her nearly everywhere, Ianto even bedding down in the classroom, where, if you were unfortunate enough to be last in, and had to sit on the chair next to his basket on the floor, he would sometimes clamp his teeth into your ankle. He was the teacher's disciplinarian. "Don't fidget. Pay attention to my mistress." Not that girls didn't pay attention in Geography. Besides being a martinet herself, Miss Orsman's lessons were always eccentric enough to hold your attention, if not always devastatingly interesting. She drove to school in Minnie the Morris from somewhere south of Pontypridd where she lived with her friend Miss Lloyd, she of the sideways smile, specially cultivated, so it was said, to show off her gold teeth. Miss Lloyd taught History and had apparently been engaged to Miss Orsman's brother who had died in the war.

Physically, she had two noticeable features. The first was her large, well strapped up, immobile bosom, which sometimes wiped things off the bottom of the board while she reached up to chalk in a contour, O.S. symbol or river name at the top. In fact, the lower half of the Geography room board was always smudged — land merged with sea, towns sprawled, ox-bow lakes joined back up with rivers — and Miss Orsman's jumpers, blouses and cardigans were constantly re-decorated at the front with coloured chalk. Her other outstanding characteristic was her jowls, so puffy they almost buried her nose, which wasn't very large anyway, and we wondered sometimes how she managed to breathe without hindrance. In profile, all you could see was a small point of nose and a large ration of cheek which hung down to merge with an assortment of chins. If Miss Orsman turned suddenly or shook her head, the lower half of her face would still be quivering several seconds later. And it was partly this that set us giggling when we were singing *Taps* in Guides. All eyes would be mock-modestly lowered as we stood, trying to restrain twitches of smiles but furtively nudging each other, for the closing rendition: "Day is done, Gone the sun, From the hills, from the sea, from the sky. All is well, Safely rest...," then, as we sang the last line, "God is nigh", as one (wo)man, the company's eye would be raised to our Commissioner in eager anticipation. Miss Orsman would square her shoulders, stand quite erect and toss her head upwards and back in what seemed a grand, but rather exaggerated salute to the Almighty, publicly professing her fervour. For a moment her eyes would be closed or staring at the ceiling as though mentally transported in the manner of Southern States negroes ecstasied by some loudly persuasive Bible puncher. This started us off giggling, but to see her chops and chins quivering like jelly for seconds on end set the seal on our mirth. If she wished to make an announcement immediately after emerging from her quaverous euphoria, eyes were once more cast floor-wards and a circle of Guides with shaking shoulders could be seen tightly clasping their hands together as they attempted to control their suppressed laughter. Miss Orsman must have noticed and wondered at our hilarity, but was never reproving, only mock patient as she briefly waited for order. She probably thought of us simply as silly little girls — which we often were. Despite, or probably because of her idiosyncrasies, she was held in much affection by those who came into contact with her, in school or in Guides.

The part of the evening that our clique looked forward to most was the post-Guide meeting when half a dozen of us, including some Secondary girls, Jean Ishmael and Netta Jenkins, whose milkman father Fred had an Encyclopaedia Britannica, would hang around Porth Square and talk to a group of Secondary boys. They wore light and dark blue woollen scarves around their necks on cold nights — smiling, swarthy Brian Phillips, wavy-haired John Davies, lithe, hyper-active Jeff Saulter, serious Gerald Lloyd, shy Bryn Densley and suave, flirtatious Gerald Richards. These were the faithful ones, mostly choristers at St Mark's, always on Porth Square at 8 p.m. on a Thursday, though others appeared and disappeared at intervals. Usually we'd carry on the chat, jokes and laughter over a cup of coffee upstairs in Bacchetta's café. Sometimes we were joined by the quiet twins, Aldo and Mario Bacchetta, when they could escape their elder brother Ron's managerial eye. Afterwards we'd walk down deserted Hannah Street, shrieking and fooling around, then on up Police Station hill, but never paired off, although everyone fancied everyone else in turn. On such occasions, Margaret Algate might say to me, "Don' say, will you. I've been told a secret an' I been told not to tell anyone, but Jeff Saulter wants to go out with Margaret Howells, yeah." I'd answer, "Margaret Howells likes that boy in school, whassisname?"

"Marcus Morgan?"

"Oh p'raps she likes him too. No, Peter something. Two names."

"Oh, I know, Peter Scott-Lewis."

"Yeah, that's it."

"Why don' Jeff Saulter ask her then?"

"Oh well, 'e won't mun. 'E asked Pat to ask me to sound 'er out. But it's supposed to be secret. Brian Phillips likes you."

"Oh, go on, 'e don't."

"'E do. 'E told Jeff Saulter an' 'e told me. 'E said 'e said in school yesterday."

And so it went on, circumnavigatory, hearsay flirtation that never came to anything, but provided us with much diversion and happy, quasi-confidential chit-chat. Margaret Algate knew everyone as well as their secrets. She was one of those girls everybody confided in to spread a story or rumour, knowing full well that if they swore her to secrecy, she couldn't resist telling sundry, if not all, and the information would disseminate as intended.

On numerous occasions she said to me, "Mary, I've been told a secret about So and So. Ve..ry interesting, I might add. I've been told not to breathe a word to anybody, but I'll tell you 'cos you're my friend, see. But promise you won't tell a soul. O.K?" My answer usually was, "Look Margaret, you know I can't keep secrets 'cos I forget they're supposed to be secrets, so you'd better not tell me."

"Oh well, never mind then," she'd answer, looking frustrated and disappointed. Then, after a pause, "It's about So and So's boyfriend actually, or perhaps ex-boyfriend after this. If I tell you, will you promise not to say?"

"Oh Margaret, I'm not promising and I don't really care if you tell me or not. I 'spect I'll hear about it in the end anyway."

"Oh, orright then, you've persuaded me. I'll tell you. Well see, you know...?" and out would come the information, soon to be public knowledge all over Porth.

We went on many outings with the Guides, both for duty and pleasure, usually both combined — distributing books from a trolley in the wards of Porth Cottage Hospital on a Sunday morning, singing carols at Old People's Homes at Christmas, flag-selling for various charities in Hannah Street, making up and delivering food parcels for the needy from the proceeds of jumble sales. We marched behind the Flag in processions on Armistice Sunday and, on Scout and Guide day, to a service in St John's church, Cymmer. Once we learned and practised some songs which we recorded in the Reardon-Smith lecture theatre in Cardiff for the sound track of a film on Guiding. We were accompanied on the cello by Lady Davies of Llandinam. She was a friend of Miss Orsman and suitably impressed we were too, at meeting our first real Lady — so impressed, in fact, that when this charming, normal person spoke to us individually we were totally discomposed, blushing and tongue-tied and we couldn't say two consecutive, sensible and articulate words to her. She must have thought the Guide movement's intake, singing apart, had hit rock bottom in the Rhondda.

Day outings were good fun but weekends away were exciting. We prepared for these long in advance, searching around for a rucksack to borrow, for you could hardly depart on such a thrilling venture with an attaché or suit case. Mothers were persuaded to stump up for a pair of stout walking shoes or we had to borrow those too, if nothing was forthcoming financially. We ironed and washed everything and ensured that the precursor of the polythene-filled sleeping bag, made out of an old sheet specially for the occasion, was properly sewn up the sides and had no holes in the worn parts likely to cause embarrassment or draughts.

The south Wales Guide movement owned a single storey, purpose-built building overlooking the sea and adjacent to the second most extensive expanse of dunes in Europe, at Wig Fach near Porthcawl. This fine dwelling place was called Gorwelion. From its raised front courtyard with flagpole was a splendid view of Newton Bay with the treacherous Tusker Rocks visible, directly in front, at low tide. The town of Ogmore-by-Sea could be seen on the headland to the left while to the right was the eastern extremity of the vast caravan park of Trecco Bay, always full to bursting during miners' fortnight in July. The house, long and low, nestled against woodland which sheltered it at the back and protected it from the northerly meteorological onslaughts.

One weekend in March, the company, albeit a truncated version, was going to have a Guide camp here. We arrived by bus, sitting three to a seat so as to make room for the public, with our paraphernalia cluttering the racks and the aisle, and were deposited near the entrance to the Happy Valley Caravan Park. Then we set off into the unknown, down a country lane, casting envious glances at the luxurious looking, curtained and cushioned caravans in the adjacent field.

"Aaw, is it far, Captain?" queried one less than intrepid young adventurer.

"No, just around the corner. And don't complain. The walk will do you good."

"I wasn't complaining Captain, just asking, 'cos I got a blister."

Several corners, and no doubt several more blisters later, we arrived at the rather prepossessing house atop its acre of land above the dunes, above the sea. Captain, on the way down, had disappeared into a whitewashed cottage to collect the key, while we struggled on, led by non-committal deputy Jane.

"Have you been here before Jane?"

"Mmmm," she said, nodding.

"Is it nice?" Hope asked.

"Mmmm."

"Will we be allowed into Porthcawl?" Hope persisted. This was not so much Porthcawl itself, as the Coney Beach fairground, but naming the town sounded less reckless. No vocal response was generated this time, only slightly pursed lips showing veto and slow head shaking. Jane *was* able to articulate as we'd seen her talking to Captain, but we assumed her day job was exacting and she rested her mind and voice in her spare time. Whatever, conversation with her was an uphill task. If someone had asked her "Do you hire out sunbeds?" or "Can you push a gallon of water up a pipe with a fork?" her answer would have been "Mmmm."

At one end of the house was a comfortable flat for those in charge, separated by a kitchen and a large communal room from the small bedrooms with wooden bunks and from the wash-rooms for the rabble at the other end. There was no apparent form of heating, apart from a fairly comprehensive fireplace in the main room, which looked as though a fire was the last thing it expected to see. The lack of carpets and wallpaper gave the interior a bleak air. Still, we were only there for a weekend and a fire in March wasn't necessary. Gracious me, no! Tough, hardy girls like us didn't need namby-pamby heat! Activity would keep the blood circulating and us warm. After all, we might be there for a change, but it certainly wasn't intended to be a holiday. We were there to learn — probably how to survive in the wild again — without despoiling the environment. We soon dis-covered we also had to work, as we were despatched into teams of cooks, cleaners and washers-up. Provisions had been pre-viously delivered: hundreds of eggs, dozens of loaves, a sack of potatoes, tins of corned beef and large chunks of cheese, butter and lard. Bunk beds were bagged and argued over.

"Bags I this one!"

"Oh no, Judith, you're too heavy for the top bunk. Look how it sags! I won't even be able to turn over 'cos of the bulge. You'll have to have the bottom one O.K.?"

We were famished and ready for the food we had to prepare. Wisely, we had been instructed to bring sandwiches for lunch, and those who had any left, tucked into them, rapidly devouring the food to thwart the bad conscience induced by those who had eaten theirs on the bus and were now envious, starving on-lookers. We raised the flag on the forecourt, saluted it and played games on the field. No exploring of the vast dunes was allowed, as there were red flags flying about the place, not signifying it was dangerous to bathe, but that men were shoot-ing at targets, or rabbits, or people, if they got in the way. No-one could be seen, but quick, sharp bursts of rifle fire cracked now and then and towards Ogmore, one could see dark objects hanging from scaffolding like gibbets, presumably the butts. "The war's over. Why are soldiers shooting at things and stopping us going on the dunes?" Pam asked crossly, fancying a leisurely stroll down to the beach in preference to the frenetic team games on the sloping field.

"They're not soldiers as far as I know. It's nothing to do with war. It's just blokes with guns shooting. Sportsmen," Captain explained.

"But they're only shooting at bits of wood or something. What's the point in that?"

"Well, you know, like little boys putting up tins on fences to throw stones at and knock down. Only these are men," offered Margaret Algate reasonably.

"I want to go on the dunes," said Pamela.

"You can't," said Captain. And that was that. So instead we went in and started making tea, which was to be scrambled eggs on toast. Forty eggs were casually cracked and tossed into a massive pot and the Margarets Howells and Algate, armed with efficient looking whisks, almost disappeared into the receptacle after them, bumping their heads together as they espied and chased whole yolks needing to be smashed up. Willing hands brought salt and pepper and most of the company came in turn to peer at more eggs than they had ever previously seen being beaten. The Primrose patrol was in charge of toast making, some grilling, some scraping off the carbon and some margarining. The Bluebells gathered around to ladle thirty spoonfuls of tea into a big, brown enamel teapot. Eventually, everything was eagerly consumed. There was only one complaint, from Gillian Morgan, "Ugh!, there's all shell in my scrambled egg. And one side of the toast is black. Who was supposed to be scraping the toast?"

"I'll have it, if you don't want it," Hope offered kindly.

Another weekend expedition — a summer one for a small group of around twelve — was organised by Miss Orsman and Miss Lloyd, also a Guider, to Ogmore-by-Sea. We were to experience real camping — in tents — for the first time and everyone was hopping with excitement for the romantic, open-air sleeping under the sky. We didn't realise how accurate the vision would be — not much sleeping, but plenty of sky. The tents were very basic affairs, primitive even, made of khaki canvas material with no sewn-in ground sheet or fly-sheet to protect us from the weather, cows, sheep and flying bits of tree. Still, it was June so the weather shouldn't be a problem. In Geography we had learned that the prevailing winds over the British Isles are the south-west variables. That weekend they changed into the south-west constants and when the wind blows on that particular bit of coast, it really does blow the cobwebs away. If you didn't have a sizeable stone on your possessions, they disappeared out through the tent flaps and scattered perversely all over the field, invariably heading for the cliffs and the sea. We were three to a tent and although no-one wanted to be the pig in the middle, to opt for that position was the wise move, even if your feet did stick out through the entrance. Lateral bodies tended to freeze all along their outer sides and woke up, if they managed to get any sleep at all, numb from shoulder to toe. For sleeping purposes, we had brought a sheet sleeping bag and a blanket each, which we shared over all three occupants, so again the pig in the middle was covered and relatively warm, while the flankers were exposed alternately, depending on the movements of the aforementioned pig and whether she preferred sleeping on her right or left side. The night air rang with cries and protests of:

"Keep still Pat, you've pulled all the blankets off me."

"Oh, move over will you? I'm half out of the side of this blessed tent."

"Ouch! Watch your bloomin' elbows. That was my eye!"

"Crikey, I'll never get to sleep. This ground's like iron!"

"Where's my shoes gone?"

"What you want your shoes for? You're in bed."

"Well, I don't want them now, silly. I'm just worried they're outside. What if it comes to rain?"

"It won't. It's June."

Famous last, optimistic words to echo a childhood plea when it suddenly rained in summer and playmates scampered home, abandoning a fascinating game, "Don't go. This rain's not wet. It's only a sun shower." Come the middle of the night, a pitter-patter quite close to our heads elicited a worried whisper from Margaret Algate, "Mary, Marjorie. Are you awake?"

"No," came two simultaneous groans.

Margaret, ignoring them, carried on. "Well, I think a cow's got into the field and is going to the toilet outside our tent." Marjorie sat bolt upright, taking the bedclothes with her, ready to flee if Margaret's prognostication was correct, while I, semi-comatose, tried to peep out through the tent flap on my side. The grass was certainly wet, but smelled pleasant enough."No, s'not a cow, thank God," proclaimed Marjorie, " 'S drizzling a bit, tha's all." We settled down again, turning, wriggling, writhing, tugging at blankets, impossibly trying to find some warmth and comfort on the unyielding, sloping ground. The drops got gradually more insistent. There was a permanent quality about them. No-one spoke. In fact, no-one appeared to be breathing, just listening, waiting for the inevitable. Finally, voices could be heard in the other tents and there was a wail from Margaret. "Oh, I'm wet. The rain's getting in 'ere." Frenzied activity ensued as we squirmed out of sleeping bags to the accompaniment of tearing noises and crawled around on our knees, bumping heads as we searched for shoes, jumpers, coats — anything to get warm and keep relatively dry. Keeping completely dry was out of the question, as now a rivulet was entering the accommodation at one end and flowing out through the entrance, occupying much of the intervening space. We huddled, partially clothed in an assortment of garments belonging to various owners, on either side of the stream, watching it in horrified fascination by the light of a torch. The beams of flashlamps danced outside, urgent voices and squelchy footsteps could be heard.

"Are you all right in there?" came Miss Orsman's voice.

"No Miss," we answered bleakly in unison.

"We're flooded out Miss," Marjorie continued, calmly and philosophically.

Miss Orsman's head poked through the entrance. "Oh, goodness me...! Well, get out of there you silly things."

"But it's raining...." Margaret began.

"Get out! We'll have to move the tent. We can't leave it there." Finally, several cold, damp hours, or so it seemed, later, the tent was re-erected on a level spot, Margaret was given a spare winceyette nightie nearly as big as the tent, that belonged to Miss Orsman, to replace her wet pyjamas, and we settled down again, clutching each other for warmth, just as the rain stopped. Miss Orsman and Miss Lloyd returned to their tents (with sewn-in groundsheets and camp beds) to finish the night.

The following morning, we awoke to sunshine in a cloudless sky. After breakfast, which took so long to make over a camp fire that it was nearly lunch-time when we finally finished it, we went down to the beach where we sat on rocks and under Miss Orsman's conductorship wearily sang, 'Am gang gooley gooley gooley gooley wash wash, ging gang goo, ging gang goo.' Passing residents and visitors eyed us as though we were creatures from outer space....

Many years later, I heard Miss Orsman and Miss Lloyd quarrelled and parted, each going her separate way. Shortly after the rupture, Miss Orsman died leaving everything to the vicar who moved into her house where he apparently lived with his fancy woman.

CHAPTER SEVENTEEN

Languages and School Holidays

Although some of the older staff disapproved if you walked to school with a boy, pupil or otherwise, I nevertheless sometimes did if my mates Hope, Pam and Marjorie were away sick or visiting an auntie, or if I'd missed the bus up from Trehafod or if it simply didn't come.

On one particular morning in January, Neville Pugh, who lived in the colliery under-manager's house in Pleasant View opposite us, had sat next to me on the bus and I walked up from Porth Square with him.

"What languages do you do?" he asked.

"Only French now."

"I did French for 'O' level too (he was in Form Six). I'd like to have taken Welsh though."

"Why didn't you then?"

"Well, in our school there's a choice between French and Welsh, and to make sure not everybody chooses French, they decide for you. No choice really, unless you insist or get a letter from your parents."

"Well how do they decide who does what?"

"They ask you what your father's job is."

"Eh?"

"Yeah. Like this. David Herbert, what's your father's work? Bus conductor, sir. Right, Welsh. Wayne Thomas? Estate agent, sir. French. Keith Gillard? Solicitor. French. John O' Leary? Miner, sir. Welsh... and so on."

"Why do they work it out like that?"

"Well, I suppose they think that if your father hasn't got a swanky job you couldn't afford to go to France, so there'd be no point."

"Have you ever been to France then?"

"No. I've been to Lansdowne Road though."

"Lansdowne Road? Where's that?"

"Oh, it's in Ireland. I don't s'pose many girls have heard of Lansdowne Road." I certainly hadn't and Neville proceeded at length to enlighten me. Boys are often strange creatures.

This method of selection for language study bothered me and I was delighted to find one's fate wasn't decided in the same way in the Girls' school. Had I been a boy, I would surely have been in the Welsh camp, having weekly to learn a poem I didn't understand and lists of verbs I thought were poems, as my father was only a carpenter and part-time shopkeeper.

Musing on these thoughts going into school, I came across a cluster of excited girls around a colourful notice featuring cut-out pictures of the Eiffel Tower and Notre Dame cathedral. It said *"Vacances de Pâques 1951. Séjour d'une semaine à PARIS pour celles qui apprennent le français. Visites aux monuments célèbres et à l'opéra. Journée à Versailles. Prix £25 qui comprend l'argent de poche. Voir Mlle. Llewellyn."*

I was in 4B by now, so could more or less understand the notice. All around, girls were enthusing and making plans.

"Gosh! Paris! Great. I'm definitely going."

"Me too. I hope my father can get £25 from somewhere."

"Cor, France. I don' 'spec my mother'll let me go. I haven't even been to London." As of course, the vast majority of us hadn't, it only being six years after the end of the war.

My mother was fairly sure I could go but couldn't say definitely until Dad had come home and they'd talked about it together. Once she'd announced this, I knew I'd be going, as Dad let me have whatever I wanted within reason and left decision making to Mam. He would say, "I don't mind what you do as long as it's not dangerous, you're careful, and I can have a bit of peace." He would also sometimes say, puzzlingly, "I don't mind what you call me as long as you call me early." These were his two sayings. So the following morning, before I left for school,

Mam simply asked, "When do they want the cheque for this Paris trip?"

That term couldn't go by fast enough. I worked harder at French than I'd ever previously worked at anything, learning bookfuls of irregular verbs and long lists of vocabulary, even useless things like *'pondre'* — to lay an egg, *'la méduse'* — jellyfish and *'Le joug'* — yoke. I developed a crush on my French teacher, Miss (Mary) Davies, who constantly praised my efforts. In the French terminal I came top for the first time in my County career and didn't need to lie in wait for my report to alter it.

One Saturday afternoon a few weeks before the trip, Mam and I went to Cardiff on the bus to buy me some new clothes. As far as I was concerned this was totally unnecessary as I always loathed shopping for clothes, always feeling happier with familiar skirts, jumpers, jackets and dresses that Mam mostly bought in my grateful absence. Mam loved shopping expeditions though, and, horrified at my objections, insisted, "You can't go to Paris with old clothes! What's the matter with you?" So I trailed patiently along after her to Roberts', David Morgan's, Mackross, Seccombes', Marments' and Howells' while she tried various garments on me.

"I do like this green skirt, but then the heather tweed is very pretty. Which do you like best Mary?"

"I like them both the same."

"Well, which one shall we buy?"

"I don't mind."

"Aw, come on, *you've* got to wear it. Say which one."

I'd do a quick 'eeny, meeny, miny mo ' and point to one.

"That one."

"Are you sure now?" Mam would ask.

"Yes, that one."

"Mmm. I think I'd rather the other one."

"Well let's have that one then."

"No no, we'll have the one you like best."

"But I don't mind which, honest." And so it continued, the conversations being more tiring in their monumental irrelevance than the shopping. But Mam enjoyed dressing her doll, even if the doll didn't at the time appreciate her generosity and kindness. On such trips, the best part for me was having tea in the 'Continental' where they had a small orchestra upstairs. When I was very small, I used to get up in my hat and coat and dance to this orchestra, twirling around on my own, oblivious to every thing, particularly the amusement of the other customers. At fourteen, I felt embarrassed to think of my former foolishness and ignored the music, concentrating on the correct worldly behaviour in a restaurant, while at the same time eliciting maximum enjoyment from the cakes. The waitress would bring a silver pot of tea on a tray, china cups and saucers with 'Continental' written on them, a plate of thinly sliced bread and butter and strawberry jam and another plate of about six different, individual pastries. You only had to pay for the cakes you ate. Mam would eat one and I'd have three or four, sometimes five.

Mam took the opportunity to buy me a white and brown, dog-tooth check overcoat which I had absolutely no intention of taking to Paris as we had to wear blazers on the journey for easy recognition, and I certainly wasn't carrying it. In fact, some others in the party had been trying to persuade me to take a week's provision of sweets and chocolates, so I envisaged my case nearly as full of goodies as clothes. When I put this argument to Mam about the coat, she said, undaunted, "Oh well, never mind. It'll be your new Whitsun coat for church."

Mothers, sets of parents, whole families even, accompanied their Paris bound daughter, sister or niece to Porth station on the appointed morning. There was hardly a dry eye on the platform. It was a scene more reminiscent of a decade earlier, when soldiers were going off to the war, rather than an exciting, pleasurable holiday departure. Girls were feeling homesick already, their faces pale and drawn as they secretly wished they'd never heard of Paris and had chosen Welsh not French. Younger sisters and brothers clung on to their hands, chins quivering with pent-up tears. My mother was looking at me as though she would never see me again and kept repeating, "Take care, won't you?". The only person who didn't look as if she was about to face a firing squad was Miss Llewellyn who, smiling and brisk, bustled about ticking people off on lists, reassuring relatives that Yes, she would see that Jennifer took her tablets, Yes, she did have Joan's spare pair of glasses, Yes, she did have the individual and the collective passports and Yes, we would be back in a week's time at 5 p.m.

Everybody felt much better once the train had left the station even though kith and kin had waved and craned their necks until it was out of sight and one silly little brother, moving along with the train, had run out of platform and, dangerously, on to the line. Remaining tears were mopped up, carriage windows adjusted, sweets passed around and entrancement lay ahead. I was the only one from Trehafod, lower down the line from Porth, and felt a bit sad to see my house from the train, its green shop door abnormally closed at 10:30 in the morning.

"There's my house," I said and everyone crowded at the windows to have a look. Redundant, sick or retired men always stood with one foot on the bar at the railings opposite the shop, talking and gazing at the wide panorama of the valley, and there were a few as we passed.

"Is that your father?" asked Pat Williams.

"No, he's in work," I answered.

"Let's wave all the same," suggested Margaret Algate, so down the window came and the surprised fellows were treated to the sight of a dozen, green Porth County blazer-clad arms wildly gesticulating to attract their attention. Languidly they waved back, showing a modicum of interest but waving more out of politeness than curiosity as they put the world to rights.

By the time we'd reached Cardiff Central, all thoughts of sadness and homesickness were behind us as we descended on the station's sweet kiosk. It being Easter time, we bought up all their supply of Cadbury's creme-filled chocolate eggs at 5d each. In fact, all along our route to Newhaven we were like a plague of locusts as we pounced on small shops and stalls, devastating them of their creme-filled Easter eggs.

The train journey to London was like a little holiday in itself and I think that many in the party would have been quite happy to return to Porth the following day, feeling they'd had their moneys' worth. Few among us had previously encountered a corridor train, so there was nearly an eighth of a mile of novel, shaking, ever changing, populated coaches to explore. After Miss Davies boarded at Newport, to much enthusiastic welcome, and an equally enthusiastic interest in a male companion who was standing at the platform seeing her off on the trip, the party was complete.

Green blazers were on continuous move through the train, in twos or small groups, locating the toilets (a constant fascination to young girls), peeking into the guards van, negotiating the shaky, pleated tunnel area between coaches, making repeated forays to the buffet car for biscuits, chocolate, egg rolls and orange squash, squeezing sideways past smokers, leg stretchers, lovers or scenic viewers in the corridors. Rarely did anyone sit, even to consume a packed lunch, and it could truthfully be stated that we walked several miles of the railway journey to Paddington.

Adult passengers, seeking to relieve themselves, would hover impatiently outside the 'engaged' toilets, their irritation increasing by the second as merry laughter and girlish voices issued from within:

"Not much room for all of us in here is there?"

"Well, it was only made for one, I 'spect."

"You go out then, if you're squashed."

"No, I want to go to the toilet."

"You can't. We're slowing down and you can't go at stations. It says."

"Where does it go then?"

"What?"

"It. You know, when you go to the toilet."

"Well, that flap thing lifts up and it flushes on to the line. Nowhere else for it to go really."

At this point the waiting adult would correctly visualise four heads peering aghast down the lavatory pan.

"Oh, no!"

"Ugh!"

"D'you mean to say the railway lines of Britain are littered with......?"

"Yes!"

Laughter and giggling breaks out and the lingering adult scowls and stamps up and down the corridor before resignedly leaning against the window to stare, unseeing, at the passing scenery or busy station. Eventually the sound of a bolt being drawn, more bumping and chortling and "No silly, it opens inwards. All move back". The by-now desperate adult glares in disapproval and amazement as four or five grinning girls, trying to look sophisticated, with a light smattering of illicit powder and lipstick on their youthful faces, emerge from the tiny room.

The adventurous mood had been totally superseded by the anxious one by the time we disembarked at Paddington station. Leaning sideways with the effort of carrying heavy suitcases and struggling among the crowds to keep the teachers in sight in this huge, noisy place with people rushing to and fro, we felt very small and insignificant indeed. To get lost here would surely be forever and no-one in this swarming metropolis would care one jot. So we huddled round our 'loci parentis'. Gazing wide-eyed at everything as if in a dream, we travelled on the swaying, rattling, wheezing Tube to Victoria where we were to stay overnight in an hotel.

Normal sleep that night was out of the question, for tomorrow we were to be in a foreign country for the first time. And not only that, but in one of the most fascinating cities in the world. Apart from the excitement of that, we had been put in a large room or small dormitory sleeping six and there were people talking and wandering around all night long. London rumbled on outside much as it had during the day and there was a lot to see going on out of the windows. Eventually, most of us fell deeply asleep from exhaustion just as it was getting light, only to be woken up an hour or so later to catch the boat train to Newhaven.

The day passed in a sleep-walking haze as we were shepherded hither and thither, off this and on to that, out of one thing and on to something else. We waited patiently around, nudged cases a bit further on, dozed on our feet. Lunch of chips, steaklet and something green, registered to drooping eyelids on the ferry, and later, people were being sick, although the crossing was calm and far steadier than the London Tube. Toblerone bars replaced Cadbury's Easter eggs for those who had the energy to go in search of them and some girls took off their blazers and bought beer in the bar.

Dieppe was a revelation. The ferry berthed, and next to the dock stood a train! Wearily, Hope said, "Pinch me if I'm asleep, or is that a train in the middle of the street?" Several took up the invitation, although she was not, in fact, dreaming. After a slight delay to do with tickets, passports and disembarkation cards, we climbed and lugged cases up steps on to what seemed the highest train ever. Once aboard, we had a fine view of the state of the top of the French head. Thus far, no-one had understood a word of what anyone was saying and even Miss Llewellyn's French had completely changed from the sort of French she used in school. Worryingly, the sounds didn't even appear to resemble those used in Porth. There was a lot of nasal snorting, not to mention shrugging, pursing of lips and waving of arms.

However, a few reassuring street signs, *"Boulangerie. Props. A et G Fouchaud"*, *"Vins, Gros et en Détail"*, *"Alimentation générale"* confirmed we were truly in France, and were enthusiastically, if not entirely correctly, translated by the wakeful. "Bakery owned by A and G Fouchaud. Fat, detailed wine. That's a funny notice. How can you have fat wine?"

"Don't be silly. It doesn't mean that!"

"No, you know, it's um....What do they call it? Fruity or full-bodied wine, that's what it is, and that other sign means General Alimentation."

"No, you don't say! Well, who'd have guessed that? It takes a clever person to translate that. Ten out of ten to you."

Mock aggression, such as pretending to bash the ironic person's brains out, followed, and the train moved off through the streets of Dieppe. "Funny place, this France," I thought, and that was the last thing my tired brain registered until I was aware of Hope screeching, "Wake up, wake up! We can see Paris." Nearly everyone was in the corridor and Miss Llewellyn was indicating a distant, impressive, white building that looked like a wedding cake on a hill glowing pink in the afternoon sun. "That's the Basilica of the Sacré Coeur. We'll be going to the top of that," she said.

We stayed at the Hotel Jean Bart, number 9, in the rue Jean Bart, quite close to the Luxembourg Gardens and not far from the top southern end of the exciting 'Boul Mich', the busy, *mouvementé* Latin Quarter of Paris. We went everywhere on foot. We couldn't have walked more if we'd visited the Alps in Savoie and the next time I had new shoes in Gamlins, Pontypridd, I'd gone up from a size three to a five. Our bodies were transported to the walking area by Métro. We bought 'carnets', little booklets of tickets, and plunged down wide steps in the avenues, marked by charming Victorian-type signs saying '*Métropolitain*', into warm, garlic-smelling tunnels. Despite hurrying we would normally be in time to see the iron '*porte automatique*' swing across the platform entrance and an empty train clatter off after a violent slamming together of compartment doors. Then the '*porte automatique*' would open to allow us on to the platform, where we translated posters, put francs in machines for '*le chewing gum*' or gazed at the electric rails of the track while waiting for the next, invariably full, train to arrive.

"Keep away from the edge of the platform."

"What would happen if you fell on the track, Miss?"

"You'd look very foolish."

"No, I mean, is it dangerous?"

General laughter with anonymous answers greeted this naïve query.

"Cor, daft question!"

"Oh no, it's rather pleasant being run over by a train."

"Well, what do you think?" Miss Davies replied.

"Well then, are those rails electrocuted?"

"You'd be if you touched them because they're electrified."

"Cor, what would happen exactly?"

At last, Miss Davies, to put an end to the constant questioning, would be persuaded to provide some gory details for the attentive audience. "First, there'd be flashing sparks as you screamed and writhed in agony, then you'd glow blue and red before going black, purple and shiny all over. Your clothes and hair would catch fire and we'd have to send for the '*sapeurs pompiers*' to douse the flames. But by this time you'd be well and truly dead, SO GET BACK FROM THE EDGE OF THE PLATFORM!"

Our nearest Métro station was Boulevard Raspail so we got quite well known to the personnel there who would smile and nod benignly on our approach. Occasionally they would say something to which we'd answer, "*Oui Monsieur* or *Madame*", our reply sometimes occasioning broad grins or laughter. The French are a friendly lot.

We mostly ate our dinner, *'le déjeuner'*, at restaurants wherever we happened to be. Miss Llewellyn told us what we could have, or what price not to exceed, then paid everyone's bill. If it surpassed a certain frankage we had to stump up ourselves. Some girls, to be on the safe side, had the thin French chips all week with something innocuous like a tough-skinned, fat, red Frankfurter sausage which was tasty enough once you'd managed to penetrate its protective covering. As the week wore on, girls became more adventurous, choosing *'le steack-frites'* or *'un roll-mop'*, sometimes with horrified results. 'Ugh!' would resound round the restaurant as someone sliced into their meat and the teachers hid their faces behind casually raised hands and pretended they were not of our group. "Ugh! Look at all this blood running out! I can't eat this. It hasn't been cooked!", and the injured party would sit disgruntled, not even eating the chips, only pecking at a chunk of bread, which was always in plentiful supply. Bread was eaten with everything. If Barry Island is the kingdom of the chip, France is the kingdom of the crumb.

Roll-mops, which turned out to be soused herrings, were given similar treatment and left disconsolately at the side of the plate for the kitchen cat or the next customer.

Once or twice, we went into rather disquieting self service restaurants which hadn't then appeared in Britain — not in Porth anyway. Surprisingly, these weren't so popular as you couldn't practise your French on a grinning waiter also trying to practise his English, ("Weell yoo meet mee toonaight pleeze"); they were always crowded; you had to dash for a seat, sometimes losing your food off the tray and spilling your mineral water. Occasionally, it was necessary to share a table with a French person. They didn't appear to use knives, just a fork chasing the food around the plate in one hand and a chunk of bread in the other chasing the fork. If you were a slow decider or looker, you passed the food you wanted in the quickly moving press of the queue, then couldn't go back for it and ended up with bread, yoghourt (plain), *petit suisse* and a radish for your meal. Sometimes, if you weren't doing something right, the harassed waitress doling out the food behind the counter would bark at you, attracting all gazes, mostly unsympathetic, in the mêlée. She wouldn't be appeased or laugh at a *"Oui Madame"*, but would bark at you again, completely putting you off the food you didn't have.

In the evenings, we ate at the hotel, an altogether more satisfying experience, after the first few days anyway. The hotel Jean Bart didn't cater especially for English tastes in the fifties, as do the majority of continental hotels accommodating British schoolchildren of the Comprehensive era. These latter, no doubt striving for international appeal in the nourishment stakes, provide chips in some shape or form with every meal — stick chips with steak, fat chips with omelette, round chips with chop. Apart from the provision of oil rather than vinegar, (which is of a red hue when brought to the table by the surprised waiter when demanded by the British pupil) one might well imagine oneself to be in Blackpool and not abroad at all. Not so with the Jean Bart chef. Whether he could only cook *à la française,* whether he wanted to educate the junior British palate or whether his pride prevented him from forsaking an almost total commitment to the cuisine of his native soil, we didn't know, but eat French food we did, or starve. We had *'cassoulet'* — beans. "Are these Heinz?" someone asked a non-plussed waiter, "I'm not eating them if they're not"; *'choucroute garnie'* — thick slices of smoked sausage, tender chunks of fat bacon and shredded white cabbage cooked in wine with cloves; small brown lentil beans with *'paupiette de veau'*, succulent white veal inside a wrapper of ham; delicious, pale green and white artichokes with slices of leg of lamb; young green beans with *'coquilles St Jacques'*, scallops, oven-baked with a covering of cheese. Potatoes were provided in varied and imaginative forms: baked in milk with shallots and mushrooms; delicately sautéed in butter; puréed in cream with cheese; oven-baked in cone shapes so that the outside was crisp but the inside soft but firm; mashed, rolled in breadcrumbs or batter, and fried. We ate aubergines, artichokes, asparagus, courgettes — vegetables we had never previously heard of, let alone seen — and a fair dash of garlic so that we became part of the scene, odourwise anyway. Different cheeses with romantic names were presented for our delectation or distaste, often disgust, at every *'dîner'*: *Reblochon, Tomme, Roquefort, Brie, Cantal, Morbier,* and smelly, runny *Camem-*

bert, (usually returned whole but explored) and we learnt to mash sugar with a fork into the soft *'petit suisse'* cheese, then mop up the plate with bread. We were introduced to yoghourt and sweetened that too with spoonfuls of sugar.

Pamela Nicholls observed, "We're doing some funny things here. My mother'll never believe that I was mixing sugar with cheese. It's nice too."

"I know," replied Anne Towers from Form Three, a year behind us, "and mine would have a fit to see me wiping my plate with bread. Hope I don't get into the habit. She'll think I've been living with the Rodneys."

One meal-time early on in the week, the waiter carried in a large dish of baked ham in a white sauce with mushrooms, another with tiny, roasted new potatoes and a third with courgettes cooked in butter and garlic.

"Hallo, what's this then?" asked Shelagh Burke. "Fried cucumber slices tonight girls. Who's starving and desperate?"

The ham and potatoes disappeared like the proverbial snow in the ubiquitous ditch. Hope, usually hungry and always ready to eat, put a spoonful of the undisturbed vegetable on her plate, which she consumed, warily at first then enthusiastically, following it up with several more spoonfuls. "Mmmm. These cucumbers are okay." The rest of us at the table tried some and, soon, that dish was empty too.

Our waiter, Philippe, returned for the plates, smiling to see them empty.

"Goood, *hein ?*" he said.

"Oh, très bien," we replied.

"Encore?" he asked.

"Oh merci," we chorused.

His face fell. *"Régime?"* he asked, looking disconsolate.

"Oh oui oui," we articulated. We waited, and to our great disappointment, he brought the third and fourth courses, the *'salade'* and cheese. "Where's the cucumbers and roast potatoes?" we asked him but he had no idea what we were talking about and shrugged his face.

The next evening there was an especially delicious marshmallow pudding with what appeared to be cold custard sauce. Philippe hovered with a bowl of seconds. *"Encore?"* he asked pleasantly. We weren't going to be caught out this time. *"Merci, merci,"* the table enunciated clearly, nodding furiously like the Dickensian aged parent, Wemmick. To our amazement, he looked disappointed, shrugged and moved off to the next table.

"Oy, come back. *Oui oui,* we want some."

He turned, paused and pointed at the bowl. *"Oui, encore?* You want?"

"Oh oui, oui, oui," we chirruped like a styful of porkers.

He and his smile returned and with hand signals, facial expressions and leapings about like a ballet dancer, he explained, *"Faut dire 'Oui, s'il vous plait' "*, carrying imaginary spoonfuls of food to his mouth. Then, looking sadly at the bowl and shaking his head and free hand, *"Faut dire 'Non me rci' "*. We clapped his performance, our ultimate comprehension and the return of the marshmallow pud. The French are a logical, practical nation. They only say "thank you" when the bird is in the hand, but tempt him out of the bush with a canny *"s'il vous plaît"*. It was one more step along the road of international understanding.

CHAPTER EIGHTEEN

Still in Paris

What is it about the French that compels or rather propels them to mount every summit in sight? In London there is one climb up to the Whispering Gallery in St Pauls, but one walks *around* Westminster Abbey, the Tower, the Houses of Parliament, Covent Garden, the Cutty Sark. Come to think of it, in London you can only *look* at many prestigious edifices — Eros, Marble Arch, the Bank of England, Nelson's Column — (with the recent exception of Buckingham-Palace) nobody invites you to inspect them. When your feet get tired of standing you just go and sit on some convenient wall, fountain rim or bench. Not so in Paris. After one day, the question over breakfast croissants and coffee was, "What are we going up today?" We had to serve our apprenticeship in altitude and got higher gradually, starting with the relatively innocuous (in terms of height that is) Notre Dame cathedral. In other terms, it is the most beautiful building in the world, clearly reflected as it is in the still waters of the Seine, standing solidly on its riverside site but with a simple majesty, as though it had grown there out of the earth or been lowered down from Heaven. The flying buttresses right around the nave, the fine central spire no doubt ending in a pin-point, with its delicate tracery of sculptured stone, the copper statues, a fluorescent light green with the patina of the centuries, appearing to descend the roof in prayer, and the two solid towers above the West door, must surely create a feeling of security the hearts of those who seek refuge there from the rigours of the world, delight in the hearts of lovers of refinement and culture and awe in the hearts of tourists.

We walked to Notre Dame from our hotel through the Luxembourg Gardens and along the Boulevard St Michel, with its diverting attractions slowing us up, then down to the river and over the bridge on to the *Île de la Cité* where the cathedral stands. After being given twenty minutes to look around, we were to meet on the Place du Parvis fronting Notre Dame to make the ascent up the south tower and around the roof. Half an hour had passed and a little second former, Myfi Smith, was missing. Back into the cathedral, so high it seemed almost open air, a small search party went to look for her. The plump, bespectacled figure of Myfi was found sitting in the north transept on one of the wicker seated cathedral chairs. Her face tear-stained, gazed as though hypnotized at the magnificent, stained glass Rose Window, high in the wall of the south transept. The sun highlighted the deep colours, causing multifarious rainbows to glow in the gloom of the church.

"What are you doing here, Myfi?"

"Just having a sit down and looking at that (nodding at the Rose Window). I think it's lovely I do."

"Did you think we'd gone without you?"

"No."

"Well, um... you're crying."

"No, I'm not," she said as a tear dropped off her chin.

"Is everything all right? Did you think you were lost?"

"No. I just like that window, that's all."

"Well look, we're going up the tower now, up the stone stairs and Miss Llewellyn is going to get the tickets."

"I'd rather stay here, I would. Can I?"

"Don't you want to see the lovely view all over Paris?"

"No. I'm counting the colours in that. I was up to twenty five when you came," she said as she licked up another tear.

It was a touching moment. Whether she was weeping because she was tired, thought she was lost, overcome by the occasion, homesick or something mystically else, no-one knew. Twelve year old Myfi missed that particular aspect over Paris but there were plenty more to come as we constantly headed skywards. Miss Davies, later in the week, made an unofficial trip back to Notre Dame with Myfi and a few others so she could have another look at the stained glass window. We also nicknamed her Myfi Rose.

We breakfasted daily around 7:30, so we could get our ready if not eager legs out on the streets and maximise our sightseeing, pounding the pavements of Paris. Bleary-eyed and somnolent, we stood around on the narrow pavement outside the hotel waiting for everyone to arrive, when someone yelled, "Look out!" Girls leapt out of their sleepiness on the the pavement off the road, fearing some great vehicle must be bearing down on them. Some, startled out of their minds, foolishly jumped off the pavement into the road as, hurtling along in the gutter, came a fast-moving stream of water carrying discarded paper bags, chocolate wrappers, Métro tickets, receipts and other assorted rubbish with it. Some of our party were too slow waking up and stared down in horror at a tardy foot, Persil-white sock and Clark's sandal sodden and plastered with wet paper and dusty detritus. The gutter river disappeared as fast as it had arrived down a hole in the side of the pavement and the road, if not all its occupants, was left clean.

The next morning we were ready for this evil little torrent, and on subsequent mornings, tracing it back a hundred yards or so, had races with paper boats made from the breakfast serviettes. We ended up betting a few francs on the winners. If we'd been there any longer someone would probably have ended up running a book.

On one of the marathon sightseeing days, we started off with an intellectual morning in the Louvre museum, though many would have preferred to stay in the Tuileries gardens outside, where small boys were pushing or mechanically guiding toy yachts around on the artificial ponds and getting very damp in the process. It was a child's paradise, with mini, musical roundabouts; white jacketed, straw-hatted gentlemen with pushcarts selling lollipops and ice cream; hawkers selling small bags of seed for the hovering birds; others selling little toys — kaleidoscopic coloured paper balls on elastic, tin yo-yos, whistles, wooden bats and spongy balls, plastic boats and childrens' sunglasses. Toddlers ran around sampling the odd mouthful of gravel when their anxious, fussing mother or nanny had her eyes averted or her mind and mouth otherwise occupied in conversation. Grey and violet pigeons were everywhere. Clouds of them scattered at one's approach and cannily re-assembled like starving urchins at the sight of anything vaguely resembling an abandoned crumb. There was a lot of interesting French life going on and you had to keep a cautious eye on the feathered friends.

"Oh damn," said Shelagh Burke, "look what that bird's done on my sleeve."

"Supposed to be lucky," offered a relatively unsympathetic best friend, Mary Norman, as she edged away from an eager looking pigeon who seemed to be fancying her as a prospective victim, "you can wash it off in the pond."

"With what?"

"Haven't you got a hanky?"

"With my hanky? Ugh! What if I need to blow my nose? Or cry?"

"Why should you want to cry?"

" 'Cos my feet are tired already and we haven't started yet."

We were warned not to get lost in the vast Louvre, as some bored and over-dressed Dauphin did for two days in the seventeenth century, because we were meeting for lunch in two hours and anyone late or lost would also fast. We climbed the stairs to admire the oldest known statue, that of the Winged Victory, one of whose feet had been found in the 1930's in the Mediterranean. The other was missing altogether. We stared in amazement at the Perfect Woman — the Venus de Milo — and hoped we'd never be as fat, not to mention armless, and giggled at statues of naked gods of classical mythology minus their fig leaves.

"Aren't they smooth?" said Jennifer Jones, running a hand over the marble, and surreptitiously touching the private part.

"I saw you," said Pamela.

"Oh, there's rude, Jennifer," added Pat Williams in mock horror to a blushing but giggling Jennifer.

"*I'm* not rude. It's *him*. Exposing himself like that. He should have a pair of pants on. My mother would be disgusted, she would. Paying all this money for me to come here to be exposed to!"

"They didn't have pants in those days, silly," said Pat amid much laughter.

"Well, a loin cloth then, or a G-string, or whatever they wore in ancient Rome. They didn't go round naked now did they?"

"Actually, they didn't wear anything under their togas. They were always sort of...ready for action," Pat went on.

"Oooh, who's being rude now? I don't believe *that,* any road."

"Yes, it's like Scotsmen with their kilts," chipped in Pam, "you know, they've got a little pouch to hold their kilt down and..."

"Do you mind? This conversation is getting far too naughty for me," said Jennifer marching off in mock high dudgeon to almost bump into the thighs of another naked statue with a profusion of curly hair. "Oh, my God...," said Jennifer, blushing, covering her cheeks with her hands and looking for a quick escape.

To much laughter, chuckling and silly chat, we made our way to the Mona Lisa gallery where a dozen artists with easels were trying to capture the enigmatic look with largely disastrous results.

No-one had to fast, and the mixed delights of the afternoon were a mile trudge from the small Arc du Carrousel in the Tuileries, along the glittering Champs Elysées, past the Place de la Concorde where we had a sit down, up to the Arc de Triomphe.

Two gendarmes eyed us suspiciously, unfriendly pistols at their hips, ready for the draw no doubt should any Porth County girl wish to desecrate the tomb of the Unknown Soldier. Myfi wasn't as impressed with the tomb as with the Rose Window.

"Cor, there's a fire coming out of that hole," she said.

"It's the everlasting flame," explained Miss Llewellyn.

"Does that mean it never goes out then?"

"Yes. There's a gas jet feeding it."

"How long has it burned for?"

"Since the end of the first World War, but I don't think it burned during World War Two," whereupon, and to no obvious effect, Myfi stood at the grave side and blew towards the flame with all her might, puffing out her plump little cheeks until she was puce in the face. We climbed to the roof of the Arc from up inside one of the legs, then admired the *Etoile* of avenues from the top. The most exciting thing was the bird's eye view of vehicles tearing around the Arc as though they were racing around Silverstone, their drivers blowing klaxons, shouting, waving their fists, crossing lanes and making rude gestures to each other before their cars shot off like jet-propelled black pats down some avenue leading off the Arc.

As sometimes the interval is the most enjoyable part of a play, so it was with our party in Paris. After a hard foot slog of sightseeing and before pressing on to the next dome or spire, we would make for a pavement café for well-deserved refreshment and a sit down. "You mustn't order anything alcoholic," Miss Llewellyn constantly re-affirmed as welcoming tables, chairs, awnings and white-shirted, black-trousered waiters hove in sight. "I can't risk your getting tipsy and having an accident or doing anything stupid." So, with resigned looks, we would order fruit juices — *cassis, pamplemousse, grenadine or limonade, orangeade* or *citronnade*. On one occasion, sitting at the far end of the *terrasse* from the teachers and partly hidden by a bush in a box, Hope rebelled and decided she was going to buy some white wine which wasn't dissimilar from *limonade* but came in a different-shaped, betraying glass. After all, we'd seen French children, younger than us, at the wine. "You can't order that Hope," I said, "you'll cop it if they catch you."

"No I won't, 'cos I'll ask for a straw and they'll think it's pop."

"Do you know the word for straw?"

"Yes, I do see, *'paille'*."

" *'Paille'* is straw for cows, silly. I bet there's a different word for drinking straw."

"Yes, I 'spec there is in this nutty, froggy language," chirped in Pamela, also at our table. "Go and ask Llew. She'll know."

"Yes, but that'll draw attention to us."

"Us!" I said, "I'm not having any to get into trouble."

After a spoilsport, stuffed-shirt type look from Hope, I slightly redeemed myself by suggesting we ask the next table along to ask the next to ask the next until the item of vocabulary reached Miss Llewellyn. After a load of muttering, a word came back to Anne Towers. "Something like *'chameau'*," she said.

"Oh, they could have listened carefully," complained Hope. However, when the waiter eventually arrived at us, Hope ordered *"Un verre de vin blanc .... et un chameau s'il vous plaît."* The waiter stopped in his jotting down the order. *"Comment?"* he asked.

"Je voudrais un verre de vin blanc avec un chameau."

At this, a grin broke across his features and he suddenly laughed aloud attracting the attention of not only the café customers but the passers-by as well. *"Ha ha. Un chameau! Ha ha. Pour porter le vin?"*

"Er..er.. *une paille?"* Hope added hopefully miming a trombone-like movement to and from her mouth. Realisation dawned.

"Ah! Ah! Un chalumeau," he said histrionically, *"chalumeau."* Then looking puzzled again, *"Du vin avec un chalumeau?"* he said, unbelieving.

By now, Hope's resolve for wine had completely dissolved. "Oh, *non, non,* forget it, *une limonade s'il vous plait."*

The fellow sighed. *"Une limonade. Avec chalumeau?"*

"Oui, oui, that's it, *c'est ça."*

He moved off, shaking his head, muttering something about *"Anglaises"* and by the time Miss Llew came across to investigate, we were all blameless if not innocent.

Our quest for France's nectar, however, did not go unfulfilled as most evenings after dinner were free in the sense that we could write cards home, practise speaking French to each other or go to bed early to be well rested for the following day's slog to the next lot of monuments. We were free, but of course, confined to the hotel. The teachers weren't much in evidence until ten o'clock when they circulated around the bedrooms to ensure we were settled for the night. Rumour had it they were ensconced in their rooms doing what we had been forbidden — drinking alcohol. Until we discovered the fire escape, the chief evening entertainment was riding up and down on the lift and summoning it from various floors until it was red hot. That, and shouting from the balcony outside the window to girls on other balconies.

Pamela and Anne Towers shared a room at the back, next to which was a door with a lot of French on it. One day they opened it, and to their delight, found a fire staircase. During our week at the Jean Bart that fire escape was constantly in use between 8 and 10 p.m., with girls stealthily and on tip-toe creeping up and down. Myfi, who was only in Form Two and indifferent to nocturnal wanderings or wine-tasting, came and sat in Pam and Anne's room in her dressing gown to open and close the fire door and keep guard. What exactly she was supposed to do on guard was unclear.

"What shall I say if Miss Llew comes?"

"Just tell lies, Myfi."

She was quite happy with this arrangement as we all bought her sweets and chocolate. So much, in fact, she had a surplus to take home as presents.

There was a café around the corner from the hotel, but after some girls had had to flee and hide at the sudden and un-expected approach of two familiar figures also seeking post-prandial liquid refreshment, that particular establishment was avoided. However, a block away was the Boulevard Raspail...

We were never caught, although Myfi returned to Wales with a slightly less pure soul than the one she'd left with. In fact, she was rather pleased with the lies she'd thought up, which became more fantastic as the week wore on. "Margaret was feeling sick Miss Llewellyn, so the others took her to the door for a breath of air."

"What, all of them...? "

"Jennifer had a phone call from her pen-pal and they've all gone down to the phone with her."

"There was a lost dog barking down in the street and they've gone to pat it." It was just as well we'd found the fire escape later rather than sooner for the sake of Myfi's virtue.

We slept much better, I'm sure, for our taste of the forbidden, fermented juice of the grape even if the reality wasn't as delight-ful as the imagined. In fact, it wasn't as nice as lemonade, but we all enjoyed the illicit outing, and at least we didn't go off with boys from Ashford, Kent, staying at the hotel Fleurus in the Rue du Fleurus around the corner, like the Sixth formers who were supposed to be looking after us did.

Miss Llewellyn had made plans for two evenings of the week's holiday and the first was a visit to the Paris Opera to see Verdi's 'Rigoletto'. We had all heard of the celebrated Paris Opera which ranked on a par with Covent Garden, the Metropolitan in New York and La Scala, Milan and we had seen the impressive, ornate building a few times as we scurried to and fro across Paris. We had even seen dreamy-eyed young girls with upswept hair, ballet shoes slung over their shoulders, sauntering delicately there as though walking on gossamer on pointed, outward-turned feet. For like Covent Garden, there is a ballet school at the Paris Opera.

No-one had ever previously seen an opera, but despite the merest mistrust of the unknown, and the esoteric unknown in this case, everybody was looking forward to the evening out. It meant dressing up in our best taffeta frocks, (mine was maroon with a large white check and a collar which stretched out almost to my shoulders) clean white ankle socks and brown sandals specially polished for the occasion; an evening ride on the Metro; a sight of the sophisticated, night-time Paris. Excited speculation was rife.

"D'you like opera?" Margaret Algate asked me as we clung on to the grab straps in the crowded, swaying Tube train.

"Well, I dunno, really. I don't know much about it. I 'spose so. I had to learn *Musetta's Waltz Song* for a piano exam once. That was O.K."

"Oh, I never heard of that. My Dad's got a record of *The Pirates of Penzance* and there are some nice songs in that. And he's always singing *A Wandering Minstrel I*. That's opera, he says."

Miss Davies was hanging on nearby. "D'you like opera, Miss?" I asked her.

"Mmm...On the whole I prefer listening to orchestral music. But some of the Italian arias are superb. *La Donna e Mobiles* is in this one. I expect you know that."

"No, never 'eard of it," we answered like true Fourth Form ignoramuses.

"Oh, of course you have," she insisted and proceeded to hum, "dum dum dum, dum te dum. Dum dum dum, dum te dum." I met Margaret's eye and we suppressed smiles.

"Is Verdi Italian?" Margaret went on.

"Oh yes."

"So there are going to be superb arias in this?"

"Mmm. Well, I only know that one."

In the event, the outing was more appreciated than the performance and once again, the interval was the high spot when we could all parade around the foyer, get a tub of ice-cream and look at the glamorous Parisian evening crowd. In the theatre, the opera glasses you could hire by putting a 100 franc coin in a little machine on the back of the seat in front were only cursorily used to look at the stage, as more interesting things were going on all around: a man edging closer to a haughty looking woman with mahogany coloured hair in one of the boxes; an incredibly handsome young man in evening dress sitting across the aisle; Pat Williams surreptitiously stuffing herself with sweets and not sharing them with anybody; a fat lady snoring in a seat under the balcony. Once, on my opera glasses perambulation, I came eyeball to eyeball with Miss Llewellyn sitting in the row behind and her deep frown in my direction impelled me to turn quickly and concentrate on the stage for five minutes, but I had little idea of what was going on. As Hope had indignantly exclaimed to much ssshhing at the start, "Hey, this is in some foreign language! How are we going to understand this? And the programme is in French!"

Eventually, after what seemed several hours of the second half, there was loud applause then the lights went up to illuminate a row and a half of sleeping girls in taffeta frocks with two slightly embarrassed but tolerant ladies in their midst.

The wedding cake basilica was next on our visiting list. Not only were there millions of steps to its summit but it seemed thousands just to get up to its front door. However, the narrow, steep streets up through Montmartre were an ideal place to buy presents and souvenirs to take home. We were allowed an hour to dawdle and browse up to the terrace in front of the Sacré Coeur. Interest in purchases and price comparisons were constant.

"What did you buy in there?" Jennifer asked Hope, Pam and me as we emerged from a small shop, jam-packed with souvenirs.

"I bought the Sacré Coeur in a snowstorm, look," said Pam taking a round object out of a paper bag, shaking it and sprinkling us with something wet. "Oh blow, the water's coming out. The plug's not in properly," she complained, examining it carefully. "I'll have to put more water in before I give it to my mother. It cost me three hundred francs too."

"The snow looks like coconut," said Jennifer.

"Well, you wouldn't expect it to be real snow, dope."

Hope showed the tiny blue and cream plastic camera she'd bought which clicked through a dozen views of Paris, and I displayed my brass coloured, metal model of the Arc de Triomphe and a totally useless turquoise silk handkerchief with a heavy beige embroidery of the Sacré Coeur in one corner.

"Hmm. Pretty," Jennifer said critically, "But you couldn't blow your nose in that. It's too small....and slippery," she added.

"It's not for blowing your nose in, silly. It's for looking at."

Someone else had bought a pen with a transparent body which when used or held upside down revealed pictures of Paris. Another girl had two very gaudily painted sketches of Notre Dame and the Eiffel Tower. Jennifer, if anything, had the weirdest present — a piece of wood with a bright green painting of the Sacré Coeur which she said glowed in the dark. The most disappointing was a key ring, dangling on the end of which was a cream plastic skull with two false ruby eyes. On close examination we could make out 'Made in England' stamped on the back.

We wearily climbed up to the highest gallery of the Sacré Coeur and down again, then rushed gratefully to sit at a café table for our ostensibly non-alcoholic tipple in the Place du Tertre. Some of us had discovered 'un kir' — white wine with blackcurrant in it, which was an innocuous pale purple. We spent three times as long here as we had in the basilica, fascinated by the Bohemian-type artists with their long hair, floppy bow ties and thumb held, colour-splashed palettes as they painted the white, oriental building, the view, the square or each other. Some sketched tourists in charcoal as they sat self-consciously facing the artist and a crowd of critical onlookers whose eyes moved from sitter to artist as though they were watching a tennis match.

Hope, no doubt imagining herself framed on her front room wall and fancying herself as a rival to Mona Lisa, went around a few, pointing and asking *"Combien?"* However, she couldn't understand most of the figures quoted and when she did, the man having told her in English, it was more than the total pocket money we'd been allowed.

Although our confidence and ability to speak some sort of French generally improved during the week, my clumsy attempts had possibly the most unlikely outcome. Around the corner from our rue Jean Bart was a pastry-confectioner's.

Mouth-watering glacé fruits were displayed in the window, together with various varieties of wrapped bonbons, but what especially attracted me was the packaging. Differently shaped and coloured, rigid and floppy cellophane bags and boxes tied with ribbon of various hues were on display in the window. The sweets were expensive, at least twice the price of those in Britain and particularly in our corner shop, where Dad passed them to the customer unceremoniously served in a small square or cone-shaped white paper bag, deftly twisted at the top to temporarily secure the contents. I felt my parents would be interested in the French method of presentation, apart from having the actual sweets to savour. So it would be a kind of double-edged gift — on a commercial and personal level. Treble-edged really as my parents rarely ate sweets or chocolate and I would probably be the chief beneficiary.

I marched confidently to the shop after breakfast one morning, hung around uncertainly for a minute outside, practising what to say. After I'd mentally repeated the phrases, I took a deep breath and sidled in, trying to look invisible.

"Ah, bonjour Mademoiselle. Vous désirez?"

"Hmm. Hmm. Um...er...*Je voudrais des bonbons s'il vous plaît. Des bons bonbons, dans un bon paquet*..er I mean um..*dans un joli paquet avec er...*". The hesitant flow dried up completely. The man behind the counter began to smile, no doubt at my stumbling French, and I glanced around, grateful it was early and there were few people about to witness my foolishness.

"*Oui.....*" he answered thoughtfully and rather unhelpfully, "*Vous voulez dépenser combien?*"

My mind raced. Ah yes, "*Combien*". I knew that. He was asking me about money. I had a little collection of warm coins and crumpled notes in my hand which I counted up quietly in English. The man still smiled. I counted 796 francs. Oh God, what was that in French? I looked frantically round for help, but there was no familiar face. Why had I started on this mad scheme? I should merely have stayed with the others and stuck with the leaking snowstorm like Pam Nicholls or the English-made skull with ruby eyes. You just had to point at those and pay. No negotiation was necessary. I knew "*tant pis'* was 'never mind', so should I just say that and make a quick exit out of the fast filling shop? The man was still smiling benignly as he waited. *"Um...er... Il y a sept cents francs et neuf et six"* I stammered, blushing, all concept of complicated French numbers having fled my head, and indeed most vocabulary with them. I felt too confused to speak any language. By now, more customers had come in, the whole shop was taking an interest in the proceedings, gazing from me to the shopkeeper and back again, frowning in an attempt to understand, nodding sporadically and the man was laughing openly at my plight. His next words will stick in my mind for the rest of my days.

"Oh dear," he said trying to control his laughter, "what part of Wales do you come from love?" I looked at him in open-mouthed amazement. Good God and Hooray! He was speaking English! And with a Welsh accent! "Anywhere near Swansea?"

"No," I answered, my facility for speech having magically returned, despite my state of shock "from the Rhondda. Trehafod. I'm here with a group from school."

"Well, I could have sworn from your French you were from Swansea. I'm from Fforestfach myself. Originally, that is, see. But I married a French girl."

I don't know what sort of French they speak in Swansea, but I had a lovely box of sweets tied up with ribbon to take home, and the rest of the girls, hearing the news, bought up most of his remaining stock because they could transact in an English they could understand even better when spoken with a Welsh accent. I'm sure he gave us all reductions so it was a lucky day all round.

The long awaited ascent of the Eiffel Tower — that symbol of Paris, as the tricolor flag is of France — finally arrived on our last day, to be the climax of a holiday we would fondly remember for ever. Our legs, having tackled most of Paris — the infinite steps, cobbled streets, wide pavements, riverside quays, bridges, cathedrals, museums, assorted monuments, shops, gardens, restaurants, cafés and avenues — were stronger and most likely longer than those we'd arrived with, and ready for anything. Stories about the Tower abounded. "D'you know what Miss said? Some man rode a horse up the steps to the top," said Anne Towers.

"What for?" Jennifer wanted to know.

212

"I dunno. P'raps he had a bet on with somebody. P'raps the horse wanted to see the view. How do I know? Stupid sort of question, Jennifer."

"Stupid sort of thing to do if you ask me," was her dismissive, pragmatic reply.

"And Miss said someone strung up a wire right from the top down to one of the buildings and walked along it with a pole," Pam piped in.

"Was he killed?" Hope asked enthusiastically, hopeful for a few gory details.

"No, I don't think so. He prob'ly did it for money."

"I expect he had a little parachute hidden on him somewhere. I wouldn't do that without taking a parachute," Hope reflected improbably.

Miss Davies came in on the conversation. "Shortly after the Tower was built, some woman jumped off the top and instead of plummeting straight to the ground and killing herself as she had intended, her skirts billowed out and she wafted into the Seine. She drowned instead, poor thing." For some reason, this piece of regrettable historical information was greeted with unsympathetic girlish giggles.

We caught the Métro to Trocadéro and cameras clicked at the view of the Eiffel Tower from the smooth, broad walkway between the twin buildings of the Palais de Chaillot.

"It's not a very nice colour. Looks as if it's covered in oxtail soup," someone observed.

"It's special, anti-rust paint," Miss Llewellyn told us,"and maintenance on it is non-stop. Once they finish checking and painting it, it's time to start all over again."

"I hope it's safe," Myfi worried.

"Well it does wobble at the top in high winds, but they usually close it then." Miss Llewellyn was a mine, or tower, of information, even if the information wasn't always completely reassuring.

Wobble! Gracious! That didn't sound too safe! Girls looked at each other in dismay and swallowed in their anxiety.

"Yes," clever Mary Norman interposed, "if it didn't wobble it would snap. You see, metal must breathe and..."

"Look!" Jennifer's voice rang out, "I don't want to hear any more about it wobbling and snapping and breathing, or I'm not going up it, so there! Frightening me to death you all are with this talk. What would my mother say? Paying all this money for me to come here, then me risking my life going up a swaying pile of...of...puffing meccano. Talk about something else please." Everyone laughed at Jennifer's feigned bossy practicality, the teachers smiled and though nervous, she queued as eagerly and excitedly as anyone at the foot of one of the four squat legs for the large lift to the first stage.

Everyone was surprised at the speed with which the ground was left behind, as the lift sped diagonally skyward through the maze of metal. On the way up we passed tourists climbing the steps which, though winding and see-through, looked an altogether steadier mode of ascent, I thought, feeling sick as we whizzed by sideways in an overhang position. Gratefully, but gingerly, we emerged on to the first platform to gaze in wonder at the tops of buildings: the Arc de Triomphe with its converging avenues and mad ant traffic on one side, majestic Notre Dame with the silver Seine sliding past on another and the Sacré Coeur glowing rosily to the east up on its mound.

Apart from the view and the array of metal joists beneath us, we might as well have been in a small, covered square on the ground with an open walkway around the perimeter, as there were small, chic shops, mostly selling expensive souvenirs and a large, impressive restaurant, closed and empty but with a lot of greenery besides the usual furniture.

I imagine it must have been the thinner, rarer air affecting us, perhaps it was contained excitement being released at last, but everyone was behaving as though tipsy. Hope, her grandfather's phrase book in her hand, was going around speaking to strangers, telling them silly, irrelevant things such as *"Il faut se méfier des abeilles"* (You have to watch out for bees) or asking them equally stupid questions such as *"Pardon monsieur, voulez-vous me diriger a l'oculiste?"* (Excuse me sir, which way is it to the oculist's). When I asked her what she was doing, she simply grinned and said, "Practising my French, of course." It was, however, one-sided conversation as she got no answers, only odd looks. Myfi was lying on the floor poking her finger down a space in the metal towards a rivet which she said she was testing; Shelagh Burke was taking photos of everyone in sight, strangers included, and someone who shall be anonymous spat over the side as she said she was interested in the physics of flight. And this was only the first floor!

Eventually Miss Llew rounded everyone up and we nervously boarded the lift for the top. This rose at a far more sedate speed than the sideways hurtling one, which was just as well, as the ground now seemed miles below us. We passed platform two and carried on to a little stage half way up to change lifts for the summit.

"Don't look down!" warned Hope, Jennifer, Margaret and Anne simultaneously. Immediately everyone's gaze shot downwards into space to see what they were missing. "Oh," said Margaret Algate, "I feel sick."

"No you don't," Miss Davies answered firmly, "you're imagining it."

We rose gently to the topmost part. Once there, people edged like slow crabs to the periphery of the glassed-in viewing balcony. For five minutes Myfi couldn't be persuaded to leave the security of the wall of the central pillar. No, she didn't want to move as her back had to be against something solid and no, she didn't like views. Finally, with a girl on each side holding her hand, she was persuaded to advance to the viewing area where a sharp intake of breath expressed her feelings, either as to the condition of her stomach or appreciation of the vast panorama. "It's not as good as the Rose Window though," she immediately decided. Soon, she was walking uninhibitedly around like everyone else, looking at the little shops and buying chocolate for nearly double the price it was a thousand or so feet below. Steps led up to an open viewing platform, but the lower vantage point was high enough for some. Hope was indignant because she couldn't go to the ultimate top where there was a broadcasting station.

"Cor, the cheats. They make you pay to go to the top and it's not the top at all!"

"You can't go into the radio station, silly. There's people working there," Pam argued reasonably.

"How many?"

"Well, I don't know. Half a dozen, I expect. I shouldn't think there's room for many more. But people can't go disturbing broadcasts can they?"

"I wouldn't disturb them. Just want to see the view from the very top, that's all."

"It can't be much different from here. You can see practically to the Atlantic and the Mediterranean from this height!"

Paris stretched out at our feet and into a circular horizon, straight as arrows roads, cutting through buildings, plouging into the distance to places too inummerable and varied to imagine. In this eyrie, you felt you only had to reach up a hand to touch the sky. An aeroplane taking off from one of the Paris airports flew level with us for a while. People walking in the Champ de Mars were black dots and vehicles small rectangular boxes. The Seine was an unmoving blue mirror of sky with a random flash of sun on the water or a reflection of white cloud, giving the impression of a shoal of basking fish. Now and then, the sunlight would catch a window or a car windscreen in some suburb miles away to semaphore a quick, unknown message through the clear air. The silence above this moving, living, working, trading, learning, loving mass of humanity was eerie. But soon bodies were back down among the throng, though spirits remained aloft and contemplative in the bustle. For most, this visit was the climax of the holiday and making it on the last day left us feeling we'd seen and done everything worth seeing and doing. Was there anything in life to cap that?

For me in fact, the highest of the high spots had occurred a couple of nights previously. We'd gone to the *Théâtre des Champs Elysées* where a delightful man called Charles Trenet strode on stage, rakishly wearing a hat perched towards the back of his head, and sang an equally delightful song called *La Mer*. Even before the Eiffel Tower, I was hooked — on Paris, on France and everything to do with it.

We were veterans of travel on the homeward journey. There was no running around the train like unworldly schoolgirls, no squeezing of half a dozen bodies into the tiny train toilet for a giggle. We languidly took in the scene as the train ambled through the streets of Dieppe, and could even understand a lot of overheard conversations. Few notices and shop signs gave us any trouble now, though Miss Llewellyn had to explain about *'Vins, gros et en détail'* (Wine sold in bulk or bottles). No-one or their suitcase got lost on the boat, but a few, looking slightly

216

green, declined their chips and *steak haché* lunch. At Newhaven, there was some anxiety untypical of seasoned travellers. "Oh God, I hope they won't make me unpack my case. I've got a bottle of brandy for my father," said Shelagh Burke.

"You fool. You haven't!" her friend Mary consoled.

"Well yes. You know, that little flask I bought. It's only small."

"You'll have to pay a lot of money if they find it."

"Oh no she won't," Miss Davies, overhearing the conversation interposed. "They'll take it away altogether because she's under eighteen. And they won't be too pleased either."

"Oh no! I won't have anything to give my Dad then," moaned Shelagh.

"That's nothing to worry about. What if they take you for questioning or put you in jail or something?"

"Oh Mary, don't. You've got me really worried now and I'll look guilty as well. I can't help it. It shows on my face."

Similar worried conversations concerning perfume, wine and packets of French *Gauloises* or *Gitanes* (although I could understand why the authorities didn't want those smelly things in the country) were taking place all around, but in the event, the wide-eyed, culpable looking band of scared schoolgirls was waved through.

A strange incident occurred in London the following morning as we waited, blasé, world-weary international travellers on the pavement outside the hotel for the teachers to settle the bill. A leaflet-carrying, middle-aged woman pushed through the crowd of us and stopped in front of me.

"I've come to save you," she said.

"Oh, thank you," I answered. "From what?"

"From yourself. Read this leaflet and you will find the true way, the path ahead." She shoved a pamphlet into my unwilling hand and after mumbling a few more words, departed, ignoring everyone else.

"Cor, who was she? What she want? What she give you Mary?"

On inspection, it turned out to be a paper booklet of the religious type distributed by the Jehovah's Witnesses, the Latter Day Saints or some similar God squad. But why had she made a bee-line for me in the crowd when there were around thirty of us?

217

"It must be your evil aura, Mary," joked Pam. I certainly didn't want to be singled out for a fanatic's attentions, so I crumpled the paper into a ball, aimed for a nearby bin and tried to forget the irritating encounter. I pondered the incident though, on the train back home, thinking of the insight on the world we'd received from only a week abroad; the realisation of the many and different cultures from our own. The hugeness of the world and the vast numbers of people in it was as mind-boggling as star distances. Perhaps my 'true way' in life was going to be linked with this trip, the 'path ahead' inextricably bound up with France and French. Was this to be my future? Time would tell.

Acknowledgements

Many people have been instrumental in helping Snobs and Sardines to see the light of publication and I should like to give them my thanks; to former schoolfriends who prompted recollections of those days, particularly Marjorie (Woosnam) Grey who also dictated the words of the school sports song to me over the phone; to Graham Woosnam, Deputy Head of Porth County Comprehensive for his help with photographs; to Glyn and Doreen Jones for their sympathy with my problems and worries with the book when things weren't going according to plan and their encouragement; to Margaret and Brian Smith without whose help with the Amstrad word-processing system I'd have been utterly lost; to Mick Felton of Seren Books who suggested I write the book in the first place; to Amy Wack and Cary Archard, also of Seren Books; and to Tom Hutchinson for the superb cover drawing. Above all my grateful thanks and love to my children — Richard, who has been a tower of strength throughout, and Sarah for her encouragement to me in difficult days to finish the book, who typed up most of the manuscript and photocopied it, and finally to my late husband Michael who patiently listened to the three-quarters written by September 1991, made helpful suggestions, and laughed in all the right places.

Mary Davies Parnell
September 1993